I0203450

Sweat, Blood & Dust

Age 16

Sweat, Blood & Dust

The Military Career of Charles Napier during the
Peninsular War & War of 1812

ILLUSTRATED

Sir William Napier

LEONAUR

Sweat, Blood & Dust
The Military Career of Charles Napier during the Peninsular War & War of 1812
by Sir William Napier

ILLUSTRATED

FIRST EDITION

Leonaur is an imprint of Oakpast Ltd

Copyright in this form © 2017 Oakpast Ltd

ISBN: 978-1-78282-684-2 (hardcover)
ISBN: 978-1-78282-685-9 (softcover)

http://www.leonaur.com

Publisher's Notes

The views expressed in this book are not necessarily
those of the publisher.

Contents

Parentage	7
The Rifle Corps	20
His Father's Death	32
To the 50th Foot	48
Copenhagen Expedition	57
Battle of Coruña	76
On the Coa	97
On Campaign	134
American War	160
Craney Island	184
Exchange to 50th Regiment	203

CHAPTER 1

Parentage

Born at Whitehall, 10th of August, 1782, Charles Napier was eldest son of the Honourable George Napier and Lady Sarah Lennox, daughter of the second duke of Richmond. This nobleman, grandson of Charles the Second, married Lady Sarah Cadogan, daughter of Marlborough's favourite general. Their union was a bargain to cancel a gambling debt between the parents, and the young Lord March was brought from college, the lady from the nursery, for the ceremony. The bride was amazed and silent, but the bridegroom exclaimed— "Surely you are not going to marry me to that dowdy?" Married he was however, and his tutor instantly carried him off to the continent. Lady Sarah went back to her mother, a daughter of Wilhelm Munter, States Councillor of Holland.

Three years afterwards Lord March returned from his travels, an accomplished gentleman, but having such a disagreeable recollection of his wife that he avoided home, and repaired on the first night of his arrival to the theatre. There he saw a lady of so fine an appearance that he asked who she was. "The reigning toast, the beautiful Lady March." He hastened to claim her, and they lived together so affectionately, that one year after his decease, in 1750, she died of grief. Her daughter, also named Sarah, born in 1746, was likewise beautiful, and when scarcely eighteen, George the Third offered her his hand; she refused, he persisted, and was finally accepted, partly because of his apparently sincere passion, partly from the influence of her brother-in-law the first Lord Holland: but then politicians worked on royal pride, hurt by the first refusal, and the monarch fell back.

Charles Napier, sickly as a child from the misconduct of a barbarous nurse, was probably stinted of natural growth, being of low stature and slight, though both his parents were tall and strong, his

7

father gigantic: but rigorous temperance, through life inviolate, gave him an iron constitution, evinced by immense mental labours and the endurance of strange sufferings in every variety of climate. When he was three years old, his father settled at Celbridge, a small town on the Liffey, ten miles from Dublin, where he was close to Castletown, the magnificent house of Mr. Conolly, who had married Lady Sarah's sister. Lady Louisa Lennox. Near Carton also, the abode of the Duke of Leinster, who had married Lady Emily, another sister, mother of the high-spirited but unhappy Lord Edward Fitzgerald. A fourth sister was Lady Caroline, the first Lord Holland's wife, and mother of Charles Fox. These cousins were all sixth in descent from Henry the Fourth of France on one side; but Charles Napier traced his lineage on the other to the great Montrose, and the still greater Napier of Merchiston, inventor of logarithms: hence the blood of the white-plumed Bearnois commingled with that of the heroic highlander in his veins, and his arm was not less strong than theirs in battle.

The sins of the fathers are visited on the children. Lord Napier, grandson to the mathematician, lost his lands fighting for Charles the First; he reclaimed them at the Restoration from Charles the Second, but was offered, it is said, a dukedom without revenue instead: it was refused, total neglect followed, and the faithful man died absolutely destitute—even starved. Now a descendant of the ungrateful dissolute monarch, whose merry life made others so sad, was united to a descendant of the despoiled lord, and they and their children were to struggle with poverty. Had the confiscated lands been restored the Napier inheritance would have been vast; for the lost estate is said to have comprised all the ground covered by the new town of Edinburgh up to the tower of Merchiston.

As a child Charles Napier was demure and thoughtful, and his expressions generally had a touch of greatness: thus, when only ten years of age he rejoiced to find he was short-sighted, because a portrait of Frederick the Great hanging in his father's room had strange eyes; and because Plutarch said, Philip, Sertorius, and Hannibal, were one-eyed, and Alexander's eyes of different colours: he even wished to lose one of his own as the token of a great general; unknowing then that none of God's gifts can be lost with satisfaction. But a longing for fame was with him a master passion, and in his childhood, he looked to war for it, with an intense eagerness: yet nothing savage ever entered his mind, his compassionate sensibility was that of a girl; it was displayed early and continued till death.

When he could but just speak, hearing for the first time the caw of a single crow, probably a melancholy one which infancy could detect, he stretched forth his little hands, and weeping exclaimed with broken infantine accents *What matta poor bird? what matta?* And only by repeated assurances that the bird was not unhappy could he be pacified.

Danger he sought as conducing to reputation, but indifference to it was not, as supposed, any part of his temperament, he was of very sensitive fibre; yet with astonishing force of will he could always call up daring and fortitude to overbear natural timidity. Unlucky as to accidents, they beset him from childhood to latest age, he was never deterred thereby from striving in all perilous feats of youth, in youth, and daring actions becoming age, in age. Once, in leaping, he struck his leg against a roughly-revetted bank with such force as to tear the flesh from the bone in a frightful manner; he was but ten years old and the wound was alarming, yet he sustained the pain and fear with a spirit that excited the admiration of stern men.

His moral resolution was very early shown. A wandering showman, a wild-looking creature, short of stature but huge of limb, half naked, with thick matted red hair and beard, and a thundering voice, was displaying his powers on the Esplanade at Castletown. A crowd of people gathered, and, after some minor displays, the man, balancing a ladder on his chin, invited, or rather, with menacing tones ordered a sweep to mount and sit on the top, but the boy shrunk in fear from the shouting gesticulating ogre. Charles Napier, then six years old, was asked by his father if he would venture? Silent for a moment he seemed to fear, but suddenly looking up said yes, and was borne aloft amidst the cheers of the spectators.

Again: at ten years of age, having caught a fish when angling, he was surprised by the descent of a half-tamed eagle of great size and fierceness, which floating down from a tree settled upon his shoulders, covered him with its huge dark wings, and took the fish out of his hands. Far from being frightened he pursued his sport, and on catching another fish held it up, inviting the eagle to try again, at the same time menacing the formidable bird with the spear end of the rod. Plutarch would have drawn an omen from such an event.

About this time, he was taken to the Hot Wells of Bristol, where Mr. Sheridan, being acquainted with his father took much notice of the boy and once offered him a present of money, which was instantly rejected.

Papa told me never to take money, and I will not have yours: but I thank you.

Sheridan was surprised, and rather characteristically said to the father "Your boy is a fine fellow but very wonderful."

In 1794 Charles Napier obtained a commission in the Duke of Wellington's regiment, the 33rd, but was soon transferred to the 89th, then forming part of an army assembling at Netley camp under Lord Moira. His father was assistant quarter-master general to that force, and the boy was taken there: thus, without joining his regiment he was early initiated in the ways of soldiers, by which his natural genius for war was quickened. When the camp broke up for foreign service he was sent back to Ireland, and exchanged into the 4th Regiment, but instead of joining was placed with his brother as day scholar at a large seminary in Celbridge.

At this school he was noted for a gentle but grave demeanour, as if he felt that he was an officer not a schoolboy, and he was very sensitive to wrong or insult. His master, a passionate ill-judging man, once struck him, and unjustly, whereupon he retired into a dark closet of the school-room used for holding cloaks, and remained there weeping with shame and anger for hours: nor did he recover serenity for a week. This keen sense of wrong was deeply infixed, and was a result not of selfish pride, but love of justice, being as easily excited by wrong to others. He never quarrelled or fought, but soon the quiet reserved boy, who seemed to shrink from rough fellowship, displayed his commanding character.

Ireland was then seething in the heat of coming insurrection, yeomanry corps were generally being formed, and suddenly Charles Napier proposed to organise his schoolfellows as a volunteer corps. His father hesitated, yet finally assented to the trial, pleased and surprised at the boldness of the proposal; which was indeed no ordinary one, for nearly all the scholars were of Catholic families, neither rich nor zealous in support of a government which reviled their religion, and oppressed them with class legislation. Such a mask of loyalty was however a safeguard, and young Charles, through the sons, persuaded the fathers. Soon, under his organisation, were provided by the parents, without an exception, uniforms, colours, drums and wooden fusils having bayonets well hardened, weighty weapons and formidable if well wielded. But then arose a party desirous to give the command to John Judge, a boy destined for the priesthood and in every way a formidable rival. He was older, stronger, more learned than Charles; he was the best fighter, the most accomplished in all games, and moreover a vigilant generous protector of the weak against the strong; but he was also a well-judging generous lad, and instantly suppressing the agitation, avowed his inferior military knowledge and claimed only to carry the colours.

There was in the vicinity, some two miles off, another seminary called St. Wulstans, of higher pretensions as to learning and gentility, and essentially Protestant, as that of Celbridge was Catholic. It was situated in a fine park, bounded on one side by the Liffey, on all others by a high wall under which run the high road. Hither Charles Napier, mounted on a little Arabian mare, which he rode well, led the Celbridge volunteers one evening, meaning no offence, but simply as a common march. The St. Wulstan boys swarmed on the wall, which could be easily scaled from the inside though not from the road: at first, they looked with curiosity, but soon with anger, scoffing and hooting; shouts of defiance were returned, and then the column was pelted, to its great disadvantage: it was the entanglement of regular troops mobbed in a defile by armed peasants. The volunteers called out to storm the wall, but their young captain sternly forbad them to break the ranks, continuing the march amidst volleys of dirt.

Soon the road crossed the great gates of the park, which were suddenly thrown open, and a crowd of the irregulars rushed out, seemingly intent to close in fight. The volunteers faced to the right with levelled bayonets, and the contest would have been serious, for on each side were lads of eighteen and nineteen years of age: but then Charles Napier displayed his temper. Riding between the two bodies he told his troops that to charge unarmed boys would be cowardly, and vehemently ordered them to resume the column of march: this was effectual, for the levelled bayonets had made an impression on the others.

At another time, two of the volunteers, one Charles Napier's brother, being insubordinate under arms, were by his orders seized, tried by a drum-head court martial, and sentenced. The brother would not submit to punishment, and the stern commander ordered that he should be drummed out of the corps. This was instantly carried into execution, but in a disorderly manner, with hooting, and when the mob closed on the recusant, he suddenly whirled a large bag of marbles like a sling, cast them into the crowd, and then charging, broke the drum and forced one boy, conspicuous in insult, to a single combat: the fight was not interrupted, but he was overmatched and so badly hurt that the lookers-on withdrew him, and, as he still refused to yield, generously restored him to the ranks.

During the fight and restoration Charles Napier maintained the dignity of command unmoved; but at home, in the evening, sought with all imaginable solicitude to assuage his brother's feelings, offering him all his most cherished possessions. It was an epitome of his whole life: stern in duty, compassionate in feeling, generous in temper, in all unselfish. The control thus exercised over his schoolfellows cannot be regarded as an ordinary matter. Many of them verged on manhood, all were precocious in thought and passion, from the excitement of the times, and inimical to the government, and their real feelings may be judged from an event which happened somewhat later, when he was nearly sixteen.

Thomas Cooley, a murderer, pardoned for turning informer against the disaffected, was naturally abhorred in the place, and one morning the schoolmaster's nephew burst into the schoolroom frantically exclaiming, *Cooley's murdered, boys! Cooley's killed! Hurrah! Hurrah!* This was instantly responded to with shouts of triumph, and dancing on the tables; not because he was himself a murderer, but that he was a government spy. He had been killed in the night, and with him his mother, eighty years of age: the sight of her grey hairs dabbled in blood, had an effect on Charles Napier which he did not cast off for a long time, and it first made him deeply reflect on the consequences of civil war, which he afterwards always held in abhorrence.

Amidst terrible scenes he was nurtured: for previous to the outbreak of 1798 the soldiers were let loose to live at free quarters; the yeomanry, animated by a sectarian fanaticism, were exceedingly ferocious; and magistrates, for the most part partisans, acted with great violence and cruelty. Poor men were frequently brought into Celbridge, dead or dying of wounds, having been wantonly shot while labouring in the fields by passing soldiers or yeomen, and there was no redress. On the other hand, houses had for a long time been nightly assailed by the disaffected in search of arms, and on both sides the fiercest passions were in full play: at a later period, the government twice ordered the burning of Celbridge, and each time it was saved by the elder Napier's energy.

Here let the heroism of Susan Frost, a Suffolk woman, be recorded. She had saved Charles Napier when he was an infant from a vile murderous nurse, and ever after watched over him with inexpressible affection; instilling lessons however in her broad Doric that would have been applauded at Sparta. During a visit of the family to England, she had been left with some of the youngest children in Celbridge, at the time when gentlemen's mansions were constantly assailed, as before said, for arms. Celbridge House contained many, and one night was surrounded by several hundred Defenders—such was the name they went by then. They expected no resistance from a few maid servants and an aged serving man; yet the house was strong, and the old man, Lauchlin Moore, acting under the imperative Susan Frost, defied them.

Gathering the children in one room, she stood at the door outside, armed with pistols, while Lauchlin shouted out refusals to the savage cries for arms, and threats of death if they were withheld. Passing from room to room on the watch, he was constantly fired at when he crossed a window, but was inflexible to their menaces, and a deep stone area served as a protecting ditch to the lower apartments: the Defenders then procured a beam, and began to batter the hall door, whereupon Lauchlin more than once proposed to deliver the arms, but always Susan cried 'No! no! never! never! Let them take what they can, I will not give.' The firing was constant, the windows were all shattered with bullets, the massive door was yielding, and with shouts the assailants were pressing the assault: all seemed lost, when suddenly the tumult ceased, and the Defenders went off.

This was owing to Susan's generalship. On the first alarm, she had dispatched a maid servant by a back way to Castleton House, about a mile distant; and though Mr. Conolly's family was also in England, the bailiff, Sergeant Crask, a fine resolute clever old soldier, who had served at the siege of Gibraltar and in America, immediately armed a dozen of servants and came so unexpectedly and skilfully on the flank of the Defenders as to scare them, notwithstanding their numbers.

Susan Frost was a woman of wonderful spirit and strong natural sense, full of noble sentiments, compassionate and charitable, but passionate and vehemently eloquent in a rough way: she was just fitted to fashion a child of high aspirations into a hero. Nor was Lauchlin Moore a bad coadjutor. Warm-hearted and impetuous, he poured forth his feelings with a fervid eloquence, strange tones, and stirring action, that was very impressive, though sometimes bordering on the ludicrous, and interspersed with deep saws, such as, that it was death by the law to stop a cannon ball on its road! with other wise sayings of that nature, ending always like an Eastern with, Glory be to God! however misappropriate to what went before. He knew the ancient legends of Ireland also, was a good horseman, and a brave old fellow with a loving heart, and always sought to nourish magnanimous feelings.

When the insurrection of 1798 broke out, many families took refuge in Dublin. The elder Napier would not do so. In that time of trouble and terror he fortified his house, armed his five sons, and offered an asylum to all who were willing to resist the insurgents. About a dozen came, and with them he long awaited an attack, which was often menaced, yet never made, although an insurgent camp too strong to be meddled with by any military force available at the time, was but a few miles off. Finally, he removed to Castletown, where a company of the Derry Militia, of which Mr. Conolly was colonel, soon arrived to reinforce the irregular garrison. The elder Napier was, from his kinship and knowledge of war, virtually accepted as the commander of all, and frequently scoured the country, Charles Napier being always at his side.

One very dark night they came suddenly upon an armed body; both sides halted, and a fight seemed impending; but, suspecting the truth, Colonel Napier instantly gave a loud military order as a test, and a cry of recognition was heard: the grenadiers of the Cork Militia were in front! At that moment the moon shone out, and Charles Napier, very diminutive for his age, was seen with his small fusil charging bayonets in opposition to Tim Sullivan, the biggest man of the Cork Militia. Tim looked down in astonishment an instant, and then catching his small foe up in his arms kissed him.

After this adventure, the grenadiers garrisoned Celbridge, and Tim Sullivan especially patronised his *inimy* as he called Charles, always swelling out his own gigantic proportions when he pronounced the word. The officers were Captain Rowland and Lieutenant Hewitt, men of steady loyalty but incapable of perpetrating or suffering their men to inflict the slightest wrong on poor people; they were, therefore, well esteemed in the place; but their military position was perilous, having with eighty undisciplined soldiers, themselves inexperienced, to hold and defend a town, small indeed but generally disaffected. Colonel Napier offered his counsel, which was accepted, and he immediately constructed some field works with such skilful adaptation to the locality, that eight thousand insurgents in the vicinity never dared a trial beyond some firing at the out-sentries.

When frequent defeats had abated the insurrection. Lord Camden was replaced as lord-lieutenant by Lord Cornwallis, of whom Napoleon said, that a dozen men so honest would redeem a whole nation. He repressed the ferocity of the domineering Orange faction, and calmed the general commotion; but there remained of course many high-spirited outlaws, and around Celbridge roved one of local celebrity, Tarrant the Robber, He was a strong courageous man, and withal a generous fellow in his way, feared indeed, yet not disliked.

Several attempts to capture him failed, and Colonel Napier, although not a magistrate—he would not be one in those days of violence when justice was the last thing thought of on the bench—often sought to encounter him, having Charles Napier as usual by his side. He also failed, but Tarrant was so pressed as to surrender, on condition of voluntary exile, and said, circumstances corroborating his assertion, that he had more than once from different lairs covered both father and son with a blunderbuss, yet would not fire from pity for the boy: he was a rebel, not a villain, a robber only from necessity.

Such were some of the leading events of Charles Napier's early life, recorded to show how the germ of his great character was precociously quickened; but henceforth the gradual expansion of his mind shall be developed by himself; for so constant was his correspondence, so frank, so copious his journals and private notes, that his story can be told almost as an autobiography. His first letter, extant, tells of an amusing village romance, as cleverly managed, if not so poetically told, as that of young Lochinvar. He had been temporarily left in charge of his father's house, and thus wrote.

February, 1799.—We are all well, and have not been molested: the arms are perfectly clean, and I will send them to Castletown tomorrow, but could not hear of soldiers going before. Val Dunne is married to Nichol's daughter and the particulars are diverting. Lumley the stocking-weaver was to have been the husband, and went according to arrangement to wait at the parson's house for his bride, Val having undertaken to hand her down the street in due form: but at the bridge he had a chaise in waiting, and into it miss and her gallant stepped and drove to Dublin, where by another parson they were married.

Of the people involved in this tale, the father was a gigantic blacksmith, rich, and with burley notions, corresponding to his purse and large proportions of body: he wanted to force his pretty daughter into marriage with the pale-faced sneaking suitor who was thus baffled. Val Dunne was a bold handsome carpenter, having some right, it was

15

whispered, to be called captain when pikes were numerous: he was the wild flower of a family noted for strength and comeliness, yet more so for the wonderful age and awful appearance of a great grandmother. She by her own reckoning was one hundred and thirty-five years old! but the scenes she had witnessed, if her recollections were as accurate as her descriptions were vivid, would prove her to have been more than one hundred and forty-five! She said the Irish massacre was spoken of as a recent event in her childhood; and that Cromwell's warfare was going on when she was able to speak and understand.

To sit in the sun at her porch was what Molly Dunne loved; and an awful weird-looking woman she was: a Michael-Angelo model for the witch of Endor. Large, gaunt, tall, and with high sharp lineaments, leaning on an antique staff, her head bending beneath a cowled Irish cloak of deep blue, her eyes fixed in their huge orbs, and her tongue discoursing of bloody times, she was wondrous for the young and fearful for the aged. The departure of the Lord Dangan for the battle of the Boyne was her favourite theme. How he, beautiful and brave, rode forth at the head of his tenantry from Celbridge, then called Kildroched; how nobly he was furnished with burnished breast-plate and waving plumes; and how he was brought back a bloody corse, by the few surviving men of his band. She was indeed a woman of awful age and recollections.

Educated amidst such scenes and such people, Charles Napier's mind had been early and sternly awakened to questions of war and government, not by books but realities, when in 1799 he entered public life as *aide-de-camp* to Sir James Duff, commanding the Limerick district. His military ardour was then high and strong, he looked forward to battle and fame, and his entrance into public life was without alloy; for Sir James transferred an old friendship for the father to the son, and Lady Duff became a second mother to him; both being attracted by the combination of simplicity and gentleness with humour and enthusiasm in his temperament. He was soon joined by his brother George, a lieutenant in the 46th Regiment; and for some time all went on agreeably; but, always unlucky as to accidents, Charles, when out shooting broke his leg, and so badly that for some time life as well as limb were in peril: yet he would not let his state be made known to his family until the danger was passed; and the following account, written in aftertimes, displays the vigour of his character.

When seventeen I broke my right leg. At the instant there was no pain, but looking down I saw my foot under my knee, and the bones protruding; that turned me sick, and the pain became violent. My gun, a gift from my dear father, was in a ditch, leaping over which had caused the accident; I scrambled near enough to get it out, but this lacerated the flesh and produced much extravasated blood. George came to me; he was greatly alarmed, for I was very pale, and we were both young, he but fifteen.

Then came Captain Crawford of the Irish artillery, and I made him hold my foot while I pulled up my knee, and in that manner set my leg myself. The quantity of extravasated blood led the doctors to tell me my leg must come off, but they gave me another day for a chance. Being young, and vain of good legs, the idea of *hop and go* one, with a *timber toe*, made me resolve to put myself to death rather than submit to amputation, and I sent the maid out for laudanum, which I hid under my pillow: luckily the doctors found me better, and so saved me from a contemptible action. Perhaps if it had come to the point I might have had more sense and less courage than I gave myself credit for in the horror of my first thoughts; indeed, my agony was great, and strong doses of the laudanum were necessary to keep down the terrible spasms which fractures of large bones produce.

The doctors set my leg crooked, and at the end of a month, when standing up, my feet would not go together: one leg went in pleasant harmony with the other half way between knee and ankle, but then flew off in a huff, at a tangent. This made me very unhappy, and the doctors said, if I could hear the pain they would break it again, or bend it straight. My answer was I will bear anything but a crooked leg. Here then was I, at seventeen, desperately in love with a Miss Massey, having a game leg in prospective, and in love with my leg also: so, I said to the leg carpenter. Let me have one night for consideration.

All that day and night were Miss Massey's pretty eyes before mine, but not soft and tale-telling; not saying *Pig will you marry me*, but scornfully squinting at my game leg. There was Miss Massey, and there was I unable to do anything but hop. The *per contra* were two ill-looking doctors torturing me, and the reflection that they might again make a crooked job after the second fracture, as they had done after the first! However, my dear Miss Massey's eyes carried the day, and just as I had decided, she and her friend. Miss Vandeleur, came in the dusk, wrapped up in men's great coats to call on me: this was just like the pluck of a pretty Irish girl, and quite repaid my courageous resolve: I would have broken all my bones for her.

So, after letting me kiss their hands, off my fair *incognitas* went, leaving me the happiest of lame dogs. The night passed with many a queer feel, about the doctors coming like devil imps to torture me. Be quick, quoth I as they entered, make the most of my courage while it lasts. It took all that day, and part of next to bend the leg with bandages, which were tied to a wooden bar, and tightened every hour day and night; I fainted several times; and when the two tormentors arrived next day, after breakfast, struck my flag, saying Take away your bandages for I can bear no more. They were taken off and I felt in heaven. Not the less so that the leg was straight! and it is now as straight a one, I flatter myself, as ever "bore up the body of a gentleman or kicked a blackguard.

There was in Limerick a great coarse woman, wife of Dr. ———. When she heard of my misfortune she said Poor boy I suppose a fly kicked his spindle shanks. Being a little fellow then, though now, be it known, five feet seven inches and a-half high, this offended me greatly; and as the Lord would have it, she broke her own leg just as I was getting well. Going to her house with an appearance of concern, I told the servant how sorry I was to hear that a bullock had kicked Mrs. ——— and hurt its leg very much, and that I had called to know if her leg was also hurt. She never forgave me.

Soon after his cure, Charles rode from Limerick to Dublin, a hundred and ten miles, on one horse, between sunrise and sunset. This animal, called from his symmetry *Models* was the counterpart of his rider; for he also had broken his leg in training, and though a very little fellow, was brim-full of spirit and endurance: neither horse nor horseman complained of fatigue. Such he was even then, and his letters from Limerick shall now display the strange customs of the day, the freedom of intercourse between him and his father, and the sentiments of justice and honour which governed his ambition, even at that age.

I dine with Sir J. Duff today, so you see I must be very well. The doctors tell me, that if the blood collected at the place where the bone was broken had not dispersed, my leg must have been cut off; or if it had been saved I should not have been able to walk for several years, and never as well as before. You need not dear father tell this to mama or anybody, but my escape was miraculous: the smaller bone was broken much lower than the shin bone. There was a duel fought here today, between a Clare man, whom I know very well, and an officer of the 89th Regiment. There were certainly three or four thousand people looking on, and the officer told me, that if the word had not been given too quick, he would have shot the other dead.

I am exceedingly obliged to Colonel Clavering, and to you, for the compliments at the end of my mother's letter. Certainly, I should like very much to get a company in Colonel Clavering's Fencibles, if it neither stopped my promotion in the line, nor took me from Sir J. Duff, except to go abroad; nor put a stop to the promotion of the lieutenants of the regiment, which would be unfair. I have just heard that a new expedition is talked of in England, I must contrive to go.

His brother William obtained a commission this year, and in the latter end of it he was himself appointed to a lieutenancy in the 95th or Rifle Corps, which was being formed by a selection of men and officers throughout the army: for this he willingly resigned his staff situation, to which his brother George succeeded. When preparing to join he discovered a kind, but to him offensive solicitude on the part of his general, which he thus fiercely repelled.

December, 1800.—Douglas, my brother *aide-de-camp*, told me yesterday evening, that he heard Sir James read to Lady Duff the letter he wrote to you, advising you to get me leave of absence from the Duke of York, on the plea that I was not fit for duty. I am sure you will never consent to do anything of the sort, which you must think, and which you may be certain I think, would be disgraceful and unbecoming the character of a British soldier. Sir James would not have done such a thing for himself, and could not have considered much when he proposed it for me.

His departure from Limerick terminated what may be called the first epoch of his life, for his entrance into Sir James Duff's family was but a change of home, so kind and considerate was the reception he met with there.

CHAPTER 2

The Rifle Corps

The Rifle Corps was organised at Blatchington by Colonel Maningham. Under him were the Hon. Wm. Stewart, and Major Callendar, the latter a distant cousin of Charles Napier, who now found that the greatest secret of war is discipline, and never forgot it: he discovered also that to know soldiers requires experience, and that it is a most important part of war. His captain, Cameron, scarcely older than himself, became his friend, for accordance of opinions soon opens the heart of youth, and his new life was agreeable, but his letters for the first six months are lost. Those which followed indicate a mind uneasy under a monotonous discipline, after the stirring scenes of his childhood.

Here be it noted also, that the manners of the time were coarse, especially in Ireland, where the loyal, such was the phrase, like the cavaliers of old, adopted obscenity, drinking, oaths and long hair as badges of their politics. Now Charles Napier was abstemious in the extreme, proud to his last days that he had never fought a duel, gambled, or been intoxicated; but to avoid a habit of swearing when more oaths than other words were used in society was difficult, and at times his letters shew this more than good taste will approve.

In September, the Rifle Corps marched to Weymouth, and he commenced a correspondence with his mother, which never slackened until ended by her death.

Weymouth.—Colonel Stewart employs me as an engineer, and we are going to have a sham fight for the king. Callendar is to get a lieutenant-colonelcy out of the regiment: he is on leave now, and has ordered his horse to be sold. Much as I admire Colonel Stewart, if service was in question it would please me more to be under Geordie Callendar than him; for I see he has not Callendar's abilities, though more of a dashing, showy man. If they drew together we should probably be the best regiment in the service; but unless Callendar were senior, that cannot be, for he will not bear control from anyone he has not a high opinion of, and Stewart makes it a rule to strike at the heads. With him the field officers must first be steady, and then he goes downwards: hence the privates say. We had better look sharp if he is so strict with the officers.

This view of Stewart's abilities was afterwards justified in Egypt, at Albuera, and at Maya, for at all three, he, though one of the most gallant soldiers that ever wore the British uniform, failed from fiery zeal overlaying judgment.

Southampton, Oct.—After a march of 25 miles I came on here, in my way to Goodwood, to see my dear sister Emily, and have only to tell you I am just out of a very foolish quarrel, having been obliged to send a challenge, which was accepted, but the king's being at Weymouth prevented an immediate meeting. We were irritated, and never thought of that, but the other officers stopped us, to avoid ruin for principals and seconds. We then agreed to be quiet until his departure, which happened yesterday, and our arrangements were then made: but again, the officers interfered, saying we were both passionate and wrong, and must shake hands. We were uneasy, thinking it might appear shyness, yet thinking likewise it would be foolish to oppose the opinions of all our brother officers; and still more foolish to knock one another over: this last, between you and I was of weight, and we shook hands.

Blatchington, Oct.—Your letter, dearest mother, surprised me by supposing a wish to keep the foolish quarrel a secret from my father: by no means. But no more of this; it is hateful to think how near foolish passion was involving me in a desperate duel."

The peace of Amiens, now being negotiated, alarmed him for his future destiny.

About this peace! As charming for England as it is ruinous for her soldiers. What can one do? My plan is to wait for a few months, and see what powers continue at war; then exchange with George to half-pay, and get into some foreign service. As to remaining an English full-pay lieutenant for ten or twelve years! Not for the universe! Sometimes my thought is to sell my commission and purchase one in Germany or elsewhere: but my secret wish cannot be fulfilled, which is to have high command with British soldiers. Rather let me command Esquimauxs than be a subaltern of Rifles forty years old!

October.—A pretty message the Comptroller—(his father was Comptroller of Army Accounts Ireland)—sends me, he was a subaltern at twenty-seven. He must be content with my being one nine years before nineteen, instead of after. Had he been in Germany he would probably have been something better than a brevet colonel: it would be a good thing to get on half-pay, and go to Germany for six months, where I could learn more than by mounting guard here. Colonel Stewart wants me to go to General Jarry's school; saying he would get me leave, though only granted to captains and field officers. I would rather get six months' leave, as the only way of learning our profession is to have French and drawing masters; and a good officer to ask questions of in explanation of difficulties. Now masters are to be got in Dublin as good as at Wycombe: and the Comptroller can give me as good, probably a great deal better instruction than an old foreign lieutenant-general, who would not have been here, if he is such an excellent officer.

This judgment was sound: The High Wycombe teaching at that time, more than verged on the ridiculous. One of the students, being invited by Sir John Moore at Shorn Cliff to move his brigade as a test of his acquirements, coolly answered that he had not been taught to direct less than one hundred thousand men!

November.—What gives you the least hope, dearest mother, that Cameron can be a major, or I a captain, for 30 years if there is peace, or for six if war? Poor Cameron! he has had some news which makes him very low indeed, and vexes me: he will not own that he is grieved but it is too plain. Joy dearest mother! A secret you must not tell to any, the Comptroller excepted, for none of my secrets are ever to be kept from him. Cameron will purchase; and no captain above him can: he is going to persuade his guardians to advance the money. His spirits are rising; so are mine, at seeing him going to Scotland for money to purchase, instead of wandering here in grief. I am just now, myself, absolutely dressing for a third ball since being here! Do you think of sending me a strait waistcoat? My leave of absence

22

will come in two months. Shall it be spent in Dublin? Or three months in France, and then getting it renewed for four months in Germany? It will be easy to live abroad on my pay. Sometimes I think of going to Dieppe for three months, and then to Sackville Street to see you, come home to Blatchington, marry, and tell my father-in-law and children, forty years hence, confounding lies of my doings, as a full-pay Rifle lieutenant. How the 'Old lieutenant' sticks in my gizzard! Colonel Stewart says I ought to insist on the Prince of Wales giving me a company, or fighting me for taking the liberty of calling me Charles! Marry come up, my dirty cousin!

At present, I have so little amusement as to be tempted to buy a horse! Reading all day long tires me. I quit the mess at five o'clock, and from thence to ten o'clock gives five hours more reading. You will say, walk! There are no walks but on the Downs, and I have had six months of them, which is worse than doing nothing. There is a billiard table, but feeling a growing fondness for it, and fearing to be drawn into play for money, I have not touched a cue lately. In short, I have no reasonable amusement. Shooting was near getting me into a scrape.

Lord Gage thought we had trespassed on his manor, and wrote a letter to me and another officer which we would have resented, if, on finding himself wrong, he had not written a second and very civil one. Having government stables, the keep of a horse will not cost a great deal, and my wish is to buy Cameron's, because he can't now sell him at Lewes for his worth on account of the Dragoons' auction. When that is over I can easily sell him, and Cameron would certainly like to have fifteen guineas: to lend him that sum would be a pleasure, but he is such a fellow that, unless sadly pushed, he would not borrow even from me.

His next letter, addressed to his sister Louisa, indicates a remarkable change in his mind. What soldiers call *the mother sickness* or longing for home, now first seized him, and it will be found clinging to him during life, with a tenacity requiring all his energy to resist: the warlike man, while bearing arms in every quarter of the world never ceased to sigh for home and a mother's tenderness!

December.—I am a determined rake, in love with four misses at once! I rode across the Downs, twelve miles after dark, to dance with one of them, and then came back at daybreak. Yet would to Heaven I could get home. My prayer at night is that Buonaparte may send some thousands to Ireland, for then our regiment would go there. Make George and William say how tall they are, I am only five feet five inches and a half! However, that is taller than five or six of our officers. You write very seldom. I would give the world to see you, and shall go mad if you don't come to England, or I go to Ireland. Nobody but myself ever had such a feel for home; my heart jumps when thinking of you all together, merry in the old way.

This wishing for home makes me gad about in a wild way, for melancholy seizes me when alone in a cold barrack-room, and I cannot read with thoughts busy in Kildare Street. I should like to go to London for a fortnight and stay with Emily, but am too poor. I have no coloured clothes, and they are expensive to buy; my horse also is costly and must be sold: very sorry, for he is the dearest little wicked black devil you ever saw, and so pretty! Will the Duke of York send us to Ireland? It would set me wild, yet I am as happy with my regiment as can well be, and there are pleasant people here. Lord Gage's family are really delightful; a Mr. and Mrs. Round also are both very agreeable people, and have been very civil.

January 1st.—Happy New Year and many of them to my dearest mother. Now to ask a favour *not* to be told to dad, unless you think there will be no inconvenience to him. Cameron has been in a very disagreeable situation for some time about family affairs. Several things have happened to put him to enormous expense, and he intends borrowing money from the Jews, which must do him much mischief in the end, though he will have a very good property when of age. His guardians are angry, and used him ill because he kicked against their wishes, and they will not, it is to be feared, even advance money to purchase his majority.

Now if my father has not drawn the £100 of forage money belonging to me, which Armitt has had these eight months,—to repay the money you advanced; can he spare it for Cameron? I am sure he would soon repay it. If you think the Comptroller can do it conveniently I would be rejoiced; but if the contrary say nothing about it, as Cameron has not the least idea of the matter; and it is only to save him from having to do with those

Jews, who may ruin him. You know the Comptroller as well as I do, and if you shewed him the letter at once, he would do the thing at once to oblige me, when perhaps it was troublesome. Pray give me your opinion, as things will soon happen to Cameron which fix his happiness or misery for the rest of his life, poor fellow!

January.—So sorry dearest Louisa was I for poor 1801, as not to be able to eat my dinner. I do so hate new years, and love old ones. It is not so for new faces, for I am most wickedly in love, and have been at another Lewes ball to dance with the Miss Gages again. It is one of them, the second, that I am in love with. She is not a famous beauty, but one of the handsomest women ever seen. Beautiful figure, and that majestic appearance Lady Duff has, only with more of it to those she don't like: she takes fancies to some people and dislikes to others, and gives such repulses to forward gentry they don't know which way to stare, while she looks so wicked and haughty. Her eyes are beautiful. She is to me the most charming creature ever beheld. If she was not going to London my longing after leave of absence would be almost forgotten. I am more in love with Miss Gage even than *Giuli*; for I think of nothing else, and hate any kind of company where she is not. Pray ask me five hundred questions about her, or you will get no answers to your letters. I am devilish cunning, having persuaded Callendar to ride to Lord Gage's to wait on him, with me, by which she will be seen. This visit is my only thought; and my hope is that Lord Gage will persuade Callendar to dine. At any rate, they are going to another ball, and Lord Gage asked me to sleep at Firle Place as it is close to Lewes; so, I shall see her twice before the 12th and then we must of course call on them afterwards, which will be three times!

January.—To see you all would make me quite mad, being now half so, at being disappointed of my leave; but I dare not trust myself to think; the thought of not seeing you all makes me really sick, and it will not go out of my head that I shall never see you again. Tell mother not to be disturbed at my yesterday's letter, having really worked myself to madness I knew not what I said. In short, I am miserable, and nothing can make me happy but seeing you all: less unhappy though, since falling so in love with that beautiful Miss Gage. Don't laugh: this is not joking but wretchedness. I read at least twenty books, and write three or four letters in five minutes; that is, the books are opened and then shut, and the letters begun and then burned: then I begin thinking of you all, sometimes of Miss Gage though, with my head in the grate, until I entirely stupefy myself.

Notwithstanding this childlike simplicity of feeling and expression, he was able to meet and repel with the austerity of a philosopher the temptations of London, where he now went to see his sister Emily and Lady Louisa Conolly.

March.—My father being so well makes me very happy. I went to a few parties with Emily, but have gone to none since, being unwell; nor have I danced, lest it should make me ill again. Once only have I been at the Opera, never at the play, and I do not mean to go, not being able to afford it. No sights either, except the Shakespeare Gallery, the Historical Gallery, and a picture of Sir Ralph Abercrombie's death, the whole at a cost of only five shillings, which is not any vast expense. London is for me very disagreeable. Lady Galloway told me she had a letter from Lady Charlotte Crofton, who said she had seen you, with some fine speech, to be forgotten. Colonel Stewart has been kind beyond measure, and introduced me to his mother: your saying how much obliged I am will please him.

I really do like him exceedingly, and if he was properly trained he would be a very good officer; but he is flattered instead of being taught, and does foolish things in command. To do him justice he has none of the haughtiness which other Colonel Stewarts have, and to me is like a brother, except when commanding officer! He has begged me to breakfast with him every morning, and stay all the forenoon, saying. You know it is the devil to be made a fag for our sisters. As to seeing the Duff's, consider, one cannot here go to them at their breakfast, or after dinner, as at their own house: Lord Fife would be discomposed; my one invitation came from him, to meet Sir James Duff. Lord Fife talked a great deal of you, and my father of whom he thus speaks, *Poor dear Napier, blast him! he liked dried cod fish, I'll send him some in a frank!*

As to my old acquaintances: D—— is as friendly as possible and very pleasant, sensible, and perhaps clever; but illness prevents my seeing enough of him to judge. C—— is a very fine gentleman, and not at all handsome, having lost all his blooming complexion and fine hair; he is now a *minikin pale doll*, with his hair powdered, and a cocked hat, &c. F—— is a conceited fine gentleman, a great beau, good-natured, stupid, pert enough, and with very bad manners; wears boots with heels six inches high to make himself look tall!

The military college is worth going to, but not without being a good draughtsman, and speaking French perfectly, as the lectures are in that language. My hope is to master both in three months at Dublin, and then go, as it gives one a name, and makes people think a stupid dog a great officer. Colonel Stewart asked me today if that old uncle the duke would not purchase me a company? My reply was—could not tell, because I never asked him.

So dear, dearest mother, you think your letters bore me! Never half so happy as when pacquets of them come to read, instead of stupid books! I hate paying visits, am not fond of parties, never liked the Opera, can't afford the play, and could not stand London a week longer, if aunt and Emily were not here. The Duffs, Johnstones, Lady Castlereagh, and the Gages, are the only people to regret in leaving London. I dined with Lord Galloway, and liked them all: the girls are very pleasant, and Lady Sophia very pretty. My journey to Ireland is settled for Monday. At Lady Derby's party last night.

His mastery over his passions was shewn in these letters, for beneath the austerity displayed were impulses for pleasure strong as those which afterwards urged him to battle; his temperament was indeed vehement for all things, and he was a passionate admirer of women: but every feeling save love for his mother, was suppressed when not conducive to honest fame. The times were however favourable for the formation of stern character. Napoleon's terrible genius, menacing England with destruction, made young men think very differently from what they do in pleasure-seeking literary times.

His leave of absence was soon changed to a recruiting mission in Ireland, and that brought down on him the first of a series of unjust reprimands which he was fated through life to receive and to resist—never from any man of genius however. On this occasion, his resistance was very bold, as being by a subaltern, under twenty, to a favourite court general, Maningham, immediately about the sovereign's person, at a time when the Duke of York's imperious, and not always discriminating despotism, made the boldest tremble even in defence. Nothing disagreeable followed, and soon afterwards he rejoined his regiment at Shorne Cliff, but found it no longer an agreeable home. The best officers were away, and as happens in most newly-organised societies, some men of offensive habits and manners had taken a lead. General Maningham was seldom with the regiment, and William Stewart was become so inflated with false notions of command, as entirely to change Charles Napier's feelings towards him.

In the British Army, the regimental mind is subject to perturbations, and disposed to exaggeration both in praise and blame of commanding officers; but Stewart's uncalculating zeal may be measured thus. He ordered that all the Martello towers on the beach should be visited a certain number of times, day and night, by the subaltern on duty. Napier was the first to report. "How is this. Sir? not a quarter of the duty performed!" "It was impossible." "That word is not in the military dictionary." "But in arithmetic, colonel it is, to walk forty-five miles along a beach mid-leg deep with shingle!"

Shorn Cliff, December.—Very anxious dear mother to get away from here. I am reading Sir Robert Wilson's Egyptian Expedition. It is not well written, and seems incorrect as to names: the style is altogether bad, the plans very bad, and on too small a scale. Major Birch's are superior to any others; Captain Boordwyne showed them to me, and Birch explained them. Wilson abuses Buonaparte in the most unmitigated manner; and if what he says be true, Buonaparte must be the greatest ruffian on earth: but I can hardly credit all he says. (Sir Robert in after life admitted that he had been misled.) Ask my father if he thinks this book of Wilson's well written? there might have been better plans at least: and there was no great occasion to puff Sir Sydney Smith so violently. He harps on General Regnier abusing the English, yet in the same page scolds the French, like Susan Frost with the maids, when they call forth her delicate phrases in anger.

We are going on here as badly as need be. Two or three men desert almost every night, and not recruits either: the hospital is full of rheumatic patients, and men with colds, and coughs, caught from standing long on damp ground, and being kept in mizzling rains for hours without moving. Stewart is however killing himself as well as us, and the toss up is who will go first. I am trying my luck in the lottery—a Napier seeking luck! I begin to have a sane idea that I am mad.

Stewart and I have had a rumpus this morning. He came from headquarters to the fort of Moncrief, to inspect the arms; all the rifles had been reckoned by me, but as he seldom reckons the swords they were trusted to the sergeant; with a knowledge, however, that they were all complete. This was a very foolish thing to do with such a commander, and when one or two swords were not forthcoming, Stewart, without giving me or the sergeant an instant to recollect or inquire, got into a furious passion, bolted from the room and went straight out of the fort. I took no notice of him, neither following him, nor speaking a word to appease him; but we found immediately afterwards, that two men had gone from the room with their swords on, which accounted for the deficiency. Then the quarter-master followed Stewart and told him the fact. I would not.

The pay-sergeant also followed him, but Stewart said:—'Get home sir, and tell Mr. Napier that I'll make him march with his arms to headquarters, and will give out an order directly about it.' I knew he would be quite savage at me for not following him to explain, and for that very reason I would not do so. He got the worst of it however, for it began snowing very hard, and if he had been *asy* he would have got a dinner, as he expected; but I did not even ask him into my room, and he had a pleasant walk of ten miles in a snowstorm. He will probably give out a flourishing order tomorrow for which I care about as much as for this exhibition.

Write often to me, for though living alone is to my taste, want of society is apt to make me low-spirited. Stewart was here yesterday, and seems to think I shall be able to hold a staff situation and remain in the regiment. We are quite gracious at present to see: you would think we were brothers! What hypocrisy there is in the behaviour of men. However, now that I am not furious, let me confess his faults to arise from having much passion, much zeal, and not the least judgment. He is open-hearted and honourable in the greatest degree; but those qualities are nothing to those who serve under him, and therefore the sooner I get out of his hands the better.

March 3rd.—My letter has been delayed because a swelled jaw and mouth kept me awake for three nights, and stopped my writing, reading, eating, talking: everything but cursing and swearing. This I should not have been guilty of if married; for you know what Job's wife said to Job, and his answer: all owing to the spirit of contradiction, not to patience: had he been a bachelor he would have sworn like a trooper. *Adieu.*

He had now a promise from his cousin, General Fox, then going as commander in chief to Ireland, to take him on his staff; and as the hollow truce, called the peace of Amiens, was evidently approaching its termination, the plans for continental service and study vanished: meanwhile sickness again assailed him.

April 3rd.—Been confined to bed for four or five days with a fever, but pretty well again, though weak and with a violent headache, the remains of the illness. Twenty of my men are down with it in this fort alone: our surgeon cures me with James' powders and oranges, and I shall be well tomorrow they say: if so, well and good, but giddiness and headache remain.

4th.—Quite well today dearest mother, but weak: however Colonel Beckwith has some excellent madeira, and promises me a bottle. Lord Mark Kerr tells George, that the Duke of Leinster says I am on General Fox's staff, yet it is in my head that it will not be: this would be immaterial if it was not so near you; but that would make it a vexation not to succeed.

April 7th.—Your queries were put out of memory by illness, and my head aches now so violently that a blister is to be put behind my ear. You talk of magazines of clothes! Why I have no clothes but those on my back. I have indeed too many books, above thirty volumes: but my whole magazine, books, clothes, all go in two trunks, except my tent bed. When once out of this regiment it will not be to return, be you certain: Stewart renders it odious. As to William coming in, that can only be done through His Royal Highness; but I would not put a dog under Colonel Stewart. High Wycombe would be William's ruination; all the tricks played there have been made known to me by Neil Campbell: there are a set who keep horses, race, bet, play, everything that is bad, and learn nothing, though others do study and learn. This has taken place lately, it was not so formerly. Some of my books are in my way certainly, but cannot easily be replaced again, and parting with books is hateful to me.

London, June.—My uniform is expensive: the dress coat costs twenty guineas, exclusive of epaulettes. Nothing of mine except linen will do for an A. D. C. My pantaloons are green, and I have only one pair; my jacket twice turned! a green waistcoat— useless; one pair of boots without soles or heels; a green feather and a helmet not worth sixpence. This is the state of my Rifling kit: luckily I have credit with my tailor.

With this equipment, which was not much augmented when, in after times, he went forth to command the armies of India, he joined General Fox in Dublin, and there witnessed the rash insurrection of the generous-minded heroic Emmett. No letters exist to display Charles Napier's feelings on that occasion, for he was at home: but the murders which accompanied the outbreak, and the executions which followed, augmented his already deep abhorrence of civil strife. The vengeance of power on that occasion shocked him: it was accounted moderate, even mild at the time, yet the following extract from Mrs. Fox's journal will give another meaning to the words.

We passed the gibbet in Thomas Street, which is now fixed there, with a rope suspended, and two sentries to guard it; for so many of the rebels are now executed it is in daily use. What a horrible state for a country to be in!

Soon arose disputes between General Fox and the Irish government, and, following the invariable rule where military men and civilians differ, the general was misrepresented, ill-used, and recalled. He was however appointed to the London district, being too powerful in parliamentary friends, and the personal favour of the king, to be crushed: his staff accompanied him.

Here the second epoch of Charles Napier's life must terminate. Hitherto he had been making acquaintance with the world, rather than acting in it: henceforth he will be found experiencing its enmities and iniquities, and his correspondence takes another character as his original views of life become shaken.

CHAPTER THREE

His Father's Death

The London staff baulked Charles Napier's desire for service; efforts were therefore made to obtain a company in the Royal Staff Corps of Artificers, a hybrid body, just then being organised to combine engineering with the quartermaster general's duties; and good service it did, at home and abroad, until extinguished by a silly economy. While awaiting this promotion, his London service furnished the following correspondence with his mother.

December.—The Duke of Richmond not in town; Sir J. Duff not in town; Charles Fox not in town: there my enquiries stopped until my own concern was settled and a fine one it is. My lodgings cost a guinea and a half per week and my allowance is but a guinea! We are to have dragoons and horse artillery out on Saturday, for the inspection of his Excellency Mahomet Elphi Bey, and his Mamelukes: I will describe them and the reception of myself. Pichegru and Dumouriez will be there, and will satisfy my optics, my admiration of them being great. My reception by the duke to be noted.

Sunday.—Saw Elphi Bey and the Dukes of York and Clarence, but was not introduced to him of York. Some of Elphi's attendants are well-looking, others the contrary: he is a tall man with a ferocious countenance, good eyes, and a hooked nose. The devil thank these Mamelukes for riding restive steeds well; and God help the poor horse! His under jaw is put through an iron ring, like a solid curb fastened to that part of the bit which touches the roof of the mouth; and from the junction there runs an iron spike into the palate, towards the teeth, when the reins are pulled, while the ring is drawn up behind against the under jaw: the poor beast's jaw may thus be broke, and his mouth cut to pieces. Their stirrups are broad knives; and as to their saddle: can they fall out of one that comes nearly up to the armpits? We slept at St. Anne's Hill, and I like Charles Fox and his wife very much.

December.—Was with Aunt Johnston today. She looks so young and well, she might really be taken for thirty! She has a very small house at Brompton on a lease, and though a long way off, my hope is to see her every day. Nothing yet about my company. If it is to be in the staff corps and forces me to quit General Fox I will make a push for High Wycombe. The understanding is that a captain of artificers may be allowed to make himself a good general in spite of God's teeth, although he must not be an *aide-decamp* in spite of the Duke of York: this is fair enough, for most of our generals are more obliged to the duke than the Deity for their military talents.

Aunt Johnston was his father's only sister, a woman of extraordinary beauty, talent and energy. She had passed great part of her life in India, was a widow, and had claims on the directors for more than three hundred thousand pounds. They refused payment and, following up the wrong, endeavoured to support dishonesty by slandering the character of her husband, who had saved their army from starvation in the field. Payment would have been an acknowledgment of misgovernment, and they were afraid to be grateful or honourable.

Hence with every legal chicane, dishonest artifice, and unscrupulous use of influence, they sought to wear out the widow's courage and resources: but they had to deal with an indomitable spirit, such a one as their successors found afterwards in her nephew. Aided gratuitously with the counsel and advocacy of Lord Erskine, she, from her poor lodging of Brompton, fought her remorseless enemies for more than twenty years, gaining decree after decree, and finally forcing them to acknowledge her husband's integrity and pay her claims: but the expenses had swallowed up nearly all the money, and, exhausted by her long struggle, she died almost immediately after victory.

A singularly interesting story would be her life, and two short anecdotes will indicate her character. Going out to India, the ship, an Indiaman, was attacked by one of Suffrien's frigates; her husband took his post at a gun, and Hester Johnston, wearing round her neck a gold case containing the heart of the great Montrose, her own heart as firm as his, kept the quarter-deck, holding the hand of her son, then five years old. To those who urged her to go below she said aloud "No wife should quit her husband in danger, here will I stay and take his chance." Soon fate vindicated the declaration: a shot splintering the deck, struck down husband, wife, and child, the two latter with severe wounds, and the gold case containing Montrose's heart was broken on her bosom: yet she would not go below!

At another time, having to take her husband, when in a fever, across the desert, she was pursued by an English enemy, not a private one, but a tool furnished with a writ of caption on a false debt, and employed to kill Mr. Johnston by taking him from the covered litter and exposing him to the sun. Hester had a guard of twelve *peons, Rajapoots*, and when the miserable villain came up they drew round her in defence, though he had two hundred. Sitting on the top of the litter, armed with pistols, she menaced whoever approached with death; and when the pretended creditor advanced, fired at him with so close an aim that he turned and fled: whereupon his *peons*, also *rajapoots*, made *salaam* with smiles, and retired. Well she knew the Eastern people, and deeply into her nephew's mind worked the stories she told of cruelty and fraud perpetrated by the Company's government in India.

Charles Napier's brothers who had been placed on half-pay at the peace were now restored to active service, George in the 52nd, William in the Blues, from which he soon exchanged into the 52nd. (*George Napier of the 52nd: Personal Recollections of Service with the Light Division During the Peninsular War Under Moore & Wellington* by George T. Napier is also published by Leonaur in book and kindle format).

December.—I told General Fox, that General Moore had got William into the 52nd, and he seemed to think the Blues would have ruined him. I would like to see my brothers, but visiting employs all my time; that however shall not continue whether it loses friends or makes enemies: rather would I be laid in the Red Sea. The expense of London is dreadful, it absorbs all my pay, and here I cannot go such a blackguard figure as in Dublin. This is exclusive of casual expenses and travelling, of which there will be a great deal; six months will destroy me; and to live in dread of tradesmen, and abominate the sight of a bill is a life not to be borne: even Stewart's despotism would be better than a tailor's!

We are going to Guilford, where there is, I hear, a fine new gaol: that is to me significant. Last night I sat up till two o'clock, writing on the old subject of grievances, and lashing myself into a fury with everything. Abusing the army, pulling off my breeches, cursing creditors, and putting out the candle all in a minute, I jumped into bed and lay there blaspheming, praying and perspiring for two hours, when sleep came. What I wrote is not worth sending however, being full of jokes, politics and blue devils. I live in fear of my creditors: but that shall not last. I will not be a tailor's slave.

December 26th.—William has recovered from his fever, and is gazetted in the 52nd; would I were in the same regiment: but no more of what you call my madness. What a curse to have a turn of mind similar to mine! Misery to oneself, and teasing to others, unless disguised, which can only be with those not really loved. Great exertion or perfect tranquillity is necessary to me, who have not that superior intellect which can regulate itself: there is more of Cassius than Brutus in me.

Three days after this letter he was gazetted, in the Staff Corps, and his feelings on the occasion, feelings which remained steadfast through life, shew how entirely events govern men against their inclinations, and will surprise those who have accepted him from his enemies, *as a man of blood, delighting in carnage!*

December 29th.—Green has offered me a thousand guineas and his company in the 67th for mine in the Staff Corps. I could get a troop of light dragoons for that sum, but would sooner go into the militia than the cavalry, light or heavy. Getting this company is like receiving an obligation from a man one wishes hanged. I was before attached to the army by five shillings and eightpence; now by fourteen and seven-pence, and the felicity of being called captain. It is not my meaning that General Fox should be hanged, but the army. My comfort is the chance of peace, when I shall be Captain N. on half-pay, with 100*l. per annum*, and a much happier man than Captain N., with 600*l.* or 800*l.* on full-pay.

At one time, my hope was that a company would cure me of my aversion to the army, though nothing could make me like it; but the first feeling is not to be conquered, or surely being a captain at twenty-one would create in a warm imagination ideas of future honours, of hopes, and wishes to rise to the head of my profession, and all the deuce knows what, which such reveries lead to. But not one thought of pleasure or happiness from promotion could be forced up. No! not one would come at my call. How different are George's feelings? He will be in Paradise though up to his ears in mud at Hythe. How happy he is to be thus contented with present pleasures, and sanguine as to the future! To me military life is like dancing up a long room with a mirror at the end, against which we cut our faces, and so the deception ends.

It is thus gaily men follow their *trade of blood* thinking it glitters, but to me it appears without brightness or reflection: a dirty red! And for the future! aye! the future! What is it? Under a long feather and cocked hat, trembling, though supported by stiff hessian boots, gold-headed cane and long sword, I see the wizened face of a general grinning over the parapet of a fine frill, and telling extraordinary lies, while his claret, if he can afford claret, is going down the throats of his wondering or quizzing *aides-de-camp*. Such is the difference between a hero of the present time, and the idea formed of one from reading Plutarch! Yet people wonder I don't like the army!

While on the London staff he had been frequently thrown into the society of Charles Fox, and the young soldier used to describe with vivid humour the manifestations of the orator's natural and earnest disposition. How at cricket he would strike at the ball and recklessly run for a score, bat on shoulder, his Sancho Panza figure fully displayed and his head thrown back, laughing in childish delight amidst reproachful cries while his opponents struck down the wickets behind him. How also, when walking in the beautiful garden of St. Anne's Hill, amidst rare flowers, discoursing gravely, he would at sight of a snail suddenly stop, plant his heel on it, spin round like a *teetotum*, and then resume his walk and his wisdom, with all possible gravity.

Mr. Fox often expressed his disapproval of Mr. Windham's military notions, calling them his fancies, and predicting failure, as indeed happened. Of other prominent men he also spoke freely, and his dislike of Mr. Canning was not disguised. His young cousin often pressed him on military policy, especially on the defects of the Mutiny Act, its vagueness where precision was essential for enabling officers to act with decision and legality. To this Mr. Fox answered drily, whether in condemnation or approval was not ascertained, *That it was purposely so framed, to retain unlimited power over military men.*

Sir John Moore was then the most honoured military character of the day, and of his opinions and actions Mr. Fox liked to hear: he knew him not, even by sight, but took such an interest in his character, that one evening hearing some person relate an advantageous anecdote, as what other could ever be justly told of Moore, he threw down his cards and called out "Tell that again! I hear a great deal of General Moore, and everything good: tell me that again."

Here, in connection with Mr. Fox, shall be noticed an error touching the heroic Moore's attachment to Mr. Pitt's niece, the Lady Hester Stanhope: the real facts presenting, curiously enough, another phase of opposition between the rival orators, although both were ignorant of them. Sir John Moore was not, as generally believed, affianced to Lady Hester; his attachment to her was strong, his admiration great: but the first was only a sentiment of friendship, enhanced by her relationship to Mr. Pitt, whose personal esteem he enjoyed in a singular degree.

Admiration was a necessary concomitant of acquaintance; it was for such a man, impossible not to admire the lofty genius of a woman created to command as well as to attract, but love in the passionate sense was not there. General Anderson, his bosom friend, assured the writer of this biography, that the only person Sir John Moore thought of marrying was Mr. Fox's niece, Miss Caroline Fox; a lady who has since displayed a power of mind, and enduring fortitude in terrible trials that surpass even the creations of fiction.

To her, when in Sicily with her father, Sir John Moore did, at one time, design to offer marriage: but she was then not eighteen, and after a hard struggle he suppressed his passion with a nobility of sentiment few men can attain to. She is, he said to General Anderson, so young that her judgment may be overpowered: the disparity of age is not at present very apparent, and my high position here, my reputation as a soldier of service, and my intimacy with her father—he might have added his great comeliness and winning manners—may influence her to an irretrievable error for her own future contentment: my present feelings must therefore be suppressed, that she may not have to suppress hers hereafter with loss of happiness.

Coruña would have ended that union in blood and misery: and here also in connection with that fatal field, a fact of historical interest shall be related on the direct authority of the late Lady Castlereagh. Lord Castlereagh's duel with Mr. Canning was not, she said, in revenge for the intrigue which ousted the former from office. He was content to leave that for public judgment; but Mr. Canning offered to reinstate him, if he would consent to sacrifice the reputation of Sir John Moore: an insult well answered with a shot.

Returning now to Charles Napier, it will be found that his father's advice, and the practice of engineering, for which he had a predilection, in some measure reconciled him to his profession.

Chelmsford, February 1804.—Resolution has worked a miracle: my low spirits are thrown off in a great degree, not quite, but I am now as eager to carry all by storm, as I was ready to desert five days ago. Not that my opinion, or dislike, is changed, but that no man can make a figure in anything who does not go hand and heart to work—except in taking physic: there a want of earnestness may be useful. In for a penny, in for a pound, shall be my maxim, in spite of my aversion to old proverbs. I am now anxious to return to Chatham, having no uniform here, and coloured clothes with soldiers smell so militia like, it makes me ashamed to look a Coldstreamer in the face.

An infamous newspaper paragraph against General Fox has appeared. His passiveness puts me out of patience: he deserves all that is said, and that *will be* said, and need not flatter himself that things can sink into oblivion. The White Roses—the York family—will have a blow at him whenever matters are so arranged as to make him think they have no such intention. This paragraph is the commencement of attacks through the papers in support of the previous ill usage of General Fox; and the giving Lord Hardwick a blue ribbon, will be no small help in fixing blame on the general, which is all they want. It is provoking to see an honest old soldier so assailed by those who were saved by his pacific disposition in the first instance, not by their own wit. One of my ears should go to see his thin little brother, the Chertsey private, let loose: how he would fling at them! The general's statement ought, certainly, to be published.

It must be here remarked that General Fox's passiveness sprung from no weakness in his cause; nor from timidity, for he was a very bold man; but from an inexhaustible goodness of nature: he was totally devoid of the fire which kindles into wrath; no personal ill-usage could arouse him to fierceness, and he was forgiving to an incredible degree. Astute measures had been early taken to mollify him about the Irish affair, and he could not be stung again to anger: moreover, he blamed Mr. Wickham, the Irish Secretary, far more than Lord Hard-wick, who was certainly not an intriguing, nor a dishonest politician, nor a vindictive man.

Chatham, February.—Being, dear mother, in all the horrors of a new coat and *cocked-up-hat* I cannot write much. I fag at French, eager to learn, as most of the officers speak it, and it is hateful to be a dunce. None of them however know anything of interior regimental duty, which woeful experience has taught me; nor can there be worse hands at drill: even the major is unlearned, the adjutant superbly so. The reason is that the first comes from the Engineers, who know nothing of field exercises; and though the latter was sergeant-major of the Guards, those who rise from the ranks seldom figure in exercising a battalion. My own regimental knowledge is small enough, yet greater than that of the captain's here, and I know as much of field engineering: The *Swish* man appears to me the cleverest man amongst them, but it is said Sturgeon and Dundas, not here, are the best engineers.

This clever *Swish* man, was Wilhermein, a native of Switzerland, a fine draughtsman, military and artistic: the picture of Abercrombie at the battle of the 21st in Egypt, painted by him and Captain Pierpont, is well known from the engraving.

March.—I have sold Cooper for £70 because my London creditors want money: my mare proved unsound and went for £25. This was unfortunate, but the money procured me another horse worth a great deal, he being sold for running away with a guardsman who could not ride. Neither master nor groom dare ride him, and both told such stories of the poor horse that nobody would buy, and he came to me for half his value. He is about Model's size, but more of an Arabian than a racer, with a beautiful curved neck, and fiery as the devil, yet without vice; he run away because he knew his riders: he has found me his master.
Expecting him to be worse than *Ça ira*, I put the bridle upon him, which astonished the gentleman a little; but he has a good mouth, and it is gentleness, not violence, he wants. *Ça ira* was to him as the great devil is to a little one: he was so large and powerful that when angry he was tremendous, and would, and could easily, have broken his own neck and mine. This little

devil is like a feather to me after the great one, and is as much under my thumb as a Mameluke's horse: I hate a vicious horse, but delight in a fiery one, and have named this one Hotspur, it suits his temper.

May 1st.—Dearest father, I am reduced by pain to such weakness as only to lie on a couch, and am absolutely like a skeleton. My long nose, pale face, and black beard, forced a yard in length by hot baths, makes me worse-looking than Lord Ruthven when he murdered Rizzio; and all this is owing to maltreatment by a gallipot limb of Satan, and designedly I have strong reason to suspect. However, two of our companies go to Dover in a week, to work under engineers; so, we are to be overseers not engineers! Nicholay swears he will resign; but when the quartermaster general hears of his pets being so scurvily treated we shall be righted. I remain here sick; take no alarm, there is no danger, but baths of 120° have made me a poor scalded devil.

May 6th.—Dearest father. What a strange thing the new ministry will be! Mr. Addington resigned yesterday, and everybody talks of a regency. If Charles Fox comes in under Mr. Pitt he will deserve the accusation of being interested, and his enemies will have an excuse for saying his principles have been sacrificed to his ambition: which will, however, be but poorly satisfied under Mr. Pitt. Again, if Mr. Fox comes in as prime minister, Mr. Pitt will deserve the same abuse, and will get it. They cannot both be at the head; therefore, one should remain out and support the other, or oppose him as he sees fit.

Mr. Fox should not be an underling; he should raise himself by turning out a weak ministry, and refusing office, or emolument, supply the government with clever men having the confidence of the country. Then like an honest Englishman he should watch that the power he thus gives is not misused by men whom he alone can control. This he should do or become premier, there is no medium.

The tendency towards melancholy evidenced in the foregoing correspondence, was not a result of youthful perturbation at finding the world different from his childish conceptions, it was of his nature, and adhered to him through life; but always he will be found discarding morbid feelings with a wonderful power of will, in obedience to reason. The profession of arms, first adopted in his father's conscientious views, was to him a patriotic object at the time, and moreover was his only means of existence; hence with this double stimulant he set the strength of his brain against the softness of his heart, and bravely accepted a fate which doomed him to a life-long struggle. His resolution to meet and sustain all evils was now however severely tried, for in October 1804 his father died.

The Life of George Napier (Senior)

The Honourable George Napier was educated by the celebrated David Hume. He possessed uncommon powers, mental and corporeal: his capacity for war, for science, and for civil affairs was great, and always in emergencies he displayed a master spirit. He served with distinction in the American war, especially at the siege of Charleston, and being temporarily on the staff of Sir Henry Clinton when André was captured, instantly offered to complete his task, yet in uniform: he thought that accomplished, unfortunate officer, had failed in presence of mind, and that the game was not lost; but Sir Henry, too deeply affected by André's danger to risk another favourite, refused.

Soon afterwards George Napier lost his wife and several children, by a fever, from which he miraculously recovered himself. He was put on board ship for England insensible, and his general, thinking death certain, actually sold his commission to save the money for an infant daughter—the only surviving child. The sick man recovered on the voyage, and so found himself on landing compelled to begin the world again. Entering the Guards then, he soon became adjutant, and was, from his great comeliness and talent as an officer, much noticed by George the Third. He had also assurances of friendship from the Prince of Wales, sincere at the time no doubt, for he afterwards proposed to take the writer of this work as a page: an offer wisely and happily declined.

While in the Guards, Colonel Napier married Lady Sarah, and was by her brother, the Duke of Richmond, then master general, appointed comptroller of the Woolwich laboratory, where his ability was immediately manifested. He placed contracts on a better footing, introduced carronades generally into the navy, and after a variety of pyrotechnic experiments, conducted in person, altered and improved the manufacture of English gunpowder, fixing the proportions of the ingredients differently from those of other nations, and it is supposed advantageously. His experimental processes were briefly described in a memoir for an early volume of the Transactions of the Royal Irish Academy, and were translated into several languages.

From this office, he retired with a marked indication of character. For the Duke of Richmond, assuming that his own resignation of office should involve that of his brother-in-law, was offended to find it was not so, and haughtily remonstrated; he was however, told with still more haughtiness, that the office was military, had been accepted as such, and should not be degraded to a party holding. He kept it therefore until some curious researches were completed, which enabled him to hand over to his successor, Colonel Congreve, whose abilities he appreciated, many valuable hints and embryo experiments, especially in the composition of rockets. When he had thus asserted his dignity, to vindicate his motives from the imputation of self-interest he resigned, and settled at Celbridge, as noticed in the commencement of this work.

In Ireland, the wildness of the times and manners often compelled him to exert his great bodily strength in repression of ill-behaved men, and he thus created great awe of his prowess; but for his justice and benevolence he was so revered, that any temporary absence produced on his return bonfires and illuminations: demonstrations of attachment and respect not accorded to rich and powerful neighbours. His person and countenance were very commanding, resembling so much, the mourning grenadier in West's picture of Wolfe's death, that it was thought to be a portrait, yet was not so: the general resemblance is striking, but his figure was larger, grander in form, his eye still more falcon-like, his forehead less fleshy, showing finer blood, and his jaw more square and determined. Such he was to view, such to act, and one instance of his terrible strength, and fierceness when aroused, will indicate the turbulence of the scenes amidst which Charles Napier was nurtured.

Long before the insurrection of 1798, soldiers designated by Sir R. Abercrombie as formidable to everybody but the enemy, were allowed to perpetrate horrible outrages with impunity, and one evening Colonel Napier's five sons were in great danger from their brutality. Being with some haymakers in a field, which was separated from the high road by a walled bank, they were asked a question by two passing soldiers, who were idly answered by young George Napier: instantly the soldiers climbed the wall, and one of them drawing his bayonet announced his intention to kill the child who had offended. The haymakers, terrified by the military licence of the day, retreated, and the boys drew together in fear; but at that moment their father entered the field, his eye rapidly caught the scene, and leaping like a panther rather than a man he was quickly upon the soldiers, swaying a six-foot quarter staff which he generally carried and used in surveying.

Back the two men jumped into the deep road and stood with drawn bayonets in self-defence; his leap was simultaneous, a clash of weapons followed, and Charles Napier, calling upon his brothers to help their father, jumped after him: there was no need of aid, one soldier was rolling on the ground, and the most ferocious of them was writhing in the grasp of the avenger, who had torn his weapon away. In vain he cried out for mercy and struggled; his terrible opponent, holding him up with one hand, dragged him towards the village, striding like a giant as he was, and striking the cowering wretch at times over the head with his own bayonet, the blood starting at every stroke. A burly sergeant came up and seemed at first inclined to aid his fellow, but soon, shrinking before the wrathful athletic man's voice and gestures, accepted charge of the prisoner.

In 1793, he was invited to become deputy quartermaster general to a force under Lord Moira assembled in Guernsey to aid the Vendeans. There, thinking the spies and royalists gave coloured, or false accounts of the state of affairs in France, he proposed, after deep consideration, to penetrate himself into La Vendée and confer with the royalist chiefs. Lord Moira was much moved with this proof of zeal and resolution, as Clinton had before been by a like offer in America; but like Clinton he would not risk a friend, and refused: saying, D'Hervilly and Rochefoucault had each made a like offer, and he had declined, though their danger would have been much less. He was at that time but a captain, and with difficulty could Lord Moira force the virtual commander in chief, Lord Amherst, to fulfil a previous promise of promotion: for then, and afterwards, a blight from the highest quarters chilled Colonel Napier's fortunes, and was extended to his son.

Returning from Guernsey, Lord Moira encamped at Netley, but after a time was despatched to succour the Duke of York in Flanders, where landing at Ostend with seven thousand young soldiers he found that they must re-embark, or risk an attack from Pichegru's victorious army of sixty thousand: he chose the latter, and by a march deserving of more notice than military writers have bestowed joined the duke. Moving for nearly a month across the front of the French, sometimes even forcing his way through their scouting troops. Lord Moira was constantly in danger of being overwhelmed, but with fine skill turned what seemed an element of destruction into one of success. For the people of the country being all in the French interest, duly gave them notice of each day's march, and this being expected was thus turned to account.

Officers of the staff each day preceded the columns to order rations for seven thousand men, saying they were the advanced guard of forty thousand, for whom provisions must be collected the next day. In a few hours the troops would arrive, in number tallying with the order for rations; the coming of the main column was therefore credited, and conformable intelligence was conveyed to the French, who dared not attack such a force without previous dispositions. In this way, a march was gained day by day in safety, though with some skirmishes, and some loss.

Finally, the deceit was discovered and an accelerated forced movement became the only resource. But one night the soldiers, beaten by fatigue, lay down and refused to rise; ruin seemed inevitable, when suddenly an Irishman, starting up, cried out with a rich brogue, richer humour, and richest honour. Boys! didn't the lord give us bottled porter when we were sick at Netley, and hasn't he the right to take it out of us now in sweat? This was in allusion to a dreadful fever which had assailed the camp, arising entirely from the brutal indifference to suffering with which they had been crowded for weeks in transports unnecessarily: the medical men prescribed porter but the government heartlessly refused, and Lord Moira supplied 7000 bottles a day from his own purse! Now he was repaid. With shouts of laughter the column rose and a junction with the duke's army was effected.

After this expedition, Colonel Napier, at the latter end of 1794, was appointed to the Londonderry regiment, of which Lord Conyngham was colonel. He had only to discipline it, and did so, with a rare ability, but had nothing to do with the mode of recruiting, which he abhorred; for the men had been raised by the usual infamous mode of the times, that is to say, false promises, the officers obtaining rank according to the number of recruits they brought.

The men were told their embodiment was to be permanent, that they were only to serve in Ireland, and be discharged in seven years. Yet they were almost immediately sent to Macclesfield, and from thence to Exeter, to be drafted into the 43rd Regiment: they resisted, but were cruelly enforced to obey and cruelly punished. Colonel Napier had quitted the regiment at Macclesfield, in disgust, and regretting that he was not in Lord Conyngham's place, thinking that a vigorous resistance would have prevented the foul play.

In Ireland, his life again became private, but his capacity was so known, that when Hoche menaced war in 1796, a new military appointment, that of chief field engineer, was created, to enable him to be the directing military adviser of the commander in chief, Lord Carhampton, whose warlike genius was not esteemed: and it is not a little singular, that Lord Edward Fitzgerald, misjudging Colonel Napier's principles, afterwards looked to gain him as chief leader of the insurgents of 1798, meaning to resign in his favour. His mental ascendancy was indeed remarkable, and his sagacity also.

When young he was an intimate friend of Lord Erskine, who was a distant relation, and being in the same regiment with Napier, was often exhorted, and finally persuaded by him to quit the army for the bar. But a more noticeable example was his early perception of the Duke of Wellington's genius. Castletown society was then prominent in fashion and politics; Ensign Wellesley frequented it, and was generally considered a shallow, saucy stripling. Colonel Napier thought otherwise, and after many conversations thus predicted his greatness. *Those who think lightly of that lad are unwise in their generation: he has in him the makings of a great general.* Whether this reached the duke's ears at the time, or that Lady Sarah Napier's attention to him, in adopting her husband's opinion, gratified him, or both, is uncertain; but though the acquaintance soon entirely ceased, whenever her sons were wounded in the Peninsula, the duke invariably wrote with his despatches a consoling letter to her.

In early life, Lord St. Vincent had earnestly, though vainly, urged George Napier to quit the army for the navy, promising rapid promotion. Lord Cornwallis also, under whom he had served in America, on coming to Ireland as lord lieutenant, pressed on him the comptrollership of army accounts with this notable speech, I want an honest man; and this is the only thing I have been able to wrest from the harpies around me. It was however an Augean stable he offered for cleansing: the military accounts were four years in arrears, including the broken insurrectionary period of 1798; foul abuses prevailed, and while the fees were enormous, the work was neglected, and the retiring comptroller received six thousand a year compensation!

Such was the enormous jobbing of the time. It was therefore with reluctance Colonel Napier accepted the place, and only on condition of its being made patent, which released him from party politics and Castle intriguers, whom he regarded with disgust. His official labours were remarkable, and are thus faithfully recorded on his monumental slab, in Redland Chapel near Clifton.

He restored the military accounts of Ireland to exact order, when years of neglect and corruption had plunged them into a confusion productive of great loss to the country and great injustice to individuals. He recovered several millions of money for the public treasury, and by his probity and disinterestedness made his office a model for patriotic public servants: his first act was to abolish all fees, thus voluntarily reducing his own salary from twenty thousand, to six hundred pounds *per annum!*

In the troubles of 1798, although but a private gentleman, and embarrassed with a large family, he had stepped between the violence of the government and the fury of the insurgents, keeping a large body of the latter in check, and by resolute interposition saved Celbridge from fire and military execution, to which it had been twice doomed by the authorities. His ambition was lofty, but so chastened by honour that he would not enter the temple of fame save through the great portals, and as opportunity came not, the master spirit passed away unknown: Epaminondas would have lived obscurely if Agesilaus had not been vindictive. More than once Colonel Napier was offered, secretly, the representation of the county, but he refused, because factions were so violent and so corrupt, that he could not hope, without the influence of wealth, to steer a proud and earnest course between oppressive power and rebellious democracy, dashing both aside. He was called impracticable by ephemeral politicians, and was so to them, but while impassive to crooked ambition, every fibre vibrated to true glory.

Although a soldier, always ready for service on the principle of protecting his country, he regarded war as a dire evil: what he yearned for was power to establish a new people on his own views of legislation; and often he longed to govern Australia, then a mere receptacle for thieves, foreseeing that it might become a great state. When the vileness of the population was objected, he answered that Rome sprung from such a source, and it was an advantage, because benevolent despotism could be exercised without imputation of tyranny. His view was to raise a great community, founded on sound monarchic principles, as a counterpoise in the world to the great advancing American republic. His principles were indeed immovably monarchical; yet he was so vehement against the cruel oppressions of the times, that many persons supposed him to be at heart a democrat.

Lord Edward amongst others:—whereas he held democracy to be an ever-seething cauldron in which the scum continually rose to the surface; and he rejected with abhorrence the republican creed which presents assassination as the greatest of virtues. What he opposed and denounced was oppression, coming from any quarter. Gentle as the dews of spring he was to the poor and helpless, but rough and dangerous as the storms of winter to the dishonourable and unjust: and with overpowering force of body and of mind he could impose his will: God had made him for command.

Kingly rule he judged the best, but he was no king worshipper; he never undervalued men's right of freedom in thought and action, consistent with the public welfare: nor did the headlong progress of republics towards greatness escape his observation. But restricted sovereignty he thought absolutely necessary for keeping the foaming turbulence of democracy within just bounds, while leaving unimpeded the natural flow of energy and genius towards prosperity. His son Charles adopted his views, and both of them, with a practical paradox, while rejecting as a golden dream the notion that nations can ever become great and yet remain simple and virtuous, strove with all imaginable energy in their vocations to make that dream a reality!

CHAPTER 4

To the 50th Foot

Colonel George Napier died at the age of fifty-one, of consumption, brought on by incessant writing after a life of country exercises and pursuits. His death placed Lady Sarah in very straitened circumstances. His principal income had come from his office, and though her three eldest sons were captains, and her youngest, Henry, a midshipman, another son, Richard, and four girls were unprovided for. The future appeared gloomy, but Mr. Pitt, when made acquainted with the dead man's services in war, in science, and finance, and the great savings he had effected for the public, gave pensions to his widow and daughters. Charles Napier's anxiety was thus relieved, and after passing a few weeks at Cirencester with his mother, Lord Bathurst having kindly lent his house there to her, he rejoined the Staff Corps.

Before Mr. Pitt's intentions were known. Lord Moira wrote on the first impulse of sorrow, offering money to Charles, and promising future patronage, whenever power should be his. This, the only proof of friendship received from his Lordship, was noticed in the following letters, with a sagacity, not blunted by the rather overstrained tone of Lord Moira's communication.

My Lord.—The being obliged to join my regiment prevented me from receiving your lordship's kind letter until now. I acknowledge it with sincere thanks. Your friendly intentions towards our family I am as perfectly aware of, as of the impossibility of your fulfilling them at this moment, I should be sorry, were that to give you the slightest uneasiness, for I am more anxious we should merit your friendship than profit by it. I will not further intrude on your time, but trust you are convinced how sensible we all are of your extreme kindness. Your obliging offer to lend me money, if necessary, I thank you for, but am not in need of it.

Enclosing a copy to his mother he continued thus to her:

My hope is dear mother that you will approve of my answer to Lord Moira. His letter does not please me so much as it seems to do you. Certainly, it is very affectionate, but all great men are so used to dependants, that they think friendship from them must be interested. I have tried to show him that this is not the case with me, at the same time expressing gratitude for his declaration, that he looked on us as his children.

I am glad the Duke of Richmond has refused a loan to you. I do not like borrowing at all; it is much better to sell Celbridge than to be obliged to any human being. It displeased me your asking him, but seeing you wished it so much I would not say so. My beautiful horse is gone to be sold for what he will fetch: the money will clear me of all debt. I cannot exist while owing money, it makes me more melancholy than anything that can happen.

Bodien Bridge, November.—I do not write at night, my spirits always sink of an evening. Good spirits never come to me at night, except when with you, and then they come madly. However, no one here knows of my lowness, being apparently merry as possible. It pleases me that William has made acquaintance with Mr. Pitt, it may be of use to him. I am glad you see Lord Moira and General Moore, and that people say government should help *his* family; for thus your memorial becomes less of a favour asked, and hardly a petition. We soon go back to Chatham. Devil is not yet sold. Your disposal of the grey mare pleases me. She comes often into my thoughts and puts me in mind of happier times. (This was the little Arab he rode at school.)

December.—Dearest mother don't let my whims prevent your asking or doing anything you wish. You will not go further than is right in asking favours of anybody, and you must not talk of infringing! There can be no bounds or rules between us. Do all you like and think best. Be mistress! The greatest happiness possible for me is to compass everything you desire.

About the middle of 1805 his quarters were removed to Hythe,

SIR JOHN MOORE

where he was employed with his brother officers in excavating a military canal, and constructing works of defence, during that perilous period when Napoleon's legions swarmed on the heights of Boulogne, expectant, until the fires at Trafalgar, scorching their ocean wings, sent them to other conquests. He was thus placed under Sir John Moore, that model soldier of England, whose spirit and character exacted admiration and devotion from all sincere lovers of honour.

His was the fire that warmed the coldest nature, and urged all who came in contact with him, onward in the path of glory along which he strode so mightily himself. No man with a spark of enthusiasm could resist the influence of Moore's great aspirings, his fine presence, his ardent penetrating genius: but when did faction ever respect virtue or genius? its life-blood is the rejection of honourable emotions! Moore, like Charles Napier, had to leave his actions to the care of history, and would perhaps have left them in vain, if his heroic fall in battle and his unsurpassable fortitude in dying, had not set a seal upon his fame which even faction could not deface.

To awaken the faculties of those under him, inspiring and teaching, was one of Sir John Moore's qualifications for command. At Shorn Cliff camp he devised such improvements in drill, discipline, dress, arms, formations, and movements, as would have placed him for military reforms beside the Athenian Iphicrates, if he had not the greater glory of dying like the Spartan Brasidas. His materials were the 48rd, 52nd, and Rifle Regiments, and he so fashioned them, that afterwards, as the Light Division under Wellington they were found to be soldiers unsurpassable, perhaps never equalled.

The separate successful careers of the officers, strikingly attest the merit of the school: so long a list of notable men could not be presented by three regiments of any service in the world. In it will be found above ninety who attained the rank of field officer, or higher grades, and amongst them four who commanded armies, three being celebrated as conquerors; two adjutant-generals of the British Army, three military secretaries; sixteen governors of colonies, and the two organisers of the metropolitan and Irish constabulary; many generals who have commanded districts; one who commanded a foreign army, and several persons noted in science and literature, or by peculiar missions and organisations belong to the roll: and nearly all were of some fame in battle, though unequal in merit and reputation.

From three infantry regiments, obscure until Moore took them in hand, went forth this crowd of men, skilled to gain authority and public notice without political or family interest, save in a very few cases. Certainly, it was a great school, and Moore's teaching is thus well described by one of his scholars, and one not amongst the least capable of great actions, if fortune had not been adverse.

It pleases me that you design to notice that real camp of instruction—Shorn Cliff. There officers were formed for command, and soldiers acquired such discipline, as to become an example to the army and proud of their profession. The details of Moore's system, from the setting up of a recruit to the movement of a brigade you are well acquainted with: but though drill was an important part of the instruction, it was not, as you also know, by that alone the soldier was there formed. It was the internal and moral system, the constant superintendence of the officers, the real government and responsibility of the captains, which carried the discipline to such perfection.

My opinion of discipline is so strong, that I must speak of it. I rank it higher for the well-being of an army than any other consideration; very far above that of being present at many battles, for battles with respect to the soldiers can only be the test of discipline. When the Light Division joined the army at Talavera it had not been engaged with the enemy, while the army it joined had been engaged on the Douro and the Tagus, yet was inferior in discipline for war, seeing that its picquets were often in scrapes, and at Talavera a brigade had been surprised. But the men of the Light Division, though new to war, were looked up to from the day of junction as the *veterans of the army!* and by their discipline they sustained that character throughout the war, committing no blunders, and shewing themselves the same orderly soldiers on the breach as in the line.—J. P. Hopkins.

To this may be added that the Light Division, though always on the outposts, in most difficult situations, never lost any baggage, except on the retreat from Salamanca, when some French horsemen, pressing the British cavalry in a wood, got into the rear of the division and cut off two mules!

Amidst these men Charles Napier's strong character was soon noticed. Nothing drew him from study, he never gambled, drank no wine, had but few intimates, was mostly absorbed in thought, and though ready for good fellowship in all manly games, eschewed it in the mess room: to his mother only his secret feelings were confided.

His first letters touch on an expedition to Russia then talked of but which finally went to Germany under Lord Cathcart.

Hythe, September.—Mason is a clever fellow to teach that conscience is our greatest enemy: it is our greatest friend! You say we need not trouble ourselves when, or where the mercy we hope for will be dealt to us: methinks we should have trouble to discover where and when it is not dealt to us! but my letter is becoming *holey* as my shirts, and with them no bishop can compare: they are not however so many as the bishops, and therefore your directions to get new ones shall be borne in mind; yet to take more than two would be unwise, seeing that number can be made good out of the old ones, with help of a pocket handkerchief, which is of no use in Russia, if we go there as 'tis said, for they are not more nice than in Ireland. However, the shirt-tails must be completed, or the cold may make me like Munchausen's horse: the English ladies should give their muffs to government for lining the breeches of soldiers destined for Russia. But you will not, it is to be feared have to direct letters to Captain Napier, Czar's Head Petrowitz Street Petersburgh for some time.

October.—When I first read the *Spectator*, a very long time ago, it appeared stupid to me, very stupid; now it appears admirable. How careful we should be of giving books to a child, the best way is to let children choose for themselves; nature makes a child like what it understands. The expedition is certainly not put off, for the German legion marches through here today, tomorrow, and next day. They are fine men, and Baron Ompteda, the oldest German baron, is seven feet high, and has a brother six feet eleven inches and a quarter. Lineally descended from Goliah, or Polyphemus, I forget which, they have, if from the last, allowed the other eye to grow, avoiding singularity.

Hythe, January.—Your alarm about our country is in my opinion groundless, but as everybody says we are still in great danger, it may be a mistake of mine: yet if all England told me so it would not change my conviction. Not that I put faith in the Volunteers, but that the French cannot swim the Straits of Dover; they have not ships to transport an army, and the few they have dare not encounter our fleets: in fine we are safe since the victory of Trafalgar. Suppose it possible to land forty thousand French in England, or Scotland; much mischief would be done, much blood flow, but our country is not to be conquered by Frenchmen. You would see London puppies and shopkeepers run, and London might be plundered; but the peasants and militia would soon become soldiers able to assist the regular troops, the whole island would be in arms and the French be destroyed.

People say, if London was taken England would be lost. So, it would be, if they who say so were our only defenders; and that a London tailor and a pastry-cook were to command officers of the line as colonels of volunteers, which is the case now. Oh! wise government! The minute a Frenchman sets foot in England, these gentlemen will find that laws are easily cut by the edge of the sword, and regular officers will laugh at their pretending to command. However, we are all thoroughly alarmed, and it cannot be said much to our credit.

The people of England afraid of the threats of Frenchmen! What shall we be if they come? It would however do us some good in correcting the luxurious effeminacy of the higher orders. For, take away Lord Huntly and a few other young men, and what a set of nobles we have: they should be all sailors or soldiers now.

In truth, our princes are the only great people who set a good example; and though one cannot say much for their talent, they fight, and bestir themselves, instead of staying in London. As to our sins, God forgive us them, they are much about the same now as formerly, and do not much interfere with the fate of the nation in my opinion: except by making us rich and lazy. The times are not harder than formerly, and the Emperor Napoleon does not appear to me at all in the light of a scourge to Europe; the same numbers of men would die whether there were war or not. No! our sins are not in fault, and you mistake my religious principles, if you think I bother myself trying to see beyond the grave.

January 22nd.—A whole year has passed since you went to Ireland, and I long to see you again, but I have no low spirits now, that is all given up: no melancholy thought is allowed to enter my mind or, if one presses to enter, reading or some other occupation drives it away. If there is no occupation at hand, reflection points out the folly of letting anything make us unhappy in this life; and the un thankfulness of not enjoying present pleasures sent, because of one or two things we choose to call misfortunes. We are not indeed monks of *La Trappe*, and need not repeat *Memento mori,* or think of it with horror, yet it should he always in our minds.

It grieves me that Mr. Pitt is in a way to follow his forefathers: poor man! George is just come in, and says he is reported to be no more. God knows if it is true, I hope not, his loss just now would he great as a minister, and everything will be thrown into confusion. As to our troops in Hanover, my fear is they will fall into the hands of the French. Everybody says they will get off, yet the French are very active. Our troops, few in numbers and requiring able commanders, have their wings under ———— and ————!! Why do we laugh at the Trojans admitting a wooden horse? The government seems even to fear the activity of Lord Cathcart, who is sent to act with his army before he knows it; yet his abilities are not so wonderful as to need impediments, like the man who had his legs tied for fear of outrunning a hare.

It is madness to expect success from a small army equipped, and its movements arranged by ministers who do not know what the operations of war are, and will not ask advice from those who do. England will always fail in her expeditions, unless the minister is military and a good soldier; or, what is the same, leaves the arrangements to a good one after the thing has been fixed upon. The Duke of York should have appointed Lord Cathcart in time, and have let him know what he was to command, instead of hurrying him after his army—altogether it is absurd.

If there is a peace, my intent is to visit the continent, finish French, and learn German, which could be done in six months; this makes me eager to see you, because, if done it must be done like lightning for fear of war again: moreover, see Buonaparte before he dies I will. My idea is to go to The Hague, or Holstein, where both languages could be learned together, quicker than in France. It is in such acquirements my great deficiency as a soldier touches me: languages are absolutely necessary, and labouring at them at home is time lost. My knowledge of engineering is now more than is necessary for officers of the line, and as much as is required for my duty as an engineer on service; but not near what it should be generally: my want is greater practice, which Brown is bent on not giving us. Never saw an old bachelor worth a farthing.

Important public events, opening new prospects for Charles Napier, now gave a spur to his ambition. The Battle of Austerlitz had terminated the war on the continent, William Pitt had gone to his fathers, and Charles Fox's advent to power was marked by negociations for peace. Meanwhile Sicily had been occupied by British troops, and the Mediterranean command was given to General Fox. Sir John Moore went as second in command, taking with him the 52nd Regiment, and soon afterwards appointed George Napier to be his *aide-de-camp*. And now also Mr. Fox, at the solicitation of Lady Sarah, had given a majority to Charles; but in a Cape colonial corps, and that only by a firm expression of his will: for his failing health was so notorious, and his political enemies so exultant, that Sir Walter Scott gave public vent to their anticipations with indecent triumph at a political dinner, by a song offensive alike to good taste and feeling.

But promotion anywhere gave Charles Napier unbounded satisfaction; it was an approach to power, which he panted for as a means of promoting good. At first, he tried to exchange from his regiment to one which would again place him under Sir John Moore, but failing in that he was going to embark for the Cape, when a remarkable incident gave a new turn to his fortunes. Contrary winds had detained him at Portsmouth, and being there thrown into the society of the 50th Regiment, he so won on the officers that they proposed to him an exchange at small cost. He refused to pay money, as contrary to the regulations; but they would not be so baffled, and contrived to have him gazetted without payment; how he never knew, but it was a signal proof of regard. Bognor soon became the quarters of the regiment, and he renewed his intimacy with Sir James and Lady Duff, who lived in that neighbourhood.

He was often also at Goodwood, where the Duke of Richmond frequently employed him to make military sketches, imparting at the same time his own views for the defence of Sussex against the threatened invasion. These were not perhaps of the highest order, yet the result of much reflection and information, and calculated to awaken his nephew's greater faculties for war: soon however, this mental aid, and worldly support, was cut off, the duke died at the end of the year.

CHAPTER 5

Copenhagen Expedition

In 1807 a vehement desire for service pervaded the British Army. Officers and soldiers dreaded the coming of peace before their prowess could he displayed; and there was much irritation at the court preference for foreign troops, and the courtly cant about their superiority. Austrians, Prussians, and Russians had fled before the tricolour of France; the white, blue, and green uniforms had been trodden down in heaps, while the red was undishonoured; yet the wearers of it were told to learn from the beaten armies! What could they learn but defeat? They felt their own value, and their martial fury, continually fermenting, was augmented by daily insults; for in most parts of England, the southern counties especially, the military were treated as enemies if they were not called so.

The glory of the navy was another stinging incentive, and it was fortunate the Peninsular War came to give a vent for the fierce-gathering discontent. Yet it is remarkable that Indian triumphs excited little interest. Men's minds were so occupied with Napoleon's stupendous exploits, that Eastern generals were regarded only as a better sort of militia; even the great victor of Assaye, then commanding the Sussex district, was only a noble captain for those immediately about him: his Indian fame was almost ignored. It was, however, no slight proof of the indomitable fierceness of the troops that they recked little of reputations, boasting that they would fight any general through any blunders: bravely has that boast been vindicated.

Like all others, Charles Napier was grieved and impatient under this forced inactivity, but bent his mind to actual duty with a severe philosophy, preparing for fame or obscurity as fate might determine. His correspondence will show the gradual development of his uncommon character; and it is remarkable how constant his antipathy was to service in the East, as if prescient of the ingratitude he was there to earn.

Bognor, February 6th.—Buonaparte's defeat at Pultusk is dwindling to a kind of drawn battle, which is probably drawing and quartering for the poor Russians. As to the story you mention it is true, and was told me by the beautiful Miss Trowbridge's own charming pair of vermilions. She is like the king, and can do no wrong: in fact, she is an angel! General Fox is coming home from Sicily, leaving Moore in command. This is pleasant and unpleasant. It is disagreeable to have General Fox recalled, but shameful that Sir John Moore should have been so long only second. We hear he drilled and rattled the heroes of Maida, when he got first to Sicily, in a way they did not relish, but he has done them a world of good.

The beautiful Mrs. Barwell has asked me to her house; she is most delightful, and her manners are very captivating. Between her and Miss Trowbridge, who is a surprising mixture of beauty, good nature, and fun, the devil himself is not more flaming than myself: I go about all fire. Don't you admire the Cossack mode of tying French prisoners by the hair to their saddle-bows? It is so delicate, and careful, so just and Christian like.

March 6th.—Withermein writes from Sicily that there is no chance of service there. The second battalion of the 81st is not there; to be an Indian major is not my want.

12th.—If the report of Lord Moira going on service be true, procure a strait-waistcoat, and teach my servant how to use it. But I fear there is not sense to employ a man equal to lead the British army as it deserves; a man who will not let it be run down, or told to look at the Austrians! The Duke of York might by this time have found out that Englishmen unite German strength and persevering courage with French enthusiasm; and that our army is at present the finest material, though generally given to bad workmen. For ten years past Lord Moira should have had every opportunity of maturing his genius, and studying his enemy's: my belief is that he would have shewn himself a master: Buonaparte's marshals are clever, but with all admiration for them, they owe half their fame, at least, to fourteen years' hard fighting: that would make us good too.

Lord Moira and Moore are the only generals the army confide

in; with others, they trust to their own courage, which is not a weak staff, though more suitable to a small than large body. Small bodies see their enemies, and beating them think all right; but large armies have no idea of the operations beyond their sight: each division trusts to the commander in chief for support, and if their opinion of his talent is not high, fancy a momentary success may lead to destruction.

My brother William will not go mad, make yourself easy, on that score: I know him better than you. His scheme of going to Russia is good, if he is not obliged to borrow money, as that would be wrong. If he can get a majority by any plan, he should take it; or go as *aide-de-camp* anywhere if it does compel him to quit the 43rd Regiment. If Lord Moira command, my trust is that he will take us both: if not I also will try to join the Russians. I have never gone to sleep for six months without thinking this over. It will be easily managed; if not, the more difficulty the better, adventures are to my taste.

20th.—Have no fear of my quitting England for twenty-five years at least! no fear either of the ministers, they are on sure ground, as no others are ready to take their places. If the Sicilian army wait till the Russians gain ground, George will have grandchildren first, unless Buonaparte kicks the bucket. There is no prospect for us soldiers. Nothing more about expeditions, and I am again in love with a Miss Home: a dear little Scotch thing with a beautiful face and beautiful figure, a beautiful dancer and beautiful genius. My heart is a cinder, and as heat is said to cure heat, I stand by the fire all day to draw out my flame.

Meanwhile I think of trying the Duke of York as to joining the Russians: one campaign got out of him would make me *asy*, and suit my notions, *viz.* Go! fight. Run away! But no East Indies for me; it would be unpleasant to be hanged by a Brahmin on the top of a pagoda and to deserve it: The West Indies there is no objection to. You may tell Richard that Xenophon has become a great favourite with me, though, at first, a slight flirtation with Clearchus was begun, it ended when his head was cut off: between friends, the Ten Thousand were great *raps*, though that should not be said amongst barbarians.

I make daily strides towards becoming real commanding officers; for Stewart—not W. Stewart—though very pleasant in command, and very decided, has no objection to the bore of drill being taken off his hands. However, I do not encroach, but only strive to teach the *major*, not the men, and so learn to be a lieutenant-colonel. There is a vacancy in the 78th, and it would please me to be in Sicily, and in a Scotch regiment; but their first battalion is in the East Indies and my ambition is not for nabobism: anywhere better than the East. The distance and the service are both disagreeable. Yet my conscience is very pliable, and if it were nearer to England I would flog the natives like others do: mind however, only in hopes of giving the devil a better hold of the directors, for all will fall on their souls of course."

(It is strange that his after life should take him to the East; that he should have this very regiment, the 78th, under him there, and be by the directors' tools foully and shamefully accused of being its destroyer.)

Monte Video has proved the great bravery of our troops. It was a bloody attack, and though one cannot judge fairly from a dispatch, the general and his engineers seem to have made a bad job: their missing of the breach, and that breach a bad one when found, &c. were sad things. I knew Vassal, Brownrigg and Dickenson of the Rifles: Brownrigg's brother died a short time since, a captain in the navy.

May, Portsmouth.—*Quo fata vocant*, is the 50th's motto, and at present *fata* sends us to Guernsey, while the first battalion will form part of the expedition now fitting out, (Copenhagen expedition.) My single chance now is, the first battalion being cut off and the two eldest majors skivered: a great comfort that would be, and is my brightest prospect.

His intense love of horses, which never abated even on his deathbed, and of which some touches have been already given, now breaks out: The Molly of the following letters was the little Arabian he rode when at school.

Tichfield.—A sagacious farrier has given a decided opinion that Molly has been pricked, farriers are of a species, apt, if offended by doubt of their skill, to revenge on the quadruped: so we have agreed on the disease and cure. We embark tomorrow for Guernsey, shall be much crowded, and probably taken by a French privateer. Molly cannot move, she must be left sick: now I do not like leaving the little thing behind, nor yet risking her on a voyage, but a horse I must have, so she follows, and the chance of her being hurt worries me.

Guernsey.—We sailed, and never was wretch more sick than I was, when at night the cry of 'Privateer!' arose on deck with, 'Officers! Officers!' I was up in a minute and a ludicrous scene opened. I, the major, shouting for the men to come up, the other officers rolling about in the dark, for there was a storm and none could keep steady; the soldiers tumbling up, some sick, some loading their muskets, others doing both, and all rolling about, and falling in such heaps, as to make me think they would shoot each other before *monsieur* arrived. However, in a few minutes we got some forty into the forecastle and side next the privateer, which was bearing down and not a hundred yards off, looking very black.

She would not answer or fight, but came almost athwart our bows, when our captain called to me, 'Sir she is a privateer and trying to get to windward to board, we had better fire a shot.' No sooner said than done: a man fired by my order, but only into her rigging, as she might not be a privateer. Still she bore down so close as to menace boarding before half my men were on deck and loaded, the latter not easy to effect, from sickness and the holding on to prevent being washed overboard. However, thirty fired, just to say we did not mean to be taken, and the argument was found good: she sailed round us and went off, answering our hail with 'Guernsey smuggler.' Our seamen said smugglers avoid other ships: yet she did not return our fire, and probably, seeing so many troops, expected more kicks than halfpence.

May.—Low spirits, having only one short letter from you since leaving London: and my lovely Molly is away. Everything else going on smooth. Being oldest major here I hope to get command of a brigade of light troops; but all commands are a bore while the expedition is going on. Oh! my luck! Shall I ever go abroad? We soldiers give a ball the 1st of June, which will cost two or three pounds: would that ball and island were at the devil. I am too poor for dashing, and the Guernsey lasses are little, which I hate; ugly, which I abhor; and can't dance, which I abominate. I have been introduced however to some of the *sixties!*—descendants of old Norman robbers, who keep up the profession by smuggling and privateering for the honour of their ancestors. The shopkeepers are called *forties*—at the head of whom is Mr. ——, draper, banker, shoemaker, thief-taker and tailor, who has already coaxed me into a new pair of breeches for the ball; which causes sincere prayer for Mick Reilly for stealing my old pair.

The prettiest little terrier ever seen has taken such a fancy to me, it is not possible to get rid of her: nor do I wish it, for she has placed herself under my protection. She has the sharpest little face you ever saw, except my own, colour about the same, with japan eyebrows, large eyes like diamonds, and a jet black nose: her head is a little ball, and her legs japan.

I fear the light companies will not be assembled, but I will make something of the 50th, for never was ground better adapted for light troops: two thousand would keep it without the expensive walls they are raising. Ophthalmia is amongst us, but slight. My rounds as field officer are sixteen miles on foot, which with a rocky road and dark night is no joke: one man broke his neck.

June.—Molly is safe in my stables, fat and mischievous: her first effort was gnawing my poor little dog when put into the manger for introduction: Moll took her by the ear, and was frightened because doggie squalled. She was delighted to touch firm ground and danced for joy. I made her call on Mrs. —— and Miss ——, who have not returned the visit and she won't speak to them; wherefore they will not ask her to the ball, and that is hard, as she has not her match for legs in the island."

In Guernsey he became a freemason, left the island in June, and reached Deal in July.

Deal.—Once more in barracks and with little duty, luckily, for Guernsey duty was too much. My poor friend McLeod 78th, has been killed in Egypt, and Wm. Stewart wounded. Our first battalion is coming here, and we are to form a brigade under General Spencer, who is a very gentlemanlike and peaceable kind of man: I thought he had been famous as a dasher both in dress and talent."

At this time, the Copenhagen expedition was being embarked and with it his brothers William and Henry, the last in the navy.

July.—William marched into this place on Monday, and on Tuesday to Ramsgate, and is now on board a transport in the Downs. He is on board a small transport and quite well. You told me our destination depends on which militia regiment we recruit from; therefore, I did not work, disliking to have any concern with fixing my own fate in the dark. Meanwhile my orders are to superintend the volunteering from the militia at one of the stations. It will be a troublesome appointment, but the most troublesome of all troubles to me is having nothing to do—*a too easy chair* is the rack for me.

As to your remark dear mother, my answer is—in the army we learn, that the oldest people are first to be trusted, unless they have shewn inability for the trust! I like Lord Castlereagh's new plan of volunteering from the militia: Wyndham's plan is good for keeping up the army, and placing it ultimately on a right footing, but will not give a powerful effective force for the present emergency, which the other will do. The two plans will in time make a fine army, but Wyndham's might have been better. His general principle is good; that is, what has been adopted by him from others is sensible, his own part not so: yet what was his, and what not, we only know from conversation and newspapers, and both are bad sources to judge from.

Brabourne Lees, August.—For two or three years, dear mother, my plan has been, not to write at night, yet that must be broken now for you. I am no longer a low-spirited wretch, and am worked to my heart's content with inspections of volunteers. Sixty officers and some two thousand men are expected, with their pockets full of bounty money; morality will probably depart from these barracks for about two months, but it is a pretty command for a major. Molly's corns have lamed her again.

This is the last notice of the Arabian mare. She was consigned to grass at Castletown, where she and two companions attained the ages of fifty-six, forty, and thirty-five years, Molly the youngest.

September.—The 50th second battalion will not go to Ireland: some regiments are not permitted to take Irish volunteers, which appears as if they were especially appropriated for half hanging, and flogging, and cutting of throats; for burnings and robberies, and other little government details. What an intolerable system of ruling. I have not made much havoc here with petticoat acquaintances yet, but have been invited to *catlap*, by the amiable and accomplished Misses Carter, nieces to the mighty old maid of that name: they are excessively entertaining. Whitelock, that miserable coward, well deserves to be shot: he can hardly escape a court-martial, which will not be swayed by party it is to be hoped, and if he gets off with life he must be broke, or the army is disgraced! Nearly two thousand men have been killed, besides the dishonour; and no good done; and all owing to the personal fear of one man! This was one of your gentry who damned officers in the ranks.

Sept.—Thank you dear mother for my two brothers' letters from Copenhagen: they are worth reading. One is from a man who reflects on the scenes before him in a moral point of view; the other, with not less humanity, notes only what relates to the progress of the action. It might be thought the younger mind would feel most the horror of war; but the one has seen dead bodies, and perhaps some burning and pillage; the other has only seen the noise and spirited part of a battle, which he expected and would have been disappointed not to have seen. A dying man in pain, a bad wound, the cries of the hurt, are things he does not expect to affect him, as they will when he sees them, and as they have his brother; he is therefore all eagerness to fight and only thinks how things favour or retard success: all this is quite natural, and the other probably felt the same, but when writing his thoughts were chiefly occupied by a higher consideration. He saw the injustice of the action; he saw brave men dead in defence of their homes; he saw a people ill-used by another nation in the first instance, and in the second ill-used by individuals; his ideas are therefore raised above the considerations of success.

Why are they so raised when he is not accountable for the event beyond his own duty? Why should his mind dwell on what he thinks unjust when he cannot help it? Because his wish to succeed is not so great as his wish to save!

Volunteers pour in and business accumulates: the rascals rob all the country. I chased two fellows a few nights ago, and cut one of them down. Thank God, he is not hurt to signify, but the affair was uncomfortable for an hour or two, until a surgeon and a light shewed that his hat had saved his head, and his ribs had preserved his inwards. It could not be helped. It was very dark, and following them into a lane I could not trust to taking two men prisoners, both grenadiers, and neither drunk. He is now well, and it has had a good effect.

I am bothered with Sir Neddy Knatchbull, and other squires here, who object hugely to their game being shot. I, hypocrite that I am, inwardly rejoice at it, while with the face of a Quaker when a trooper swears in his presence, I condole with them on the *impropriety* of shooting their birds, and the *impossibility* of preventing it—the last always tacked to my pity for their grievances, as consolation. I do not shoot, but the officers who do send my friends game: so, honour and profit combine. In good faith, however, though some of the squires behave very ill and are very sulky, which is of no use for it only amuses the mess, good Sir Neddy really behaves very well.

He now rejoined his regiment.

October.—This Copenhagen affair is a villainous job, but not being a minister what is it to me? I am glad Lady Hester Stanhope is near you: she is a warm-hearted woman. Is it true that Whitelock is to be shot? He ought to be, but it is a shocking thing for his family: however, the blood of hundreds is on his head!

Nov.—There is a report that Capt. William Napier has taken sixty prisoners! But it is said also that the poor 43rd had twelve men hanged; and Lord Cathcart said twenty successful campaigns cannot wipe off their disgrace! He praises the Germans highly. Now if the 43rd has behaved so ill, it is the fault of General Richard Stewart, their late lieutenant-colonel. Nevertheless, if they have behaved so ill, Lord Cathcart is right to stigmatize them; but he talks nonsense if he thinks those Hanoverians are equal to Englishmen. I wish the fate of England lay on the issue between five thousand of them and the 43rd alone!

This story of the 43rd, was a curious illustration of the manner in which characters of regiments, as well as of individuals, are at times blasted in England by lying envious men, playing on the credulity of story-mongers. That Lord Cathcart ever spoke thus of the 43rd, or in any way injuriously of that regiment, is probably as false as the assertion of twelve men having been hanged: not one man was executed! The story was founded on an isolated fact.

Two soldiers of the regiment, one a black musician, a deserter from the French; the other a deserter, as he afterwards acknowledged, from a ship of war, outraged a woman, and were instantly discovered and tried by a general court-martial. They were condemned, but the proceedings went home, for confirmation, and were declared by the judges illegal: the men thus escaped, but the matter was mentioned in the House of Commons, with the usual errors of would-be orators, to the detriment of the regiment. The truth shall therefore be here recorded, with the peremptory tone due to the fame of as noble a regiment as ever bore arms: a regiment that has the glory of twenty successful campaigns playing around its colours, and no stigma to wipe away. Its conduct in Denmark was immaculate.

Many regiments of many nations the writer of this work has seen in the field, and witnessed many instances of exemplary conduct; but never, not even with the 43rd itself, singularly steady as its career afterwards always was in all situations, did he ever see such entire and perfect negation of wrong-doing as the men and officers of that regiment exhibited in the Copenhagen campaign. All the ground immediately around that capital was rendered a waste by the besieging corps, under the eyes of the general commanding; but where the 43rd was quartered, a little beyond the actual circle of attack, was an oasis. Not the most trifling article was there disturbed, and so strictly was discipline enforced, that one soldier, though a good man, received twenty-five lashes, for plucking a few cherries off a tree standing in front of his quarters!

As to the sixty prisoners, noticed in the correspondence above, there is also a new but true tale to be told about them. A company of the 43rd, under the writer of this, being separated from the rest of the regiment, acted on the right, at what was called the Battle of Kioge. General Leinsingen, a name well known to the readers of the celebrated William Cobbett's works, commanded, and the following atrocities were perpetrated under the name of fighting. Advancing through a thick wood, the Hanoverian red skirmishers, not their green, were in front, and a heavy fire was heard although no enemy was perceived; dead men were however soon come upon, one or two having swords;

none had musquets, and it was evident that a butchery of poor peasants was taking place. At the foot of one tree lay six unhappy creatures; they had climbed it to hide and were shot down. Five were dead, the sixth still alive, but mortally wounded, and the upper part of his arm being broken, the bone was driven half a foot out through the flesh, from the fall! Every British soldier shuddered at the cruelty.

Next day a large village was occupied, and there General Leinsingen set some soldiers to dabble in a common sewer for money, said to be hidden; and he excited others with ladders to enter a church by the roof, the doors being too strong to break open: the writer of this work saw him in the streets without his hat, stimulating the men. All this time the 43rd remained immovably abstinent, with exception of one man, who obeyed the general's call to search the sewer: he was instantly recalled by his captain, who expressed to General Leinsingen, in terms scarcely reconcilable with discipline, his disgust and determination to rejoin his regiment. He was not opposed, and all the prisoners were then put under his charge, with orders to take them to headquarters: not sixty, but four hundred were given over.

But what prisoners? More than three hundred were women and decrepit men! Few were able to bear arms! With this column, a march of three days was made, across the country, directed by the churches, which in Zealand are all on rising knolls, and seen from afar. Hourly the poor prisoners cried out, 'There is my village—my house,' and when they did so, the women and old men were released; the column was thus reduced to sixty young men who, perhaps, bore arms, but did not appear to have done so.

In 1808 Portugal and Spain rose against Napoleon, an event which excited the martial ardour of the British army almost to madness, but at first brought no relief for the monotonous life under which Charles Napier was pining. Sir John Moore was then recalled from Sicily with a large force, which had been there raised by him to the highest state of discipline for service: yet the ministers' design was to have made them escort the royal family of Portugal to the Brazils! Contrary winds and other accidents baffled that miserable scheme, projected to prevent Moore having the command of the army they were preparing for the Peninsula: nevertheless the pitiful object was pursued by sending him to Sweden without plan or instructions, on which he could act, thus placing him at the disposal of a mad monarch, and risking the destruction of the fine army he commanded.

And so intent were they on this intrigue, that when he, having saved his army by a rare sagacity and firmness, came back before their scheme was ripe, they insulted him and placed two men, unknown as generals, over his head. Nevertheless, this expedition was supposed by the public to be designed for real service, and when the 1st battalion of the 50th was ordered to join the troops going to Portugal, Charles Napier's feelings became almost unendurable. However, a vent was now opened for the raging fierceness of the army, and it was full time, inaction had become intolerable. The soldiers, maddened by the monotony of drill, and the ferocity of a discipline disgracing civilization, sought by a variety of devices, evincing extraordinary resolution and subtlety, to escape from their unhappiness.

Amongst other modes they created a bastard ophthalmia, which ruined many hundreds of the finest men, and for a long time baffled the medical officers, both as to cause and cure. Finally, it was discovered, that a soldier of the 28th was the originator; that he had taught the patient to hold his eyelids open, while a comrade scraped lime from the barrack ceiling into his eyes! Inflammation was then kept up by other means, the disease became contagious, and the result was terrible: thousands of the finest men were lost to the service.

Ashford, February.—As to Moore's putting me on the quarter-master-general's staff, dearest mother, he cannot; his interest would of course be great, but I have no right to ask for it: nor would that be a proper way. As to being placed as my father was, it is as impossible as to be made commander in chief. The system of the department is now different, and so many are fit, and so many more think themselves fit, and so many are employed, that the situation is in fact become a very extensive command, and is generally given to lieutenant-colonels who are favourites at the Horse Guards. All I want is the name, and leave of absence, with permission to go anywhere. That favour would not be great, and General Fox is the right person to get it granted: but I don't want to go to India.

March.—Our men have got the ophthalmia very badly, and are dying fast also from inflammation of the lungs, caused by the coldness of the weather and *bad barracks*; in some cases typhus supervenes, but is not contagious. There is no raging fever, cold alone is the cause, yet the men go off three or four a day: no officer suffers, they are warmer. You have, of course dear mother, by this time got my lungs into a high state of inflammation, and put out both my eyes: you shall be duly informed when the typhus begins, or if I am to go off with a good pulse. The people are very disagreeable to us soldiers; but we are taking John Bull in his own way. Some people attacked the 14th Dragoons for keeping hounds, and prevented their hunting. In return they indicted the roads, put their enemies to an expense of fifteen hundred pounds, pulled down two mills, built too near the highway, and thus taught the *gents* that if they push law to extremity for trifles we can do so likewise.

At this period Charles Stanhope, Mr. Pitt's nephew, became youngest major of the 50th, and a friendship quickly sprung up between these near relations of the great rival orators: side by side in war the young men were placed, but destined, too soon, to be divided again by the sword.

Hythe, May.—I rode here, dear mother, this morning, to see poor Sturgeon, who has lost his little wife at last, the betrothed of Emmet, but on coming thought it better not. Young Curran is here, his sister was gone before he arrived. They are going to take the body to Ireland. Mrs. Sturgeon was past hope when she first came; she seemed a perfect ghost, and could not speak without stopping to get breath at every word. Much do I wish poor Sturgeon could get on an expedition, poor fellow! He bears his sorrow too well to forget it easily: but service would employ his mind, and he would then have a chance of being set free from misery, or at least the hope of it, for the chance would be the same.

The endeavour to get killed, even if not successful, would save him much anguish, and by the end of a campaign the bitterness of grief might subside. Yet he would be better pleased to fall, the world to him is void: had his child lived he would have some interest in life. He is to be pitied, and if they should let him go to Sweden one year's active employment might make life worth keeping. His feelings may however be different, and that indolence of grief which can bear retirement and quiet may be his turn, though to me incomprehensible. My disposition is to like retirement at all times, except when in sorrow; then I long for interesting pursuits, duty or danger, or the care of others whom I love, something equal to rousing me. Trifles are not to be borne in grief, and something of interest can always be found. Therefore, I shall always be able to bear grief, and rejoice in a disposition which prepares for that pain we are all destined to bear in life, and which it is weakness to be terrified at, although requiring a full exertion of strength to meet.

The following extract touching the surgery of the day redeems the character of Sangrado.

May.—The soldiers have got pneumonia at Hythe, and are dying as fast as we folks at Ashford. Only think of the surgeon taking from one man in twenty-four hours, *one hundred and sixty ounces of blood*, and he is recovering! They say bleeding to death is the best way of *saving them!*

June.—Moore will hardly be able to attack Cronstadt, but a sudden thing often succeeds with little bloodshed, and you must be quiet and await the event; and dear mother, as thinking will do no good, let us say no more, but hope to see George back with his bellyful of fighting. We are going to send arms to Spain, we had better send legs; however it is but fair to help them to be killed as they like. The papers say Moore is still at Gottenburg, methinks he will soon return.

Being now at the head of a battalion, he accepted the duties with a deep sense of responsibility, as the following terrible letter will shew. The disgusting ferocity of discipline then common, has, thanks to public opinion, enlightened and stirred up to the holy work by Sir Francis Burdett's generous indignation, been abolished: soldiers cannot now be scourged until their blade-bones are laid bare and white as those of a skeleton! The punishment noticed in this letter was not then accounted cruel, it was a medium infliction; and his anxiety, if known, was more likely to have excited contempt than sympathy; to such a depth of ferocity will habit, enforced by brutal powe sink the noblest minds. Yet there was even then a secret sense of shame and horror amongst the thinking portion of the army: low voices were at times heard, like distant echoes to Burdett's trumpet-tongued denunciations, lamenting that such things were.

June 1808.—You know my antipathy to flogging; you know that it is unconquerable. It began from hatred of the sight, and a disgust, not yet gone, though habit reconciles one to horrible sights. This antipathy gains strength from principle and reason, as I am convinced it could be dispensed with. Still, as other severe punishments do not exist in our army, we must use torture in some cases, until a substitute is given by our government. Mark this narrative. A robbery was committed in the regiment and the thief was discovered in a few hours, for men seldom suffer an outrage on their own society: no soldier can rob another without discovery. I resolved to make a severe example.

1). Because we are chiefly composed of boys, and if the punishment of robbery were not made terrible, the temptation of gold and impunity might have a great effect on their minds.

2). Because it was only justice. The man is a pardoned deserter and a hardened villain, very little deserving of pity; and the soldier he robbed was a comrade who put entire confidence in him. It was altogether a villainous affair, and I made a great stir when the matter was reported, giving the men to believe I would drink the very blood of the offender, and flog the whole regiment unless the robber and his accomplices were discovered.

Officers and men were thus worked up, and the grenadiers, he was one of them, soon cleared their honour by producing him. He was sentenced to nine hundred lashes. Yet there was not one positive proof of the robbery, all was presumptive evidence: but I charged him with breaches of discipline, which could be proved, and my resolve was to punish, or not, according to my own judgment, a commanding officer being in truth despotic. Two days I took to consider every circumstance, thinking if he should be afterwards proved innocent, it would be disagreeable to have bestowed nine hundred lashes wrongfully. However, the thing appeared so clear my mind was finally made up, but entirely for the good of others and against my feelings. If mistaken in my judgment there was nothing to tax conscience with, for decision is absolutely necessary amongst troops. The man thought me his deadly foe, whereas he had not such a powerful advocate in the garrison, for everyone was outrageous against him, while in my mind there was not an atom of anger. Yesterday he was flogged in the square, where, no longer appearing angry, I said part of the punishment should be remitted if he would tell of his accomplices; that torture would make him speak, and the money would prove his truth; it would therefore be better for his accomplices to confess and be produced. No one spoke. When he had received two hundred lashes he was promised pardon, if he told where the money was. No! God in heaven was his witness he was innocent; many a man prayed for my honour who was guilty of many bad things, spare him in God's name who was innocent! In this manner, he went on. I was inexorable: and it is hardly credible that he received six hundred lashes, given in the most severe manner, and which he showed he felt with that acute sense of pain that some men have not, the whole time calling God and the saints to witness his innocence, praying for death to relieve him. It required great resolution to remain inflexible, but it was necessary. Was I right in thinking him guilty, then it was right to do what was done. Was I wrong, then my misfortune could not be greater merely from giving more pain; and unless I went to the full extent it must be wrong, because it would evince doubt, and with doubt not a lash should have been given.

Feeling right I was firm, but at six hundred lashes he was taken down, with the seemingly brutal intention of flogging him again on a half-healed back, which is in a commanding officer's power to do, and the greatest torture possible. He was told it should be so unless he confessed in the interim, and directions were given that he should he kept solitary to lower his spirits. My troubles were soon over: pain, lowness, and the people employed to frighten him succeeded, he confessed all, and told where the money was hid.

July.—They say Lord Moira is to command the expedition to Spain, Anstruther is going, everybody is going but me: with my untoward luck I ought not to serve. Will you let me know if you hear of any majority of militia vacant, for it is better to be one thing or t' other at once. I see no prospect of adversity to try Napoleon's genius, but a great prospect of fresh laurels, and as much patriots' blood as will make rich land and good crops in Spain, where all is noise and bubble: the slaughter of the patriots is the only substantial thing, and that will continue to be so. Still we are bound to help them, poor people. We have not indeed ruined them by our intrigues, we are guiltless of their blood, but I would rather see England sink with them than refuse her aid in so noble a cause.

Let her trust home to my brother militia-men, and send her soldiers to the last man into Spain, we may succeed: God only knows, and He is beyond our ken. That we shall make some blunder is my opinion, we always do; but the fate of Spain and Europe is settled beforehand and we shall do as fate ordains. Those fine Spaniards are to be liked, and it is fitting we should fall with them rather than leave them without help. I have heard no military man's opinion yet, but it appears madness to make diversions as they call them: if they intend to fight, let fifty thousand men be sent, and all the officers who speak the language to form their men. We have but one chance, which is to annihilate the French army in Spain before succours can cross the Pyrenees; but this requires a rapidity of action which we never exert, although we have the power.

Why should we attempt Italy? if we succeed in Spain it will be the best diversion in favour of Italy; for Napoleon will draw troops from there and the north to restore his power: then will be the time for attacking him nearer home. If he leaves Brest defenceless, as he has often done, we could strike a blow, which *you* have often heard of, before he could help himself. In this mode we might help ourselves, but his arms will crush everything in Spain that they can reach. Nevertheless, a hostile population is a powerful weapon and no man can say what it will effect.

It is remarkable that these objections to an Italian diversion, were precisely those advanced by Wellington in 1813, when the project was renewed by Lord William Bentinck and the ministers. The stroke at Brest was a favourite project with his father, and according to the *Buckingham Memoirs*, General Simcoe also proposed that enterprise, but Lord Grenville at once pronounced it to be impracticable. The arrogant ignorance, as to military affairs, which then marked the government, would be almost incredible if it had not descended with full darkness, upon the Newcastles, Sydney Herberts, and Panmures. Formerly it excited the disgust of Simcoe, Lord Moira, Abercrombie, Sir Charles Stuart, Moore and Wellington; in the present time, the disgust of the whole world. At both periods War! War! has been shouted with the ferocity and violence of savages; and yet conducted with more than the ignorance of barbarians, so far as the governments have been concerned.

Here, as connected with the subject, it may be permitted to observe, that the noble editor of the *Memoirs* in question has assailed the authenticity of a passage in the present writer's *History of the Peninsular War* which imputes to the Grey and Grenville administration the collecting of troops at Cork for conquest in South America. He says their ministry had terminated six months before, and there was no proof of such design. The authority was the Duke of Wellington, who positively and emphatically, and with decision pressed the fact, knowing the use that would be made of his communication.

The fourth epoch of Charles Napier's life shall now be terminated with a letter, not addressed to his mother but designed for her support under severe mental depression: for she was in uneasy worldly circumstances, menaced with total blindness, and had recently lost her husband, her brother, and her youngest child, a beautiful girl, Cecilia, recalled to heaven when just entering on womanhood.

5ᵗʰ, WEST KENT REGIMENT, 1812.

Chapter 6

Battle of Coruña

From the visions of childhood to the aspirations of manhood, Charles Napier's progress has been presented in the preceding pages without reserve; and it has been seen that his spirit bent very gently to all social feelings: it was not the bending of weakness though, and he shall now be shewn as fierce in danger, and as strong in suffering, as he was before tender and affectionate.

After the Battle of Vimiera he was suddenly called to Lisbon with his friend Stanhope. His colonel, Walker, then obtained leave of absence, the regiment fell to Napier, and with a marked indication of personal esteem, Sir J. Moore incorporated it in the army going to Spain, having previously rejected it while under Walker, whose harsh discipline had excited his anger. It is well known how the truly great and ill-used Moore was sent into the heart of Spain by incapable ministers, to find not armies, nor enthusiasm, nor energetic government, nor military aid, all of which he had been promised; but in their stead the greatest military genius of the world before him, with troops so numerous that their cavalry alone doubled his whole force. It is known also with what a mastery of war he extricated himself from that raging storm of war; with what firmness, he conducted his retreat; and how, turning at Coruña, he ended his glorious life amid the fires of victory.

During the retreat Charles Napier, serving in Lord William Bentinck's brigade, so justified the favour of Moore, that the 50th's ranks were full at the Battle of Coruña, and puissant was the shock with which they met the greatest assailing French column on that fatal field, driving it back with fire and steel beneath the eyes of the general, who with exultant applause gave instant orders to support the impetuous counter stroke. Had those orders been obeyed Soult's

Sketch of the
BATTLE OF CORUNNA
16th. January 1809.

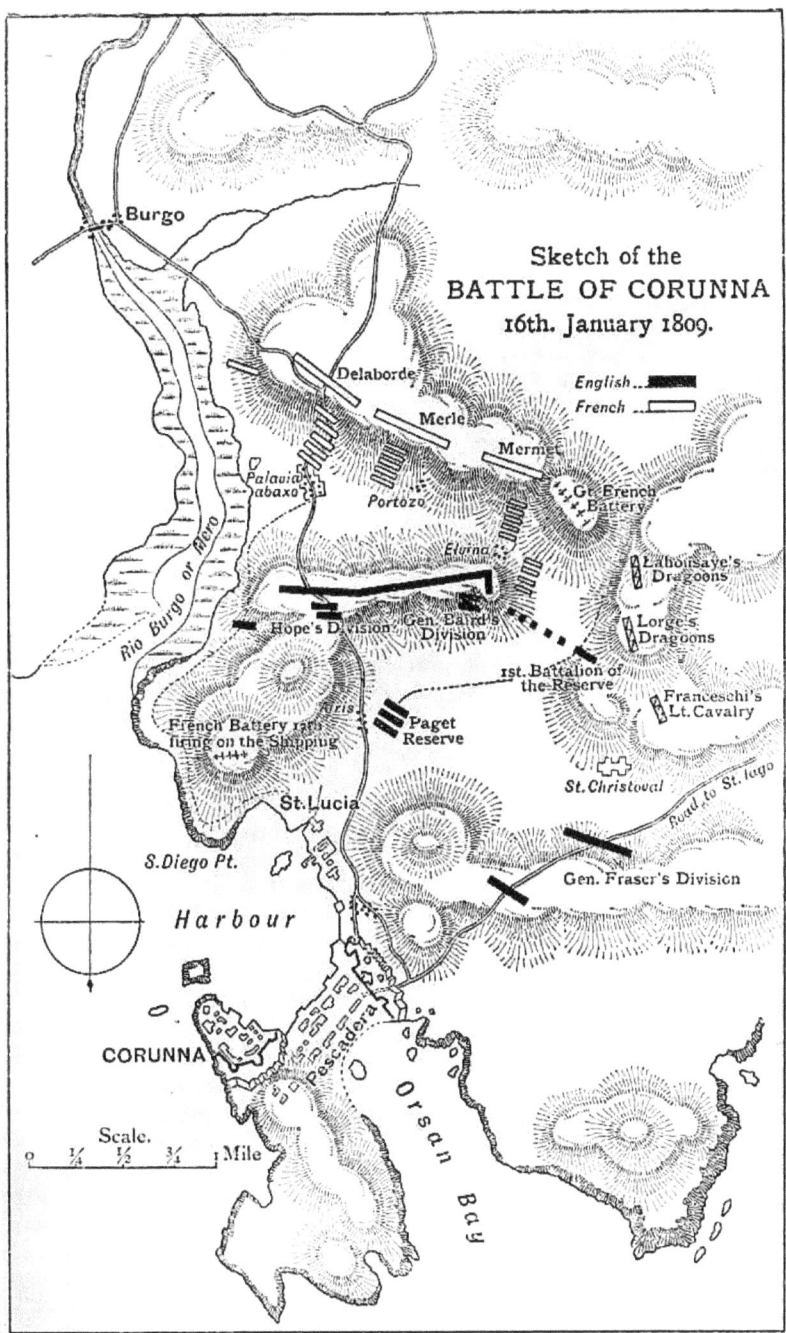

English ...
French ...

Burgo

Delaborde

Merle

Mermet

Rio Burgo or Mero

Palavia abaxo

Portozo

Gt. French Battery

Elvina

Hope's Division

Gen. Baird's Division

Laboissaye's Dragoons

Lorge's Dragoons

1st. Battalion of the Reserve

Franceschi's Lt. Cavalry

French Battery firing on the Shipping

Paget Reserve

St. Christoval

Road to St. Iago

St. Lucia

S. Diego Pt.

Gen. Fraser's Division

Harbour

CORUNNA

Pescadera

Orsan Bay

Scale.
0   ¼   ½   ¾   Mile

army would have been lost, but just then the heroic Moore fell, and error followed when the presiding spirit was gone. The 50th was not supported, and fighting amongst lanes, houses and vineyards, was scattered in small bands, when fresh enemies came down to overwhelm the broken ranks. Stanhope was killed, and Charles Napier, covered with wounds, was carried off a prisoner: far in advance, and hidden by inequalities of ground, his desperate contention was unobserved, and was in the dispatches unnoticed; but the following narrative of his conduct and sufferings, will supply the deficiency: it was written afterwards and by him marked, as

My Part in the Battle of Coruña, and that of John Hennessy"

On the 16th of January, 1809, the British Army was opposed to the French at Coruña. The Imperial troops, on higher ground, hung over us like threatening clouds, and about one o'clock the storm burst. Our line was under arms, silent, motionless, yet all were anxious for the appearance of Sir John Moore. There was a feeling that under him we could not be beaten, and this was so strong at all times as to be a great cause of discontent during the retreat wherever he was not. Where is the general? was now heard along that part of the line where I was, for only of what my eyes saw, and my ears heard, do I speak.

This agitation augmented as the cries of men stricken by cannon-shot arose. I stood in front of my left wing, on a knoll, from whence the greatest part of the field could be seen, and my picquets were fifty yards below, disputing the ground with the French skirmishers: but a heavy French column, which had descended the mountain at a run, was coming on behind with great rapidity, and shouting *En avant, tue, tue, en avant tue!* their cannon at the same time, plunging from above, ploughed the ground and tore our ranks. Suddenly I heard the gallop of horses, and turning saw Moore. He came at speed, and pulled up so sharp and close he seemed to have alighted from the air; man and horse looking at the approaching foe with an intenseness that seemed to concentrate all feeling in their eyes.

The sudden stop of the animal, a cream-coloured one with black tail and mane, had cast the latter streaming forward, its ears were pushed out like horns, while its eyes flashed fire, and it snorted loudly with expanded nostrils, expressing terror, astonishment and muscular exertion. My first thought was, it will be away like the wind! but then I looked at the rider and the horse was forgotten. Thrown on its haunches the animal came, sliding and dashing the dirt up with its fore feet, thus bending the general forward almost to its neck; but his head was thrown back and his look more keenly piercing than I ever before saw it. He glanced to the right and left, and then fixed his eyes intently on the enemy's advancing column, at the same time grasping the reins with both his hands, and pressing the horse firmly with his knees: his body thus seemed to deal with the animal while his mind was intent on the enemy, and his aspect was one of searching intenseness beyond the power of words to describe: for a while he looked, and then galloped to the left, without uttering a word.

I walked to the right of my regiment, where the French fire from the village of Elvina was now very sharp, and our picquets were being driven in by the attacking column; but I soon returned to the left, for the enemy's guns were striking heavily there, and his musquetry also swept down many men. Meeting Stanhope, I ordered him to the rear of the right wing, because the ground was lower, it was his place, he was tall, the shot flew high, and I thought he would be safer. Moore now returned, and I asked him to let me throw our grenadiers, who were losing men fast, into the enclosures in front. 'No,' he said, 'they will fire on our own picquets in the village.'

'Sir our picquets, and those of the 4th Regiment, also, were driven from thence when you went to the left.'

'Were they, then you are right, send out your grenadiers:' and again, he galloped away. Turning round I saw Captain Clunes of the 50th, just arrived from Coruna, and said to him, 'Clunes take your grenadiers and open the ball.' He stalked forward alone, like Goliath before the Philistines, for six feet five he was in height, and of proportionate hulk and strength, his grenadiers followed, and thus the battle began on our side.

Again Sir John Moore returned, and was talking to me when a round shot struck the ground between his horse's feet and mine. The horse leaped round, and I also turned mechanically, but Moore forced the animal back and asked me if I was hurt? 'No sir!' Meanwhile a second shot had torn off the leg of a 42nd man, who screamed horribly, and rolled about so as to excite agitation and alarm with others. The general said. 'This is nothing my lads, keep your ranks, take that man away: my good fellow don't make such a noise, we must bear these things better.' He spoke sharply, but it had a good effect; for this man's cries had made an opening in the ranks, and the men shrunk from the spot, although they had not done so when others had been hit who did not cry out. But again, Moore went off, and I saw him no more! It

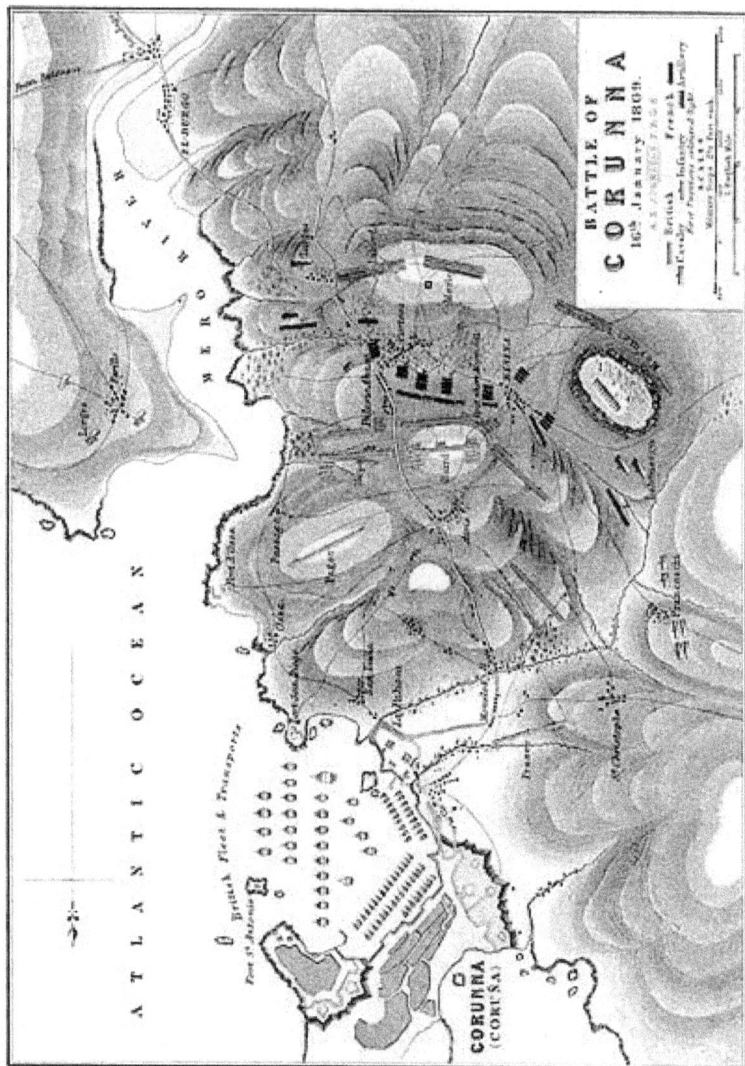

BATTLE OF
CORUNNA
16th January 1809.

was a little in front of this spot that he was killed. The French pointed out the place to me two months afterwards. There it was he refused to let them take off his sword when it hurt his wound! that dreadful wound! poor fellow! Yet, why poor fellow? Is death to be regretted when accompanied by victory, glory, admiration! Rather let those sigh who live and rot, doing nothing, and having nothing to do, until, poor miserable drivellers, they sink under a tombstone!

Lord William Bentinck now came up on his quiet mule, and though the fire was heavy began talking to me as if we were going to breakfast; his manner was his ordinary one, with perhaps an increase of good-humour and placidity. He conversed for some time, but no recollection of what he said remains, for the fire was sharp and my eyes were more busy than my ears: I only remember saying to myself this chap takes it coolly or the devil's in it.

Lord William and his mule, which seemed to care as little for the fire as its rider, sheltered me from shot, which I liked well enough; but having heard officers and soldiers jeer at Colonel Walker for thus sheltering himself behind General Fane's horse at Vimiera, I went to the exposed side: yet it gave me the most uncomfortable feel experienced that day. Lord William borrowed my spyglass, it had been Lord Edward FitzGerald's, and was a very fine one, I never saw it more. He went to the 4th Regiment and was not seen by me again during the fight; nor did I receive an order from him or anybody, unless Sir John Moore's permission to move my grenadiers forward can be called one: neither did I see a single staff officer during the battle, except Sir John and Lord William.

When Lord William went away I walked up and down before the regiment, and made the men shoulder and order arms twice to occupy their attention, for they were falling fast and seemed uneasy at standing under fire. The colours also were lowered, because they were a mark for the enemy's great guns: this was by the advice of old John Montgomery, a brave soldier who had risen from the ranks. Soon the 42nd advanced in line, but no orders came for me. 'Good God! Montgomery,' I said, 'are we not to advance?'

'I think we ought' he answered.

'But,' said I, 'no orders have come.' 'I would not wait' he said.

The 4th did not move, the 42nd seemed likely to want our aid, it was not a moment for hesitation, and John Montgomery, a Scotchman, said laughingly 'You cannot be wrong to follow the 42nd.' I gave the word but forbad any firing, and to prevent it and occupy the men's attention, made them slope and carry arms by word of command. Many of them cried out, 'Major let us fire!'

'Not yet' was my answer, for having advanced without orders, I thought to have them more under command if we were wrong, whereas, firing once begun, we could not change. At that moment, the 42nd checked a short distance from a wall and commenced firing, and though a loud cry arose of 'Forward! forward!' no man, as I afterwards heard, passed the wall. This check seemed to prove that my advance was right, and we passed the 42nd. Then I said to my men. 'Do you see your enemies plain enough to hit them?'

Many voices shouted 'By Jasus we do!'

'Then blaze away!' and such a rolling fire broke out as I have hardly ever heard since.

After passing the 42nd we came to the wall, which was breast high and my line checked, but several officers. Stanhope one, leaped over, calling on the men to follow. At first about a hundred did at a low part, no more, and therefore, leaping back, I took a halberd and holding it horizontally pushed many over the low part; and again, getting over myself, run along, followed by my orderly sergeant, Keene, with his pike. As we passed, four or five soldiers levelled together from the other side, but Keene threw up their muskets with a force and quickness which saved me from being blown to atoms, as it was my face was much burned: then all got over, yet it required the example of officers and the bravest men to get all over.

Now the line was formed beyond the wall, and I, recollecting Voltaire's story of the guards' officers laying their swords over the men's firelocks to keep their level low, did so with the halberd to show coolness, and being cool, though the check at the wall had excited me and made me swear horribly. We then got to marshy ground close to a village, where the fire from the houses was terrible, the howitzers from the hills pelting us also. Still I led the men on, followed closely by Ensigns Moore and Stewart with the colours until both fell, and the colours were caught up by Sergeant Magee and another sergeant. My sword-belt was shot off scabbard and all, but not being hit I pushed rapidly into the street, exactly at the spot where, soon after, I was taken prisoner. Many Frenchmen lay there, apparently dead, but the soldiers cried out bayonet them, they are pretending. The idea was to me terrible, and made me call out 'No! no! leave those cowards, there are plenty who bear arms to kill, come on!'

At this place stood the church, and towards the enemy a rocky mound, behind which, and on it, were the grenadiers; but no officer met my sight, except Captain Harrison, Lieutenant Patterson, and Lieutenant Turner, and my efforts were vain to form a strong body; the men would not leave the rocks, from which they kept up a heavy fire. No time was to be lost, we could not see what passed on our flanks, we had been broken in carrying the village of Elviña, and as a lane went up straight towards the enemy, I run forward calling out to follow: about thirty privates and the above-named officers did so, but the fire was then terrible, many shells burst among us, and the crack of these things deafened me, making my ears ring. Halfway up the lane I fell, without knowing why, but was much hurt, though at the moment unconscious of it; a soldier cried out 'The major is killed.'

'Not yet, come on.'

We reached the end of this murderous lane, but a dozen of those who entered it with me fell ere we got through it. However, some shelter was found beyond the lane; for Brooks of the 4th had occupied the spot with his picquet the day before, and had made a breastwork of loose stones, which was known to me, having been there, and nearly killed the evening before, when visiting the picquet as officer of the day. The heap remained, and about a dozen of us lodged ourselves behind this breastwork, and then it appeared to me that by a rush forward we could carry the battery above; and it was evident we must go on or go back, we could not last long where we were.

Three or four men were killed at my side, for the breastwork was but a slender protection, and two were killed by the fire of our own men from the village behind. The poor fellows kept crying out as they died, 'Oh God! Major, our own men are killing us! Oh, Christ God I'm shot in the back of the head!' The last man was so, for he fell against me, and the ball had entered just above the poll. Remembering then that my father had told me he saved a man's life, at the siege of Charleston, by pulling a ball out with his finger before inflammation swelled the parts, I thought to do the same, but could not find it, and feared to do harm by putting my finger far in. It made me feel sick, and the poor fellow being laid down, continued crying out that our men had killed him, and there he soon died.

This misery shook us all a good deal, and made me so wild as to cry and stamp with rage, feeling a sort of despair at seeing the soldiers did not come on. I sent Turner, Harrison and Patterson, the three officers with me, to bring them on, and they found Stanhope animating the men, but not knowing what to do, and calling out 'Good God where is Napier?'

When Turner told him I was in front and raging for them to come on for an attack on the battery, he gave a shout and called on the men to follow him, but ere taking a dozen strides cried out 'Oh my God!' and fell dead, shot through the heart. Turner, and a sergeant who had been also sent back, then returned to me, saying they could not get a man to follow them up the lane. Hearing this, I got on the wall, waving my sword and my hat at the same time, and calling out to the men behind among the rocks; but the fire was so loud none heard me, though the lane was scarcely a hundred yards long. No fire was drawn upon me by this, for a French captain afterwards told me he, and others, prevented their men firing at me; he did not know, nor was he told by me, who it was, but he said, instead of firing at him I longed to run forwards and embrace that brave officer. My own companions called out to jump down or I should be killed: I thought so too, but was so mad as to care little what happened to me.

Looking then along the field, from the height of the wall, our smoke appeared to be everywhere retiring; but the French smoke was not advancing, which gave me comfort. However, it was useless to stay there, and jumping down I said to Harrison, 'Stay here as long as you can, I will go to the left and try to make out how the 42nd get on.' No one was to be seen near our left from my standing place near the wall; but there was some brushwood, and a ridge with a hedge on the top, which debarred further sight, and the thought came to me that instead of being foremost, we might be in line with some of the 42nd—and though the 4th had not advanced, if fifty men of the 42nd and 50th could be gathered, we might still charge the battery above us: if we failed there was a house near, into which we could force our way, and as it was conspicuous from the English position Moore would send me support.

Telling this to Captain Harrison, I went off along a lane running at right angles from the one we were in, and parallel to our position; this exposed me to the English, not to the French fire, but being armed with only a short sabre, useless against a musket and bayonet, and being quite alone, short-sighted, and without spectacles, I felt very cowardly and anxious. Pursuing my course however for about a hundred yards, I came near a French officer lying on his back wounded, and being myself covered with blood and my face smeared, for two of the killed men had fallen in my arms, my look was no doubt fierce; and though I approached him out of pity, he thought it was to kill him:

his feet were towards me and as he raised his head he cried out to some comrades above him, pointing with a quick convulsive motion towards me.

Those whom he addressed could not be seen, for the ridge was about six feet high, nearly perpendicular, with the thick hedge at top; but my danger was soon announced through the roots of the hedge by a blaze of fire poured so close as to fill the lane with smoke. All went over my head, being evidently fired without seeing me, or my body must have been blown to pieces.

Giving myself up for lost, the temptation to run back was great, but the thought that our own line might see me, made me walk leisurely, in more danger indeed yet less alarmed than when going forward without knowing what would happen. The whole excursion along the lane was the most nervous affair I ever experienced in battle; nor was my alarm lessened on getting back, for Harrison and the others were gone! They could not stand the fire. I felt very miserable then, thinking the 50th had behaved ill; that my not getting the battery had been a cause of the battle being lost, and that Moore would attribute all to me. The English smoke had gone back, and my only comfort was that the French smoke had not gone forward.

The battle seemed nearly over, I thought myself the last man alive belonging to our side who had got so far in front, and felt certain of death, and that my general would think I had hidden myself, and would not believe me to have done my best. I thought also my little party had been taken. Lord William Bentinck afterwards told me that he had ordered my regiment back, in direct contradiction of Moore's design, who had, he admitted, told him not to recall me, but send men to my assistance!!!

In this state of distraction, and still under a heavy fire, I turned down the lane to rejoin the regiment and soon came on a wounded man, who shrieked out, 'Oh praised be God major! my dear major! God help you my darling, one of your own 50th.'

'I cannot carry you, was my reply; can you walk with my help?'

'Oh no major I am too badly wounded.'

'You must lie there then till help can be found.'

'Oh Christ God, my jewel, my own dear major sure you won't leave me!'

The agony with which he screamed was great, it roused all my feelings, and strange to say alarmed me about my own danger, which had been forgot in my misery at finding Harrison was gone from the corner, and thinking the battle lost.

Stooping down, I raised the poor fellow, but a musket-ball just then broke the small bone of my leg some inches above the ankle; the pain was acute, and though the flesh was not torn, the dent made in my flesh remains to this day and is tender to the touch! Telling the man of my own wound, my course was resumed; his piteous cries were then terrible, and fell bitterly as reproaches for my want of fortitude and courage. Yet what could be done by a man hardly able to walk, and in great pain, with other duties to perform? I felt it horrible to leave him, but selfishness and pain got the better, and with the help of my sword, limping and with much suffering, I arrived at a spot where two other lanes met at the corner of a church: there were three privates of the 50th, and one of the 42nd, an Irishman, there, who said we were cut off, and indeed Frenchmen were then coming up both lanes, one party from the position of the 50th the other from that of the 4th. The last appeared the least numerous and the nearest, they were not thirty yards from us, and forgetting my leg then, though I had not pluck to do so for the poor wounded man left behind, I said to the four soldiers, 'follow me and we'll cut through them': then with a shout I rushed forward.

The Frenchmen had halted, but now run on to us, and just as my spring and shout was made the wounded leg failed and I felt a stab in the back: it gave me no pain, but felt cold and threw me on my face. Turning to rise I saw the man who had stabbed me making a second thrust; whereupon letting go my sabre I caught his bayonet by the socket, turned the thrust, and raising myself by the exertion grasped his firelock with both hands, thus in mortal struggle regaining my feet. His companions had now come up and I heard the dying cries of the four men with me, who were all bayoneted instantly.

We had been attacked from behind by men not before seen, as we stood with our backs to a doorway, out of which must have rushed several men, for we were all stabbed in an instant, before the two parties coming up the road reached us: they did so however just as my struggle with the man who had wounded me was begun. That was a contest for life, and being the strongest, I forced him between myself and his comrades, who appeared to be the men whose lives I had saved when they pretended to be dead on our advance through the village.

They struck me with their muskets clubbed, and bruised me much; whereupon, seeing no help near, and being overpowered by numbers, and in great pain from my wounded leg, I called out '*Je se rend*,' remembering the expression correctly from an old story of a fat officer, whose name being James, called out 'Jemmy round'. Finding they had no disposition to spare me, I kept hold of the musket, vigorously defending myself with the body of the little Italian who had first wounded me, but soon grew faint, or rather tired. At that moment, a tall dark man came up, seized the end of the musket with his left hand, whirled his brass-hilted sabre round and struck me a powerful blow on the head, which was bare, for my cocked hat had fallen off.

Expecting the blow would finish me, I had stooped my head in hopes it might fall on my back, or at least on the thickest part of the head and not on the left temple; so far I succeeded, for it fell exactly on the top, cutting into the bone but not through it. Fire sparkled from my eyes, I fell on my knees, blinded, yet without quite losing my senses and holding still on to the musket. Recovering in a moment, I regained my legs, and saw a florid handsome young French drummer holding the arm of the dark Italian, who was in the act of repeating his blow. Quarter was then given, but they tore my pantaloons in tearing my watch and purse from my pocket, and a little locket of hair which hung round my neck; they snatched at everything; but while this went on two of them were wounded, and the drummer, Guibert, ordered the dark man who had sabred me to take me to the rear.

When we begun to move, I resting on him, because hardly able to walk, I saw him look back over his shoulder to see if Guibert was gone; and so, did I, for his rascally face made me suspect him. Guibert's back was towards us, he was walking off, and the Italian again drew his sword, which he had before sheathed. I called out to the drummer, 'this rascal is going to kill me! brave Frenchmen don't kill prisoners.' Guibert run back, swore furiously at the Italian, shoved him away, almost down, and putting his arms round my waist supported me himself: thus, this generous Frenchman saved me twice, for the Italian was bent upon slaying.

We had not proceeded far up the old lane, when we met a soldier of the 50th walking down at a rapid pace; he instantly halted, recovered his arms and cocked his piece, looking fiercely at us to make out what it was. My recollection is that he levelled at Guibert and I threw up his musket, calling out. 'For God's sake don't fire, I am a prisoner, badly wounded, and can't help you. Surrender.'

'For why would I surrender?' he cried aloud, with the deepest of all Irish brogues.

'Because there are at least 20 men upon you.'

There were five or six with us at the time. 'Well if I must surrender, there,' said he, dashing down his firelock across their legs and making them jump. 'There's my firelock for yez.' Then coming close up he threw his arm round me, and giving Guibert a push that sent him and one or two more reeling against the wall, shouted out, 'Stand away ye bloody spalpeens, I'll carry him myself, bad luck to the whole of yez.'

My expectation was to see them fall upon him, but John Hennessy was a strong and fierce man, and moreover looked bigger than he was, for he stood upon the higher ground. Apparently, they thought him an awkward fellow to deal with, he seemed willing to go with me and they let him have his own way. In this manner, we proceeded about a hundred yards beyond the corner where Harrison and the rest had left me, and found a large force under General Renaud—afterwards Governor of Ciudad Rodrigo and captured by Don Julian. He asked me my rank, and how I was taken? My reply was, taken because my regiment would not come on! I was in great anger, and altogether ignorant of Lord William Bentinck having ordered them back; for the staff officer sent by him had not chosen to come up to me.

My thought was that the regiment had given way, which made me very unjust in abuse of the glorious old 50th, for they had gone further than any other corps in the army. Had Moore's orders, for the 42nd and 4th to support us, been obeyed by Lord William, we should have carried the hill in a few minutes: that this was the cause of their going back is true, for Lord William Bentinck afterwards told me so himself. General Renaud ordered a surgeon to dress me, and he put a plaister on my head; but my leg was so swollen he could not get off my boot without cutting, which I would not allow, hoping to escape, in which case the loss of a boot would be irreparable. They took me up the hill to where the Spanish magazine on the top had been exploded.

Soon after leaving Einaudi, being supported by one of his officers and Hennessy, with a guard, we passed a large gap in a wall, on which the English fire was still very heavy. The French soldiers cried out, 'Don't cross there except on your knees, or you will be shot,' whereupon the French officer desired Hennessy and me to do so, but we refused, and Hennessy said low, 'Be Jasus they're afraid.' My desire was to be seen by our own people, and therefore my walk with Hennessy and the officer was erect, and slow; but seeing the French guard crawl on their hands and knees, I said to the captain. 'Crawl you too, or you will be hit—I can't run away.' This anxiety for an enemy greatly amused the Frenchmen, and it was afterwards told to the marshals, Soult and

Ney; Renaud also mentioned it when a prisoner in London: however, the officer would only stoop, and none of us were hit.

On the summit of the position my bodily agony was so great, that Hennessy and the French captain, seeing some straw near a fire laid me on it; my leg and side were giving me excruciating pain, it was dark, and Hennessy went away for a while with the captain: then a French officer came and stood over me, a tall handsome man; he looked at me for some time and said. 'War! war! war! My God will this horrid work never cease! poor young man, I fear you are badly wounded.' He gave me some drink, and tears rolled down his cheeks; but then he turned away and several others sat down round the fire without noticing me. Soon however came the man whose straw I had been laid upon; he gave me two kicks and dragged me by the neck off his bundle, hurting me much. I said nothing, except 'God damn you,' and two or three Frenchmen starting up took my part.

Then the tall officer returned, and was very angry, but the beast who kicked me would not let me be put back on the straw, which he claimed. The officer told them to take me into the ruin of a blown-up house, or magazine, where some officers had had a fire in the remains of a room, the fireplace being indeed nearly all that existed of the building; but he left me, and then the men took me into another ru-ined room, and threw me into the filth with which it was filled, and began to laugh at me. I was very angry, wished myself dead at once, and said something violent, whereupon they seemed to consult about killing me, and my hopes of life fled: indeed, my wish was not to live, but at that moment the officer came back with two or three more, and with two soldiers who had before left the place, I think to call them and save me.

These officers were very angry, but my understanding was faint, and my desire was to be put out of misery, for I thought we had lost the battle and my pain of body was past bearing. They however car-ried me to the other part of the building near the fireplace, and there was Hennessy. They offered me broth and wine, but I could touch nothing from the agony of my wounds, and groaned at times, for the pain was no longer supportable even before an enemy. Not being able to lie down, Hennessy held me in his arms in an upright posture.

The French officers did all they could for me, as far as kind words went, and soon one of their own officers was brought in wounded; it was the captain who had been with me when first taken. General Renaud also now sent an officer with my sword, desiring me to wear it for I had used it well. I wrote my name and rank on a piece of paper—with a stick dipped in his blood—and requested the officer to give it and my sword to Marshal Soult, with a request to speak to him. That officer did not return.

"Hennessy having occasion to go out of the ruin, set me in an angle of the fireplace, but never came back, being seized and marched off, as he afterwards told me. Before he left me he unbuckled my spurs and whispered—'The spurs are silver, the spalpeens would murder you for them.' When he did not return, my idea was, that he had made his escape, and took the spurs with that intention; at least my hope was so, that he might tell my brother George where I was, for what fretted me most was, that no flag of truce came in for me. I thought Moore was angry, that myself and the regiment had been disgraced, and therefore he would not send in, nor let George come: then the fancy came that George was killed, but my thoughts were all wild and sad that night.

(George, who was *aide-de-camp* to Moore, had not forgotten him; he had passed many hours of the night seeking for him with a torch amongst the dead, turning over body after body.)

Very wretched in body and mind was I now, and in about two hours after Hennessy had gone, the French officers went away, one after another. The fire was out and it was dreadfully cold, yet pain kept me from feeling it so much, and all that long and horrible night and next day, did I lay wishing for death, and expecting it if a stray soldier should see me. There was no roof, only a few feet of wall standing, and the following evening, about dusk, being in less pain, I crawled out, reckless of being killed or not. Outside there was a Frenchman cooking, he was a kind man and gave me some broth, but I could not eat it. He went away, but returned with another soldier and they made up a little more fire, rolled themselves in their great coats, and other warm things, and lay down.

Pain kept me waking, and the fire went out soon, for there was no fuel. I had no waistcoat or drawers, only a uniform coat and torn trousers, and the cold was dreadful, for it was January and the hill high. An oilskin was on my hat, and I pulled it off to cover my head and face; then putting my hands on my mouth warmed myself with my breath, but could not lie down. My feet and legs lost all feeling, and the wounded leg ceased to pain me, except when moved. About midnight the two Frenchmen went their way, and promised to tell their commandant of my state, yet the second dreadful night passed and no one came.

Next day about three o'clock a musician came near me, and I persuaded him to take me to his regiment, but to walk was agony. I was however very kindly received by all the French officers, who were seated round a fire, and especially so by their commander, a man with a very red face and perfectly white *moustachios* and hair; they treated me well, and finally forwarded me on to Marshal Soult's quarters. We passed through Elvina amidst all the bodies of my poor 50th soldiers scattered about; and many wounded were still alive in a house, and very clamorous for food. Scarcely able to speak from weakness, I was supported by two men, yet at last reached Soult's quarters, and being shewn into the kitchen sat down in much suffering. Monsieur de Chamont, *aide-de-camp* to Soult, came to me; he was all kindness and attention, and offered me money, which was declined, but I told him his men had been expert in robbing me; that everyone who met me as I was borne to the rear had asked '*est il pille?*' and the reply always was '*Oh pour ça oui, joliment.*'

It was impossible to be kinder than De Chamont, and that kindness was continued by the marshal and his staff, and again by Ney and his staff. On my telling Soult of the wounded starving English soldiers lying in the village, he promised to have them helped immediately, and sent me to his own quarters, where a bed was provided, and food: the latter was in truth much needed, for none had been taken since my breakfast on the 16th, and this was the 18th. The pain in my side gave me little rest, and next morning, being ordered to go into Coruña, I was put on a horse attended by a dragoon, and entered the town with the troops.

At the gate there was a crowd, and a Spaniard hustled against my leg, which put me to such torture I cursed him aloud in English, and gave him a blow on the head with as great force as the pain left me strength to do. The stupid brute knew of my wound, for I had pushed him twice away before, and shewed him how my leg was tied up. The delight of the French soldiers at my striking the Don was very great: he deserved it, but I was now very well treated. My billet was on Monsieur Barriere, a banker who lived with his brother-in-law, Marchesa, an excellent kind fellow with a pretty Spanish wife. There my state was as comfortable as kindness on the part of my host and the French officers, particularly Baron Clouet, Ney's *aide-de-camp*, could make it—but I was a prisoner!

One anecdote I have forgotten.

Before the 50th advanced, while standing under the cannonade, the balls at first went about a foot or two over our heads, the men stooped, or as it is called by soldiers ducked. Standing in front I said, laughing. 'Don't duck, the ball has passed before you hear the whiz.' The ducking however was continued, by all but one little fellow, who stood erect, and I said to him aloud, 'You are a little fellow but the tallest man in the 50th today for all that—come to me after the battle and you shall be a sergeant.' Everyone heard me, yet strange to say no one afterwards knew who he was, nor could his name be learned: we supposed he fell, and the agitation of the moment had made others forget, or not notice him.

Such were my own adventures in the Battle of Coruña, told without modesty or concealment; for I write not this for the public, but from old notes for my wife and children, with no desire to make them think more or less of my actions than the reality. I felt great fear for a few minutes at one period of the fight; yet it was not such as to influence my conduct, and at no other period did a thought of my own safety cross my mind. It was when alone in the lane and expecting to meet numbers in personal combat that my nerves were most affected; for as my short-sightedness disabled me from seeing what was going on, and what was to be met, I feared to fall unseen and unknown.

Afterwards, when wearing spectacles, the nervous feeling was not so strong, but the disadvantage of bad sight is tremendous when alone, and gives a feeling of helplessness. With all this, alarm was not my feeling when the men told me we were cut off; nervousness then ceased, and only the thought of how to break through the enemy remained: had it not been for the stab in my back, and the sudden lameness, I should have done it, for my resolution was that no man should go before me that day, and no man did, unless Hennessy. Where he had been, or came from, is to me unknown, I could never make it out from him; he spoke but little English, and explained himself with difficulty. His very strange history shall now be shortly told.

He was born in Cork, enlisted in the 50th, was not what is called a smart soldier, and at one time pretended to have lost the use of his limbs from rheumatism. Tried by Colonel Walker for *malingering*, the offence was clearly proved and, as was common in those days of atrocious punishment, he was sentenced to 500 lashes. Hennessy's fortitude was great, he bore the punishment without a groan, but would not admit he was able to walk and was carried to the hospital. The proofs being clear, he was again tried, sentenced, and again received every lash. Colonel Walker each time offered him pardon at every twenty-five lashes, if he would confess his crime and return to his duty, but he would not, and when healed, was again tried, and again condemned—this time to 800 lashes!

A church stood 500 yards from the place of punishment, and Colonel Walker said, 'Hennessy if you will run to that church and back I will forgive you.'

'No!' he said, he could not stand, he had no power of his legs! After receiving 500 lashes he exclaimed, 'Colonel take me down, be Jasus boys I can't stand it, I'll run to the church.'

He was untied and did run to the church and back, after having, from the obstinacy of his nature, borne 1500 lashes to maintain a falsehood, for he never had been ill a day! I was not in the 50th Regiment when it happened. The atrocity of the punishment, and the obstinacy of the man, must both be almost incredible to those who do not know what horrible use was made of the cat-o'-nine-tails in those days. From that time Hennessy remained unnoticed till the Battle of Coruña: his brave conduct there has been related, and now his story shall be continued.

He left me in the room, as he thought dying, and the moment he went out was seized, and next day marched off towards the Pyrenees. The march was a fearful one, for he had to retrace our long retreat, as a prisoner with a parcel of Spaniards, also prisoners. There were two or three Englishmen, and Hennessy kept a sharp look-out for an opportunity to escape; he urged the others also but they would not attempt it, and he resolved to try it alone at Pampeluna and succeeded. He got clear away and made towards Oporto trusting all to chance. As before mentioned, he had taken off my silver spurs lest the French should kill me for them.

My belief was that my friend Hennessy, thinking me dying, thought they were as well in his possession as in that of some Frenchman: if so, he was quite right, and I thought so at the time. However, travelling in great danger to Oporto, and being at one time hard pressed for food he took a spur from under his arm, where he had concealed both, and sold it. The money he got was not much, but the kindness of the Spanish peasants to an English soldier escaping from the French enabled him to reach Oporto, just before Marshal Soult attacked that city. Hennessy joined the patriot force, assisted in the defence, and, as he told me, was 'mighty spiteful against the French.'

Fate is inevitable! John Hennessy, again taken, was thrown with some Portuguese prisoners into prison, where he lay long, expecting to be put to death; but one day, hearing guns firing, he asked his companions what it was, no one knew, but the fire increased 'and my heart,' said he in the broadest brogue, 'told me it was the English, and I said to them that were near me, their bloody countrymen would never make such a fight as that;' but they were all so frightened they would not stir to make a break out with me, for the French sentry swore he would shoot any man that tried to stir. At that moment, there was a terrible battering at the door of the prison and shouting outside, so I made an offer at the sentry and beat out his brains with his own musket, which I took, as well as his accoutrements, and we all helped those outside to batter down the doors. The French were making off, but I got some shots, and when the Buffs came up I joined them, and was put into the battalion of detachments and we fought the French again at Talavera.

At Talavera, he heard of my brother George, made his way to him, and shewed the remaining spur. He thought me dead, and his joy was great when told it was not so. He would not let George have the spur, served all that campaign, and afterwards rejoined the 50th. After my exchange I did the same, and got Hennessy promoted to the rank of corporal. He then got leave of absence to see his wife and child at Cork, and carried a letter to my friend Aldridge, the collector of customs there, but then his strange nature broke out.

Travelling on foot, from Hastings he had gone straight to the collector's house, without going to see his wife and child, and when Aldridge told him that I had then gone back to the Peninsula—'Ogh! murder! is he gone back and the regiment not with him? by my soul they'll never stop behind him, I must be off.'

'Well Hennessy you must do as you please, but go and see your wife and child, come to me in the morning, and tell me what I can do for your family, if you do go back.'

'Ogh! good luck to the wife and child, I'll not go near them, *sara fut*, but off this minute.'

And he did go without seeing wife or child!

He found the regiment under orders for Spain as he expected, and in that country, at my instance, he was made a sergeant, yet was soon sentenced to be broken for drunkenness and insubordination. Colonel Stewart forgave him for my sake, I being then in Lisbon hospital with a wound. But again, Hennessy was tried, broke, and sentenced to be flogged, and again the last part of the sentence was remitted by Colonel Stewart for my sake. A third time Hennessy was tried for theft, a sad propensity in his character, and once more Stewart pardoned him for his bravery, and out of regard to me. It was useless lenity: the man was incorrigible.

When in the lines of Torres Vedras, where every man had excellent rations, John Hennessy, ever on the look-out for plunder, found a cottage with a miserable Portuguese family, half famished. There were five persons, the father, mother and three little children, and they had nothing in their wretched hovel but a few clothes on their backs, and one loaf: they were in the last degree of misery, yet Hennessy took their loaf and some articles of apparel, leaving them to die. The man, desperate from famine, followed him, and seeing an officer sought protection. Hennessy was tried and that time flogged, which he bore with his usual indifference to danger and pain.

He afterwards behaved well, for him, and on all occasions shewed the greatest courage, until in the Pyrenees a cannon ball carried off his head; and it is curious that at Talavera a cannon shot had knocked off his cap! An honourable death thus closed the career of one who had no feelings of honour in the ordinary acceptation of the word. He was wilful, obstinate, physically brave, proud of his courage, enduring in hardships, faithful to his chief, as he considered me, careless of rank when he got promotion, and robbing food without wanting food himself, when a whole family would have perished by the theft.

His strange character was an enigma not easy to explain, and his death relieved me from the constant apprehension that he would fall into the hands of the provost marshal, and die by an executioner. Had a good education given John Hennessy's firmness, courage and great shrewdness a right direction, those qualities were so extraordinary in him that he would probably have done very great things. He was indeed, a remarkable man.'

★★★★★★

In this narrative, one trait of Hennessy's character has been forgotten. The silver spur which he preserved through all his difficulties, had been given to Charles Napier by his sister, when he left her to go to Spain. It was received with this expression, "Now I am your knight." When it was taken off by Hennessy he said—"If you escape give that to my sister." The injunction was not forgotten. When the strange man first reached England, instead of going to his regiment, or to his wife or child, he travelled at least two hundred miles round to find Miss

Napier, and delivered the remaining spur to her! Some pages in the book of human nature are certainly very difficult to read!

During his captivity Charles Napier's family mourned for him as dead, yet hope lingered, and after three months the government sent a frigate to ascertain his fate. Baron Clouet received the flag and hastened to inform Ney.

'Let him see his friends and tell them he is well and well treated,' was the marshal's response.

Clouet looked earnestly but moved not, and Ney, smiling, asked why he waited!

'He has an old mother, a widow and blind.'

'Has he? Let him go then and tell her himself that he is alive!'

He also released twenty-five badly-wounded English soldiers, jocosely adding—provided they take all the Englishwomen with them, as they make our French soldiers quarrelsome.

At this period, a very bitter feeling existed between the French and English Governments, exchange of prisoners was not admitted, and Ney therefore, risked his sovereign's serious displeasure by his impulsive generosity. Napoleon however approved of the act, the captive's relationship to Mr. Fox being probably of some weight. Guibert, the gallant, humane Guibert, received a cross of the legion of honour, as a matter of course; for Napoleon, so foully misrepresented as ferocious, always rewarded generosity towards an enemy. It was, alas! a fatal reward for Guibert. The result was thus told to the writer, by a French sergeant-major who deserted to his regiment at the lines of Torres Vedras; and from different quarters afterwards came confirmation. An officer, or *sous-officier*, disputed Guibert's right to the cross, saying himself, not the drummer, had rescued the English major. Falsehood or favour prevailed, and poor Guibert, stung to the soul, madly attempted to desert, was taken and shot! The saviour and the saved are now beyond human knowledge; but if spirits are permitted to commune, they have met where it will not be asked, under what colours a noble action was performed.

CHAPTER 7

On the Coa

On his father's birthday, 20th of March, Charles Napier's captivity ended—one of many notable coincidences attending him through life, and always accepted with a half-superstitious satisfaction. Up to this period his countenance had been very comely, yet grave and sedate; his dark lustrous eyes alone giving signs of the fiery spirit within. Previously he had been inclined to care for outward appearances, although without regard to fashion; but after Coruña dress was disregarded, and his manner became eager and restless, with sudden spasmodic movements, springing partly from his wounds partly from previous ill-health. This change of manner was a mark of awakened genius: he had warred, with and against men of mighty energies, and thus becoming conscious of ability, his countenance assumed a peculiarly vehement earnest expression, and his resemblance to a chained eagle was universally remarked.

Regarded now as belonging to history, a similarity in character to the French general, Dessaix is remarkable. The latter has been described by Napoleon, as a small dark man, so absorbed in glorious aspirations, that being several times secretly and gratuitously furnished with camp equipage, he was on each occasion denuded of it in a week, and found sleeping under a gun, careless of his loss. This portrait would pass for that of Charles Napier in all points but one; he would not have lost his equipment, for order was with him a prominent quality: but he would have refused it, from disdain of such disturbance to his simple habits. In military daring and moral worth, the resemblance seems complete. Alike careless of personal comfort and appearance, both were regarded as eccentric by common minds, but were the idols of their soldiers: and while warring with absolute success against the bravest of Asiatics, Mamelukes, and Beloochees, in countries precisely similar, Egypt and

Scinde, both were by their conquered enemies, designated—Dessaix as the *Just Sultan*, Napier as the *Just Padishaw*, The French general was however never proved as a legislator and ruler. At Marengo, Lord William Bentinck, then serving with the Austrian army, saw Dessaix fall; and from Lord William's brigade, at Coruña, Napier advanced and also fell under his eye; happily not in death: he lived to render greater service for England than ever Dessaix did for France; but how differently have they been treated! The Frenchman's fame was instantly accepted as part of his nation's glory; sovereign and people strove as to which should most earnestly express gratitude and admiration: the Englishman, with higher claims, was foully insulted and maligned in life, neglected in death! What then! His fame needs not the support of courts, it belongs to history.

The actions of the great generals who sprung from the French Revolution, although laboriously decried by English politicians and writers, awakened the British genius for war, which had long slept. The English government remained indeed, to the last, in darkness and dullness; but there were soldiers who stepped into the light with undazzled eyes, and Charles Napier was not the last to comprehend the generalship of France: he studied it intently, yet for assimilation rather than imitation; seeing early, that war, though under great guiding principles, is so vast an art as always to admit the display of original genius.

The great Napoleon was however first and last a wonder to him. Early in life, deceived by the systematic vilification of that astounding genius, he felt personal hatred, and of his own unbiassed judgment always reprobated the invasion of Spain: but his sagacity soon pierced through prejudice, and the Emperor's capacity created astonishment, which increased when his own experience, as a commander and ruler, enabled him to estimate the difficulties besetting those stations. Then also he could better appreciate the frantic vituperation of enemies; and always he regarded Napoleon's captivity and death as a national stain, akin to that which soiled Rome when Flaminius drove Hannibal to suicide.

Ney had exacted parole not to serve until exchanged, a condition now rendered onerous by the shameful way in which prisoners of war were treated in England, and by an ignoble fraud practised in his particular case: two midshipmen were sent as an equivalent for the commander of a regiment who had been treated so generously! He remained therefore a long time virtually a prisoner, and did not rejoin his regiment until January 1810, when the correspondence with his mother was resumed: meanwhile the Peninsula had become the scene of great events. Sir Arthur Wellesley had again taken command, had forced the passage of the Douro, fought the Battle of Talavera, retreated to Portugal, and had become Lord Wellington. He was at this time on the north-east frontier of that country, and prepared for its defence against Massena; but with resources so little understood by his government or army, that a hasty and disastrous evacuation was expected by both.

His advance to Talavera had indeed been an error, and the subsequent retreat, with the terrible after loss by sickness, around Badajos and Elbas, had given the troops a mean opinion of his generalship: he was called a mere favourite of power, rash and unskilful. The deep design, the strong resolution, the far-seeing sagacity, the sure judgment, destined to amaze the world, were then unknown, and, with the usual hasty violence of the English public, one error was taken as a basis for generalization. Wellington was pronounced a bad general! Charles Napier's brothers were then serving with the army where hatred and contempt for the Spaniards prevailed, and similar feelings pervaded the army at home.

His mother, January 14th.—

This very hour, nine o'clock at night, last year, we took up our position at Coruña. While marching we were overtaken by the general and George, and Moore asked if it was the 50th? 'Yes sir.' 'Napier how do you do?' he said, and rode on, a doomed man!

Hastings, 18th.—We passed over the battle ground the 16th, and an unfortunate laurel tree was torn to pieces by the men, that all who had burned powder at Coruna might bear the symbol of triumph on our brows. My belief is that Lord Wellington will not fight again, unless he is mad or foolish. As to the *chef de bataillon*, it would be much more agreeable to be exchanged for him than for two *enseignes de vaisseaux*. This offer is not right. Your letter, dear mother, reached me, but not in the midst of rejoicings; I came from mess early, and, having marched twenty miles, went to bed neither in wild nor bad spirits, yet glad when thinking of my state that day year, to have a good bed, good health, freedom, and friends near.

So, thanking God, I went fast asleep, and awoke next morning

PLANTA DO TERRENO
D'ALEM DO CÔA

Grande Teso
Pequeno Teso
Serra da Francia

CIDADE RODRIGO

Caridade

Carpio

Campillo

Rio Azava

Forte dos Carros

Espeja

Quinto

Villar

Rio Duas Casas

Fonte de Guinaldo

Naves Frias

ve de Aver

o Turones

Villar Maior

Ponte de Ferrarias

Alfaiates

Sahugal

to think again of the difference and be grateful. We have little chance of going out, for every officer and man that can be spared has leave of absence until April.

January 22nd.—Got a devil of a tumble the day before yesterday, which makes me glad, because I could not do better than have my yearly accident without being really hurt: to run twelve months without some *petite chose pour passer le tems*, is not for me. Being a frosty day my horse's leg slipped, and down went horse and man. Rosinante first got up, and then I made all sorts of lovely contortions to ascertain damage: left leg badly bruised at knee, ankle and instep. Very stiff all yesterday, yet no internal bruise, this morning better. How my leg and thigh escaped crushing God knows. I fell, feet in stirrups, one leg under the mare, she lying on her side; the other thrown over her, and the reins in hand.

The ground was hard, and the holsters saved the leg for they were crushed and torn from the saddle! Well, they did escape, that will do. ——— did make the speech, at a naval officer's table; it was not to anger the 50th, but from sheer backbiting and jealousy: however, I'll be up to him. A large serpent is a reptile as well as ——— but despising it does not save one's life. That doctrine of despising I hold very cheap; meet every man with his own weapons is my creed, and failing is your own fault: but fail I will not, without a blow. Clarke of the 35th is a fine fellow. What they say of Irishmen is quite true: they are *raps* or superior animals, there are no degrees. They are unfit for jurymen, and ought to be judges or culprits. What a lieutenant-colonelcy for me if Clarke is refused! but do not utter a word about that, it would make me very uneasy, even to have it offered to me while there is a chance of his success in the matter.

February. Confound old Pivot! Sir D. Dundas. A young captain, famous for nothing but shirking duty has been made major: I would like to roast old Pivot. But don't you make Fox or anyone ask him to promote me, work him up for George if you can. He must however be touched up to let me go to the siege of Cadiz; more thanks for that than for a lieutenant-colonelcy. Will General Graham send for George, think you? I should like to see how they go on, and learn Spanish, which could be effected with three months' leave. I am very anxious about

Portugal, though thinking Lord Wellington will not venture a battle: moreover, the French won't fight, they will turn his position. Your letter of yesterday just come. They did right to tell you of the report that the armies had met; it was false, but I hate concealing what must be known in time: you need not fear any of us doing that. I don't agree with you that philosophy cannot conquer nature, but I do not want it to do so. Who would not be anxious when those they love are in danger? Last year's occurrences should do anything but frighten you, and your supposing that misfortune must come is a fault: riding out to meet evil is bad.

Yet you bear it when it does come as you ought. My trust is that your fortitude won't be tried now, and that all will be safe. I also am anxious about my brothers, but it is not an anxiety that gives me uneasiness, it only makes me eager for news: predestinarianism is too strong in me to let me suffer from these things; it is only what can be altered by ourselves that agitates me. Do not make arrangements as if something shocking was decidedly to happen: no spirits can stand that. Your sons come home full of fighting and without clothes; we shall be very merry, and if George's ardent wish to lose a *fin* be granted we shall dress his stump. I join him not in that desire, and hope to see him *statu quo ante bellum* as to legs and arms.

George Napier afterwards had his right arm twice broken in fight, and finally lost it at Ciudad Rodrigo!

April. If anything be done my brother's brigade will get full share, but hardly will Lord Wellington try to defend Portugal. God bless you dearest mother, don't think your sons are actually cut in halves! Louisa, I see seals in black already for George and William, pray order my mourning; I owe them a suit for what they did for me. Lord Mark Kerr's intelligence is bad, originating with ———— and ———— both noted bowmen, and the latter one of the weakest fools imaginable. When they told me all majors but myself were promoted I said, like an idiot, I will memorialize.

I am not apt to trouble the multitude with communications, and rejoice at being likely to lose by my folly now, though it only consists of this speech at mess 'By Jove I'll ask for a lieutenant-colonelcy too.' The mass of men are fools and rascals, or fools only, and I am sorry to find myself appertaining to the latter class. Ten agreeable letters have come to me at once: they are like the shower of manna. The handsomest one, from Lord Wm. Bentinck, I ever received; and General Clinton is also very kind. I will use no interest for my promotion, it is a right: keep all friendly help for George. They can hardly refuse me promotion now, as the other Coruña majors have got it in garrison battalions; that is the court kind of promotion: may nine millions of maledictions alight on old Pivot Davy; for all other Coruña majors are promoted. All the respect for Moore displayed in my memorial, was to put them in good humour; but really, I am more proud of having served with him in battle than of all they could give me. Shew the memoir to Lord William.

His claim to promotion was met by shuffling cold evasions: it was his right and was of course denied; but he easily obtained leave to risk his life again, that being a favour which gave him no claim, and might get rid of one. Hence in May, as a volunteer, he joined the light division, beyond the Coa, under the fiery Robert Craufurd, who was, with less than four thousand men, braving the whole French army on a plain, having only a fordable river between them! This was a place to take lessons in war, and Charles Napier's *Journal and Correspondence* show how he profited: yet it must be again noted, that Lord Wellington's great reach of genius was not then recognised. A prominent error like Talavera, followed by bad results, is easily seized by misjudging men; but nice and subtle combinations, even when successful, always escape vulgar comprehension, and sometimes even fine intellects: Charles Napier will be found not quite free from the general miscomprehension, yet his innate sense of greatness soon corrected his judgment.

Journal, April 16th. Leave of absence for three months.

20th May. After a long passage, this day saw me safely into harbour: may I reach the port now in my mind by next 20th of May! may the omen be good! I augur well of it: what we most wish for we feel most confident of, and I am sanguine.

21st. Dined with the admiral. A Spanish general and some Portuguese *noblesse* there; and also, the daughter and grandchildren of Pombal. The Spanish general told me that he was the best general they had, he thought. His name was Contreras, and he had more information than I expected in a don: he had also the honour of having been well thrashed by the French very lately. Men of three nations were at the dinner, and it is difficult to say which despised the others most; or which thought most of themselves. I have seen the church of San Roque, it is superb. The mosaics are exquisite, and the quantity of silver and precious stones wonderful, considering that the French had been in Lisbon so long! I can hardly believe their having been so foolish as to leave such riches in the hands of fanatic priests. I gave half a crown for the sight: the poor thus give alms to the rich.

To demolish such altars would be wise, meritorious, and very agreeable; Massena will surely look at the cornelian altar, the ponderous silver candlesticks, the pillars of *lap lazuli,* &c. From this over rich church I went to see the arsenal; there the Algerine slaves are chained, and are fine men. Truly I pitied them; they are slaves to worse men than themselves, for an Algerine privateer will always beat a Portuguese frigate. Poor fellows! it is horrid to see them in such hands. Hateful is slavery to me naturally, and also because I have felt what being a captive is: it is purgatory if not hell! however what God sends let man bear: *quo fata vocant*: he who is a man must follow fate like a man. The Stoic principle was good, but went too far, for they could not push practice to the full extent: Stoicism is only good when we cannot help ourselves. Epictetus would have been more to my taste if he had broken his master's skull instead of patiently letting his own be broke.

May 31st. Once more at Sacavem. On the 28th October 1808, I was here commanding the 50th Regiment. What are the pleasures of memory! I greet her *as the fiend to whom belongs the vultures ravening leak the raven's funeral song.* Standing under an olive, my thoughts were of my friend; for under that very tree Charles Stanhope had then breakfasted with me, and hope of glory, and admiration for Moore, were our themes! Two short years and lo! here am I again: but Moore! Stanhope! where are ye? Napoleon talks of peace: would to God he wished for it as sincerely as I do. Oh! that I might pluck a branch and give peace to the world, as an offering to the manes of my friend! I feel low. Stanhope! Stanhope! every turn of this road, every stone brings you before my eyes, and often prevents my seeing them: and my dear brothers! how I long to reach you. Shall I see you even now? But what brings me here? Honour! Damn honour! Falstaff is right by Jove! Yet, can one be happy without honour? No, no! Forward then, and never reason while in low spirits. Of one thing I am sure, namely, that a man is a fool to live till he is old; for he loses the greatest comfort of life thereby, and gets cornuted probably into the bargain. Enough! old bachelors are fools notwithstanding!

Coimbra, June. Portuguese troops here; they are a strong race, and will make good soldiers, but are not so now; it will take Beresford some years to make them good troops, and more English officers are wanted. We shall lose half our army if Lord Wellington risks a battle any great distance from Lisbon; and I fear the French may penetrate by the Tagus, and perhaps cut off part of our army: I am inclined to think they want to draw us on to Salamanca for that purpose. God grant I may be in all that passes and escape; I have had enough of the *malgré*, and would like some of the *bongré*, but sink or swim I will join in the tumult; twenty-five thousand British will not fall inglorious or unwept, and as death must come, it cannot be in better company. I have just heard we are to have a medal for Coruña, and it is possible I may get another here ere two months pass, *leaden* or *golden*. But all is chance, so Fates have at you: an ugly pack of witches ye are, but ye scare me not, and therefore may as well be propitious, for if not I defy you.

The view of affairs taken above was nearly the same as Lord Wellington took. That great man had contemplated a dash at Salamanca, yet relinquished it for fear of being drawn into a general action, which he was resolved not to light far from Lisbon, fearing not only the want of experience in the Portuguese troops but that the French would penetrate by the Tagus: Busaco was forced upon him, it was a political battle.

Celorico, June 14th. Passed a volcanic country to all appearance: innumerable conical hills, each covered with and surrounded by stones, are scattered in all directions. May not the name of *Celorico* come from *caloric?* Thrashed a Juiz de Fora for insolence at Penhanços.

15th. Waited yesterday on Lord Wellington, who was very civil, and signed my certificate of exchange. Dined with him. He told me the French made the most regular retreats he ever saw, at Roriça and Talavera: quaere, did he follow their example? People say his march from Talavera to Alemtejo was very bad; but those who criticise generals do not always know their motives of action, and often have motives of their own for criticising: nevertheless, we must think; and I think Lord Wellington committed a great error in that campaign by trusting to the Spaniards after what Moore had experienced; and another in advancing too far when his retreat might be cut off. He was wrong also I think in fighting when victory did him no good, and defeat must have destroyed him: his information was bad, and he trusted it too implicitly.

Again. Why did he stay in the destructive marshes of the Alemtejo until nearly the whole of his army fell from sickness? It is not easy to comprehend all this, and I have heard no good answer to it. Every officer I have seen and spoken to about the matter, has told me the same story, *viz.* that the Battle of Talavera was lost if the French had made one more attack; and that the whole army expected to be beaten next day. Now Lord Wellington might have had ten battalions more in the fight, *viz.* Lightbourne's and the two Craufurds' brigades. Why were they in the rear?

The thing is not easily explained to his advantage: he did not expect a battle, and yet, had the French delayed a few days, he must have laid down his arms, or been cut to pieces. Altogether his general operations are difficult to be defended. But his conduct in the battle shewed great coolness and the most perfect self-possession; and by what I observe, since I came here, he seems to have gained a lesson from Talavera. Still the whole of that campaign is discreditable to him as a great captain, and he appears to have deserved the epithets of rash and imprudent; not that of *fool* though, as many say; his errors seem to be more those of inexperience and vanity than want of talent. England has paid dearly in men and money for his education indeed, yet if he has thereby been made a good general the loss is less: we have very few capable of being made worth a straw though all the blood and gold in Europe and India were lavishly expended on them.

These censures were all just, militarily speaking, and the Duke of Wellington was too great to deny faults: he always admitted the Talavera campaign to be an error; excusing it principally on false information and the political embarrassments caused by the Spaniards.

17th. I see no reason to find fault with Lord Wellington's conduct now in not succouring Ciudad Rodrigo, and his preparations for a retreat are good: they might be however, I think, better, as I have seen many roads almost impassable for anybody, and wholly so for an army, which a few peasants might make good in three days, the materials being on the spot. Perhaps others are good, by which he means to retire, and that I have not seen: I can discover no fault or appearance of rashness, except the having Craufurd so advanced. His remaining so secure at Celorico is probably a consequence of good intelligence, but it appears a dangerous post if the enemy should push General Hill. I cannot help thinking the siege of Rodrigo is to entice him into Spain, and if he does move forward they will push him at Abrantes: should he be so tempted the game is up! but he will not be thus ensnared, the scheme is too evident.

Pinhel, June 19th. Dined with General Picton. The castle here, built at different times, has Moorish characters on the walls, so there are at Celorico, which some people call Roman—why I know not, for it is built without cement, and has square towers, some like bastions. The Bishop of Pinhel is said to be a sensible man; he is very hospitable, and very like Charles Fox, but better looking and not so fat: his palace full of prints, all very bad, and some not very decent for a bishop.

20th. Examined the works of Almeida. Commanded on the north-east, but may make a good defence: guns very small in calibre though large in size, one pounders chiefly, with bad carriages.

21st, Gallegos. Saw William, and George, the latter not well, heat affects him: he has I believe the best heart alive and beating, and a right good head. I hope to see both safe home after this breeze: if not they are well prepared for a longer voyage, but God forbid they should take it now.

22nd. This morning we fired five shots at a foraging party. At noon Marshal Ney reconnoitred us with some squadrons, driving our posts within the line of the Azava River. Captain Mellish—the celebrated sporting Mellish, a brave fellow, he was on the staff—and myself were at the outposts; he made a fool of himself and I laughed at him. He made our people give up two posts without a shot, and the lieutenant of the 43rd asked my advice, so did Mellish, and it was to occupy the ground again: this was done easily, as the enemy had made his observations, which he should not have done if I had commanded the post. Our position is fearfully dangerous here; we expect an attack, and having only three thousand men, and the French twenty-five thousand, shall be lucky if we get off: it is uncomfortable.

23rd. Saw the Spanish general, Carrera: he showed me his troops, and they are bad enough, like all Spaniards. Don Julian Sanchez, the partisan, has cut his way out of Ciudad Rodrigo; he is an intrepid man they say, and very savage. The French go on slowly with the siege. Lord W. wisely keeps quiet; he is blamed for this, but is right, and it gives me great confidence in the man.

25th. French opened their batteries, and the fire was returned with spirit. The enemy drove back our picquet from Marialva and Carpio, beyond the bridge and fords of the Azava. Soon afterwards a troop of our German hussars crossed the bridge and skirmished, but using only carbines and pistols, only one man and two horses were killed: the spectacle was as pretty as it was ridiculous. Such trifling work serves no purpose whatever, it risks brave men and teaches them to trifle with service; we should fight or let it alone: the latter is most to my taste. Everything convinces me that light cavalry has no business with carbines.

The Germans understand outpost work better than our cavalry, but if the English err they will fight themselves through; and though Germans are brave enough, they certainly have not the fire of our men: wherefore, taking all risks from drinking and ignorance, I would rather have two British regiments infantry or cavalry, than three German regiments, and that is saying a great deal.

26th. The 16th Light Dragoons come up. The town fires bravely: the cannonade was tremendous last night, and this morning the place is on fire. Three explosions in the trenches; but a breach is to be seen, though small. Lord W. reconnoitred in a slight way, and saw the town from Molina da Flores. Marshal Ney is supposed to have passed the ford where my brother's picquet was, and the men fired at him without George's orders, wounding one person of his suite. Had Ney been hit it would not have been creditable; it is not right to fire at people without necessity, like Indian savages. The marshal, or whoever it was, had rode up the river and crossed safely, so no end was answered by pelting him as he was going home. Brigadier-General McKinnon, Colonel Pakenham, and myself, with others, had ridden a few hours before close to their picquets, at the very same place, and instead of firing on us they only joked, and good-humouredly asked us to come across the river: when our men fired they returned the compliment, but our firing was stopped by George immediately.

July 1st. Heavy bombardment at night, and we marched from Gallegos to bivouac in the woods.

2nd. Our bivouac beautiful, like a *fête champêtre* rather than an outpost close to an enemy: the baggage got into confusion. Why do we remain in this exposed situation? Why is this fine division risked? If the enemy was enterprising we should be cut to pieces. We are not five thousand, including Carrera's force of fifteen hundred Spaniards, and twelve hundred are Portuguese. The French have twenty-five thousand, and forty thousand more within a day's march; yet we have the impudence to stay close to them: we shall be attacked some morning and lose many men.

His mother, Alameda, July 1st. We have left Gallegos at last, fortunately, or Lord Wellington would have chanced to lose his light division. My belief is that the ignorance of the French general as to our real situation saved us, but we are now comparatively secure. The siege of Rodrigo is very distressing, but Lord Wellington is resolved to give no help: very wisely. He is a much better general than I suspected him to be; that is, he has profited from his former errors: that he made them no one can doubt who hears the conversation of the army. He is not popular, less so even than supposed. However, he will not commit himself again, and that is comfort for those in England.

My brother William took a violent passion for Don Julian Sanchez, the guerilla chief, but has been a little cooled by the latter having, the day before yesterday, put to death one hundred and sixty Frenchmen, to sixty of whom he had at first given quarter! The don fights with lances, which was the first attraction I believe: he is a bold partisan, but it is to be feared very bloody. One of his men told me, if they caught Ney they meant to cut him into lengths! beginning at his feet! Ney in return has promised to hang Julian and his men, when he catches them, and has already partially performed his promise: charming warfare and mild!

We shall stay here until Ciudad is taken, and then probably the French will move on Hill and Lord Wellington at the same time. It is said the latter makes no secret of his intention to quit Portugal, and that he thinks it will be soon; but don't give me as authority, it may be only rumour. Meantime be satisfied he is not the rash man he was, or Ciudad would ere this have been relieved: it might have been for they could not stand an attack from us, and my persuasion is that the siege was little more than a battle-trap for his lordship, which he has not been caught in. Having asked for more leave, Lord Wellington has given me permission to wait for an answer, which he says will be a reprimand, and an order to go home—don't care for the first, the last must be obeyed. I have seen a little skirmishing, but being ill mounted have kept aloof, except with the infantry; for amongst the men of feet, if my nag is hurt I am still as good as my neighbours. With the cavalry, there is little to learn and I don't wish to be taken again.

If ever the Manichean doctrine was made manifest in man, it was so in Craufurd. At one time, he was all fire and intelligence, a master-spirit in war; at another, as if possessed by the demon, he would madly rush from blunder to blunder, raging in folly: the demon was strong at this period as the following letter shall shew.

Journal, July 4th. The French drove in our cavalry this morning. Krauchenberg of the 1st Hussars charged them at a small bridge; he invited Captain Belli of the 16th to join in the charge, but he would not, though he had a squadron and the other only thirty men! The French were heavily cannonaded at the bridge by Hew Boss, and we retired skirmishing across the Das Casas stream to a new position, near Fort Conception, which is to be blown up. Elder's Portuguese fired on our hussars! Rodrigo fights well, *viva* Herrasti! I fear Almeida won't do as much, yet Cox is a soldier I think.

11th. Last night Craufurd laid *a schame for catching a rot, and caught a Tartar!* He marched with twelve hundred infantry and eight hundred horse to waylay one hundred and twenty French infantry and thirty dragoons, and the latter were taken; but the infantry resisted the cavalry charge, and repulsed Craufurd with a loss of thirty-two troopers, and poor Colonel Talbot, the French marching off without the loss of a man! Had they been asked they would have laid down their arms; but Craufurd cruelly tried to cut up a handful of brave men and they thrashed him. Talbot was one of our best cavalry officers, yet the loss is less than the disgrace.

Brave actions were however performed. In the writer's *History of the Peninsular War*, Colonel Talbot is stated to have charged with four squadrons, and to have fallen *close* to the enemy; but Sergeant Major Hanley of the same regiment, himself a man of great courage and enterprise, declares that the colonel charged with only one squadron, and died *on* the enemy's bayonets! This must be the truth, for Hanley helped to carry the body away after the fight, and saw the bayonet wounds still welling blood. Talbot's quartermaster, McCormac, with eight brave troopers also fell in the same manner! Certainly, both they and their opponents were noble soldiers!

And so was William Campbell, the brigade major, known then and afterwards throughout the army for every generous quality. He was sententious of speech, quixotic of look, but handsome and strong, and his sentiments of honour were worthy of the Spanish *don*, his courage as high, yet purged of folly: he was indeed a gallant English gentleman in thought, look, word and deed. In this combat, he charged so home that his horse was killed close to the French bayonets, but being himself unhurt he arose, and though alone, slowly stalked away, disdaining haste as he disdained danger. The gallant French captain, Guache, would not let his men slay the proud soldier: thus, all was noble on both sides, and William Campbell escaped death.

At this time a message came from Ney to know why Major Napier was in the field without having been exchanged? Stung by the implied dishonour, which sprung from the conduct of the transport board about the *enseignes de vaisseaux*, he hastened to Lord Wellington, who sent him to the French outposts with a flag of truce to explain.

His mother, July 15. I went with a flag of truce to Gallegos, was blindfolded and taken to Loison's quarters. None of my French acquaintances there. Loison offered a large bet that Lord Wellington would not fight to relieve Almeida: is this a quiz, or do they mean to besiege that place? I was not blindfolded coming back, but made to gallop at full speed. Loison is a savage-looking fellow, yet was very civil, and much pleased with the brave conduct of the company which beat off our cavalry. We did not allow that we had many men, or that we were beat, but honestly avowed our admiration of his people. I heard that Clouet is with his family at Paris, and doubtless glad thereof. No chance of a battle till Buonaparte comes; but then his numbers will put battles out of the question: he will not risk his fame against twenty-five thousand English.

The 50th have been removed from Hastings to make room for militia. Our men's recovery of strength, by sea-bathing, is of no moment when compared with the wish of some militia colonel to bathe his wife and children. Perhaps the soldiers are better dead, as England has such a large army! And then Sir Francis Burdett might tamper with them, as he did with the veterans when he vainly strove to save their gardens for them at Chelsea! Yes, they are better dead.

Rodrigo surrendered the evening before Colonel Talbot was killed. Old Andreas Herrasti made a vigorous defence, and Loison told me the town was almost destroyed by the bombardment. The French committed no excesses, even the Spaniards allow this. Almeida is preparing for a siege, and poor Hewitt is not in great spirits at the prospect of being a prisoner. (Major Hewitt, brother of the Hewitt who in 1798 occupied Celbridge. He was a fine officer and his captivity was long, his life too short.) His fate is inevitable unless he gets killed; but to be a prisoner now is nothing, as exchanges are permitted; he will only have to return by France instead of the Bay of Biscay. That Bay o' Biscay! Yet rather would I be up to my neck in it than a prisoner for ten minutes!

July. I wrote to the Duke of Richmond that———— had got a majority, and his grace might as well ask for me again. If Sir D. Dundas sees that people are angry he will give in, for I know he is to be bullied, like all old men. My letter to the duke was too angry, but still if he sends it, which he will not, it might get George a step: it would indeed stop mine, but the arrangement would content me, for the next commander in chief would be more just. I hope the duke won't be angry, but I was so much so, at hearing that puppy ——— was a major, that my thought was even to tell old Davy what he was in plain terms; fear of hurting George alone stopped me; yet truly, my belief is it would have got him the step: in my own case, it should have been done, and shall be done when George is promoted. My civility shall last until he is safe, and then, setting Sir David at defiance, my opinion of him shall be written; keeping clear of insolence though, lest he should bring me to a court-martial. No one can conceive the good to the army when a little rebellion to injustice can be got up. Old Pivot can only stop my promotion, which will be reckoned shockingly unjust, &c.; moreover, he is ninety and cannot continue long in office: but all depends on the humour I shall be in.

This vehemence was well founded. Having commanded a regiment in one campaign, been foremost in fight with it at Coruña, and desperately wounded, his claim was strong; yet he was the only Coruna major left unpromoted, and men of no service were daily put over his head. *No officer has any claims*, was a saying attributed to Sir David Dundas, and his practice towards Charles Napier was conformable to the sentiment. George Napier was even worse used. Sir John Moore had avowed his intention of sending him home with the first despatches that would carry promotion. General Hope, who terminated the Battle of Coruña, knew this, and if ignorant thereof, would not have deprived the fallen hero's follower of an advantage forfeited only by the glorious death of his chief: he gave it to George Napier.

But then stepped in Sir David Baird, and though he had quitted the battle wounded, before Moore fell, gave the despatch, Hope's despatch, to his own *aide-de-camp*—a brother of Lord Aberdeen! George Napier, thus wronged, instead of being regarded as having a double claim, was further wronged by Sir David Dundas, who pushed younger officers, even of his own regiment, above him in the army: and it was not until 1811, after Massena's retreat, that with good additional service, and severe wounds, he won a brevet majority—but from Wellington in the field, not from the Horse Guards.

Journal, July 16th, Junça. Came here this morning: the cavalry have left Val de Mula, and we are now safe from a surprise, and being surrounded, which at Val de Mula was not the case, as the enemy has twelve regiments of cavalry, and on our flank and rear was an open plain. Why do we not get on the other side of the Coa? Why not blow up Fort Conception? The enemy might save that fort by a rapid movement now, if they were aware of our having dismantled it: our safety has certainly been owing to the enemy's ignorance of our true situation. Went to Almeida, and find that Cox's is decidedly not vigorous in preparing for a siege, for he gave me a bad breakfast: he cannot fight well on burned bread and bad coffee.

21st. At daybreak, the French drove in our outpost, and Fort Conception was blown up, the shock great, the destruction complete. The powder was put in the casemates in barrels, not filled up like a regular mine, and furnished a proof that the latter is not a necessary trouble in every instance: a barrel of powder slung under a bridge will destroy the arch unless a very strong one. This was well done, and our cavalry retreated through Val de Mula, skirmishing till near Almeida, about two and a half miles: we lost seven or eight horses and two men wounded, and made one charge with our skirmishers, neither able in conception nor bold in execution, doing no honour to general or men. After that a more ridiculous attempt was made with half a squadron. I saw that Craufurd's ignorance of cavalry disheart-ened the men; some of whom got near broken ground whence the French could in safety fire on them at twenty yards' distance. They were afraid to regain their own ground when Craufurd ordered them, whereupon I galloped up and called to them to follow, and they did so, and we drove the French back, receiv-ing a sharp fire. English troops must always be led, but they will certainly follow their officers, who will generally be as certainly ready to lead. Altogether we had much firing today and little danger. Craufurd does not please me as a general.

On the 24th of July happened Craufurd's bitter fight on the Coa. It was a fierce and obstinate combat for existence with the light divi-sion, and only Moore's regiments could, with so little experience, have extricated themselves from the danger into which they were so reck-lessly cast; yet it was their first battle, and Craufurd's demon of folly was strong that day: their matchless discipline was their protection—a phantom hero from Coruna saved them!

Journal, July 24th. At daybreak, our picquets were attacked. The French threw forward some infantry among the rocks, and were met by two companies of the 95th Rifles. In about two hours the enemy increased in numbers, our cavalry retired, the riflemen and Captain Campbell's company of the 52nd covering their retreat till we reached the guns, when a cannonade opened on both sides, but the enemy soon pushed men down both flanks, and our guns fell back. At this time, we could count fifteen strong squadrons of French cavalry in line, besides detached parties and skirmishers, which may be reckoned at five more—altogether about three thousand cavalry. Their infantry we estimated at ten thousand, and they had the power of bringing up thirty thousand if they pleased.

When our guns retired, the light troops kept firing until we got close to Almeida, and a gun was fired from near a tower, 800 yards from that town: a subaltern and some men of the 52nd occupied the tower, and our cavalry and artillery were drawn up in line behind. At this time, the enemy closed on our infantry, and the action there began by the dislodging of Campbell's company and the riflemen from the enclosures.

I was ordered to tell Colonel Barclay to fall back from the plain and regain the enclosures behind him, which he did, and the fire became very heavy: Barclay's horse was killed, mine was wounded, and threw me, but I remounted and rejoined Craufurd, who then sent me to tell the 52nd, 43rd and 95th to maintain the enclosures until he got the cavalry and guns over the Coa, leaving two pieces to cover the retreat. I gave Barclay, and Major McLeod, and Colonel Beckwith, these orders, but they were all hotly engaged and could no longer keep their ground, lest the enemy should turn their flanks and reach the bridge before them.

I had great difficulty to return and joined the 43rd, where I found Campbell wounded, and fearing he would be taken gave him my mare, making the best of my own way on foot through the vineyards. The fire was hot and the ground very difficult for us, but much easier for the enemy, because we made passages for ourselves, and thus made them for the French also: this caused the 43rd and 95th to lose many men. I think we retired too fast in this part: it was owing to the murderous position which kept us in fear of being cut off from the bridge; but we were thus driven in among our cavalry, and the French cavalry got up to the 95th and made some prisoners.

Now we formed in rear of the cavalry on the main road, and went down towards the bridge, firing the whole way. On arriving there, Brigade-Major Rowan called to the Rifles and Portuguese Cazadores, and part of the 43rd, to charge up a hill and to retain it, while I rode by order of Colonel Beckwith to draw off the 52nd Regiment, then nearly a mile up the river on the right: the French were trying to push between them and us, and they would have done so had they been in force enough, and that Rowan's charge had not checked them.'

The charge excited by Rowan was a very slight one: a different charge, made by three companies of the 43rd and one of the 95th, excited and led by Major McLeod of the 43rd, which Charles Napier did not see, was the one which checked the enemy and saved the 52nd.

I had little hope of reaching the 52nd alive, but escaped, though a dragoon horse I had caught and mounted was shot in the leg just as I reached Barclay, and at the same moment his cap was shot off. However, the 52nd effected their junction, passed the bridge, and took the right of our position beyond the river, down to the edge of which my brother George's company was pushed, and from thence kept up a strong fire.

The 52nd were followed over the bridge by the 43rd and 95th and Cazadores, covered by three companies of the 43rd, Dalyel's, Lloyd's, and my brother William's, and then the French pushed down to the bridge and a cannonade commenced from both sides of the river. The bridge was defended by the 43rd and riflemen, with a long and murderous skirmish, destructive as it was useless, by which many men and officers lost their lives and many were wounded—amongst the latter my brother William. Finally, this ceased, and the bloody business closed with as much honour for the officers and men as disgrace for Craufurd's generalship. His errors were conspicuous, and the most prominent shall be noted for my own teaching.

1st. He fought knowing he must retreat from an overwhelming force, and having no object in fighting.

95TH RIFLES OFFICER

2nd. He occupied a position a mile in front of a bridge: thus, voluntarily imposing on himself the most difficult operation in war, *viz.* passing a defile in face of a superior enemy, and in the confusion of a retreat! The result might have been destruction—it was great loss.

3rd. He detained the cavalry and guns in a position where they could not act, till the infantry were beaten back on them: thus, he risked the destruction of all three; for the defile became choked, and had the French charged down the road, there would have been a bloody scene. This was so evident that I rode up to my brother William, and asked him to form a square with his company to resist cavalry; the idea had already struck him, and Major McLeod and Captain Patrickson also: it was general.

4th. The position was amongst vineyards, with walls averaging nine feet high, and he ought to have thrown down enough to open communications to the rear: the want of this caused our chief loss, for while we were pulling down the enemy were firing and followed our paths.

5th. He sent no guns over to defend the passage and cover the retreat, until after the troops had commenced retiring: had one gun broke down, or the horses been killed on the bridge, the troops would have been delayed and exposed to a destructive fire from the heights around, while in a mass of confusion.

6th. He suffered the 52nd to be nearly cut off, and never sent them an order to retire, after having given them one to defend their post obstinately: his small division was therefore disjointed and nearly paralyzed by extension.

7th. His retreat over the bridge was confused, though every officer and soldier was cool and ready to execute any order, and there was no excuse for hurry.

8th. When the passage of the bridge was made he left no men to defend it; and had I not halted some who were going up to join their colours the bridge would have been for a quarter of an hour without being enfiladed, or exposed to a single musket shot. This was afterwards rectified, but the 43rd were placed in a most exposed position, when a few breastworks previously made would have covered them.

9th. He made our guns fire at the enemy's guns instead of their men. In short there seemed a kind of infatuation upon him, and nothing but the excellence of his men and officers saved the division: and as it was, the rains, which had swelled the river and destroyed the many fords, saved him from a repetition of the Franciscan convent at Buenos Ayres!

Craufurd had surrendered there, (at Bueno Ayres); and to these censures may be added that he fought on the Coa in disobedience to Lord Wellington's instructions: still he was a great officer.

His mother, 25th July. All safe beloved mother, but William is wounded in the hip. I hate to deceive on such a subject, and tell you his wound, in my belief is nothing, the ball passed through without injuring the bone; he neither suffers much pain, nor is unable to walk, which if the bone was hurt he could not do. (This was a mistake; the bone was injured and the recovery slow: two months.) It has been a severe action, and our loss great; but as yet we know nothing certain, being all fatigue and wet, for rain poured in torrents all the time: it must rain twice as much ere it washes Craufurd clean for fighting at all.

Five hundred killed and wounded will probably be not much above our loss, which chiefly fell on the 43rd: they have had thirteen officers killed or wounded; amongst the latter Tom Lloyd who has a bad clink on the head. Colonel Hull only joined the evening before, took the command, and was killed. The action was on the banks of the Coa at the bridge near Almeida, and it should not have been fought at all. Now bless you dear mother, be glad you have got off so well with three sons in the fight. There will be no more fighting, as Almeida is beleaguered.

This Lloyd, a captain of the 43rd, was known throughout the army for his genius, wit and bravery, his happy temper and magnificent person: he fell gloriously at the Battle of the Nivelle in 1813.

Celorico. Tom Lloyd has been teasing my life out with his concatenations of events, which have, he shews, in due course and of necessity, made a hole in his head, because Charles of Spain's head was without a hole for brains. Lo! again a flag of truce has just come in from Ney with compliments, to know why Mons. le Major Napier is serving, and if he has been exchanged? Ney evidently has not got my letter given to Loison; but Lord Wellington, who is very kind to me on all occasions, has again sent a flag of truce with a copy, and one of two things must happen. Either Mons. le Major will be considered as fairly exchanged, and all will be well; or Le Duc d'Echingen will judge *Mons. le Major* too precious an article to be resigned for two *enseignes des vaisseaux*, and therefore not exchanged, in which case he must proceed forthwith to *Ingleterra*. It is said there is an order to destroy all the mills around: if so we are certainly going to retreat, and probably towards Coimbra.

This anticipation of a retreat was well founded: Almeida fell, the army retired, and Charles Napier, clinging to the light division, was engaged in all the skirmishes until the English general, halting on the Busaco Mountain, offered battle. There riding in the train of Wellington, at the point where Regnier's corps assailed the position, he remained on horseback when the fire was so terrible that all the staff, and all the volunteers, with exception of his cousin the present Admiral Napier, had dismounted. He, seeing him the only mounted man in a red coat, when all the others were in blue, urged him to alight; at least to put on his cloak or he would be marked down. His answer was "No! This is the uniform of my regiment, and in it I will shew, or fall this day."

Scarcely had the words been uttered when he fell! A bullet had entered on the right of his nose, and lodged in the left jaw near the ear, shattering the bone to pieces. He was borne away past Lord Wellington, and though sinking from loss of blood, took off his hat and waved it, muttering, for he was unable to speak out, "I could not die at a better moment."

Such was Admiral Napier's account of the event, and he added, that holding him during the extraction of the ball, that painful operation was treated as lightly as the drawing of a tooth might be. Apparently dying, he was now conveyed to the convent of Busaco, some miles off; his wound was there dressed, and he found his way to Coimbra, a day's march, by next morning. He hoped to have rest and care at that place, but was hardly able to preserve his life from the brutality and cowardice, if not worse, of an army physician, not a surgeon, to whom he had been delivered.

This vile fellow, becoming cognisant of a rumour that the enemy was approaching, not only left his hurts actually unbandaged to save himself, but carried off his patient's horses, leaving him for several hours in expectation of death or captivity! His servant, an active fellow, recovered the animals by force, and bandaged his master's face again. Then he made his way on horseback under a burning sun to Lisbon, a journey of several days. The 50th Regiment, coming up to join the army, passed him on the road and gave him three cheers; and at Lisbon he was joined by his brother George who had been shot through the upper part of the thigh. Their hurts were very serious, Charles' menacing, but with an elastic vivacity he bore his sufferings, and with all manner of tenderness sought to soothe his mother and sister's anxiety. His first letter is dated the fourth day after the battle.

> *Pombal, Oct. 1st.* I am wounded dear mother: the ball passed along the cheek-bone and lodged in the upper jaw, from which it was extracted with great pain to me, although with less mischief than was expected, as it had not passed through the palate. You never saw so ugly a thief as I am: but melancholy subjects must be avoided, the wound is not dangerous.

> *Lisbon, Oct. 16th.* Your letter has given me pain and pleasure. The latter to find you bear so nobly the trial you have gone through; pain to think how much my beloved mother has been tried and still is tried!

She was quite blind, and a second daughter had gone to the grave; the letter announcing her death had reached him just as the battle begun, and being read under fire, grief was suppressed.

> The loss of our sweet angelic girl is indeed a trial for all, but for you greater than all put together. An endeavour to console you would be silly. You have taken the only way—resignation to the inscrutable decree which leaves you your sons, and called your angel girls to their father. I must not wish other than has been ordained; but had it been in mortal choice, the daughter should have wiped the tears that fell for the son. Would that I could be with you, but even away feel myself a comfort by giving you an object of anxiety without fear, for my wound is not dangerous. I am an example of the Almighty's goodness. He has shewn me the power of his saving arm in battle.
>
> Our Caroline is gone my mother, but every day teaches us there is little to lose in losing life, and much to be gained: my grief is for you. Few women have indeed sustained more cruel losses, yet few have greater comforts left; many may have more

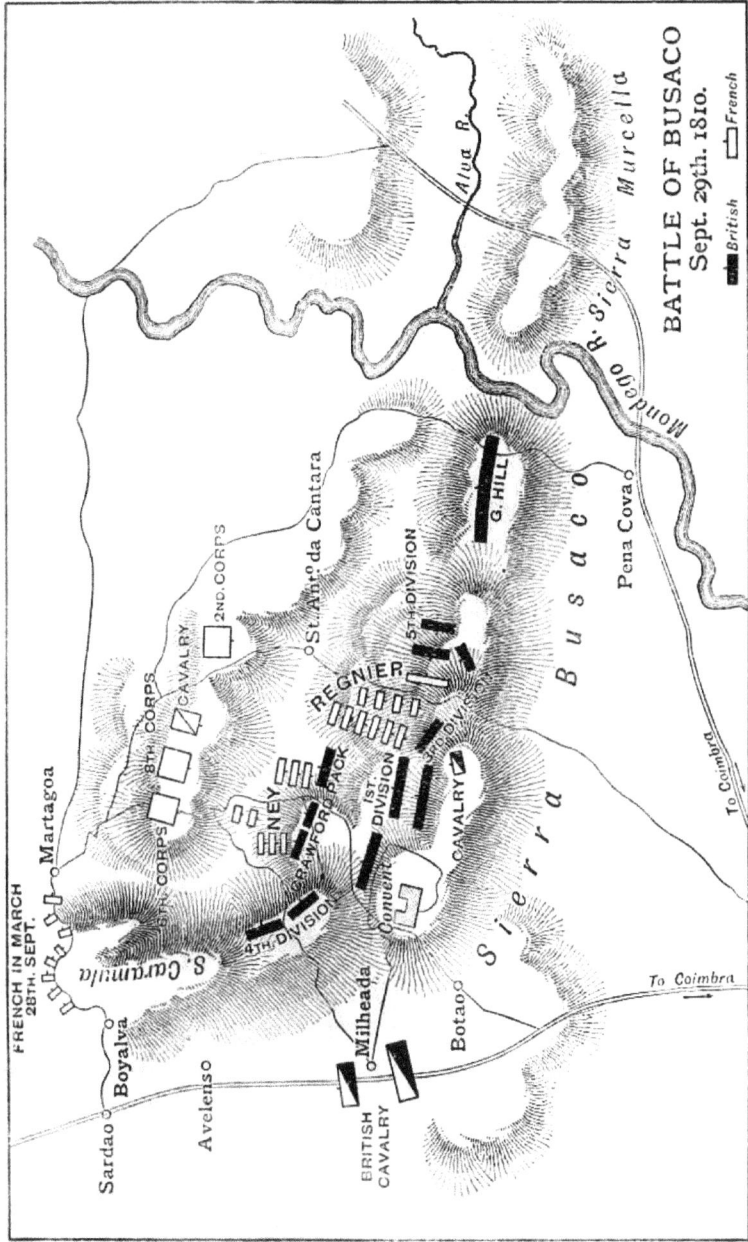

BATTLE OF BUSACO
Sept. 29th. 1810.

British ███ French ▭

Alva R.

Sierra Murcella

Mondego R.

Pena Covao

To Coimbra

Sierra Busaco

To Coimbra

2ND. CORPS

CAVALRY

8TH CORPS

6TH CORPS

St. Antº da Cantara

REGNIER

5TH DIVISION

G. HILL

3RD DIVISION

2D DIVISION

CAVALRY

1ST. DIVISION

NEY

CRAWFORD PACK

4TH DIVISION

Convent

Martagoa

FRENCH IN MARCH
28TH. SEPT.

S. Curamilla

Sardao Boyalva

Avelenso

Milheada

Botao

BRITISH
CAVALRY

apparently, but how many unseen troubles disturb them!

Oct. 20. Children and parents dear mother should be friends, and should speak openly to each other. Never had I a petty dispute with you, or heard others have one, without thanking God for giving me a mother, not a tyrant. Such as your children are, they are your work. We are a vain set of animals indeed, yet feel the gratitude you deserve, though we don't *bow* and *ma'am* you at every word, as some do. The Almighty has taken much from you, but has left much; would that our profession allowed us to be more with you: yet even that may happen, for none know what is to come, and peace, blessed peace! may be given to the world sooner than we think.

It is war now, and you must have fortitude, in common with thirty thousand English mothers whose anxious hearts are fixed on Portugal; and who have not the pride of saying their three sons had been wounded and were all alive! How this would have repaid my father for all anxieties, and it must do so for you: why! a Roman matron would not have let people touch her garment in such a case. In honest truth though, my share of wounds satisfies me: not that I agree with those who exclaim, how unfortunate! there is no shame for wounds, and no regret where no limb is lost, no faculty gone; and if there were, many lose them in less honest ways.

The scars on my face will be as good as medals, better, for they were not gained, oh! meritorious actions! by simply being a lieutenant-colonel, and hiding behind a wall. What nonsense! yet better than putting you in the dismals. Your recent loss was not touched upon in my first letter because it could not be without emotion, which would then have been very dangerous to me.

Oct. 24th. My wounds are nearly closed, but a swelling in the face and stiff jaw require care and confinement. To be so near well without joining my regiment worries me; but the doctor says Stuff, get well first, get well. His chief objection is fear of cold fixing the stiff jaw, and as even now it is difficult to eat, fatigue could not be borne.

Nov. 1st. Lord March has just come in, and tells me you have had your eyes done, and can see a little. Oh my beloved mother is this blessed news true? Great God grant it to be so! How thankful to God for this great blessing, but my anxiety is too great to write. I am afraid!

She became blind again.

Nov. 7th. As to my sufferings, there were none after pulling out the ball: so that matter is settled. (At a later period it will be seen how terribly false this was: his sufferings at the time nearly drove him mad.) Perhaps the use of my choppers will never be regained, and stiff jaws are a bore, but only painful at dinner: so at grace I put up a prayer for the fellow who shot me. My surgeon, a shrewd little Scotchman, calls me a fool for thinking of joining. 'Imposseeble! Redeeklous! Wait tull ye'er weel fly away! No patience! But go if you like—ye'll lose you neb though.' This doctor says that Lord Wellington should be hanged for the loss of men at Talavera, and that no successes can wash him clean. Now I am not for hanging, but for making him Duke of Portugal if he succeeds, anything ministers like; but I wish he did not belong to them.

Massena had now retired, it was supposed in flight, until he turned at Santarem.

Nov. 20th. My jaws are coming right, but the doctor won't let me move, which is wise. My desire is to join in the pursuit, the French will be touched up now, yet there will be no general action, which consoles George and me much. What spirits our poor fellows will be in, pursuing instead of the wretchedness of retreating, which preys on the strongest mind and overwhelms men more than anything else. Poor devils of French, they excite my pity, for they hate this warfare. What is to be my ultimate fate? A narrow escape as usual. A billet of wood fell from a garret window and grazed my cheek, so as to tear the black silk from off my wound: it hit my shoulder but without hurting I must be hanged!

Stories of a dreadful conspiracy at Lisbon, spread by the regency, at this time alarmed London.

As to conspiracy, dearest mother, be at your ease; I am a conspirator as much as the unfortunate creatures taken up; their crime is being freemasons: the regency, composed of the greatest rascals on earth, have used conspiracy for pouncing on private enemies. They called everybody they disliked Jacobins, and in two hours the wretches were dragged on board ship and no more heard of: their poor families have to thank our papers for all they know of their relations' fate! My intent is to have a slap at the regency if any of them are to be met at the admiral's, or at the envoy's, Mr. C. Stuart's: the latter and Lord Wellington disclaim these proceedings entirely. There is no more conspiracy in Lisbon than in London.

It is curious that there was at that period, precisely as much conspiracy in London as in Lisbon; and a great deal in both: not a conspiracy of the people persecuted, but of the regency, in complicity with English politicians of rank and power, who with secret intrigue, and all possible knavery and diligence, were striving to overthrow Wellington from his command. It was very vile and foolish, and Charles Napier soon found occasion for his promised *slap at the regency*. An Italian, at whose house he visited, was suddenly incarcerated from private enmity, and his wife and daughter implored for interference. The gentleman had been grievously maltreated, but his misery was somewhat alleviated by bribing the gaoler; wherefore, applying to Mr. Stuart, Charles Napier pressed the case upon him in writing; and noticing the gaol bribe said, he supposed it would be vastly augmented by the time it reached the head of the government. Mr. Stuart unguardedly sent this letter to Dom Miguel Forjas, the Secretary of State, and the subsequent proceedings are thus described.

The Portuguese prime minister, or head of the regency, told Stuart that my statement was a *lie*. Stuart told me this. I will prove it a truth said I, and taking Captain Lloyd of the 43rd, and Captain Sturgeon of the Staff Corps with me, I went straight to the palace of government and saw the minister. I told him he must choose one of three things, 1). Making an ample apology. 2). Fighting me. 3). Horsewhipping.
He said it was very unpleasant to do any one.
'Our tastes are perfectly similar,' said I, 'but having unluckily been born a gentleman I have a character to keep up, which obliges me to desire an immediate compliance.'
'Tomorrow you shall have an answer,' said he, 'for I too am a military man.'
'This minute if you please, your excellency,' quoth I.
After some more talk on his part, and a rather insolent manner

on mine, Sturgeon doing interpreter, and Lloyd looking like Gog and Magog together, Forjas said he would say, that I was right, and make an apology to me through Mr. Stuart.

'It must be given in writing, as the lie was so given,' said I.

He answered, 'If you are not content tomorrow we will fight, but read my apology first.'

'Basta, if the apology be complete,' was the reply. So, we ended. In the evening, a note from Mr. Stuart said he had received an official and complete apology from Dom Miguel Forjas, which was placed in the archives of the embassy. This was so far satisfactory, but the liberation of the old Italian gentleman, who had been, as Mr. Stuart told me, very infamously used, was still to be effected and it was so, he was let out of prison next day! He had a beautiful and agreeable Oporto lady for his wife, but the old knave kept two opera girls, being seventy: this was rather *outré*, and I told him so.

'It is gentlemanlike,' said he, 'and you may make love to them both if you like.'

'Oh! I'd rather do so to your wife.'

'I thought you did.'

'Not I.'

'More fool you, they are all three at your service.'

This was polite, but was however a lie, for two people told me he had set them to watch me; but as I went to the army immediately, his family honour was all safe for me. She was excessively handsome, very agreeable, and had the most beautiful mouth and teeth, but was a great deal too fat.

Mr. Stuart, no mean judge of men, and having in his own father the model of a heroic British officer, when speaking of this quarrel with Forjas, said, that Napier had a head and heart equal to any enterprise however difficult or dangerous. But this was only one side of his character: to step gaily from the sublime to the ridiculous was a part of his peculiar idiosyncrasy; an exuberant peculiar humour, rioting like a merry devil in a nun, always possessed him, and in adverse circumstances most strongly. He delighted to find himself and others in ludicrous situations, but generally described them with too much of Rabelais' richness for record: however, the following account of a Barmecidal dinner is free from that objection.

Having accidentally met some friends he invited them to walk home to dinner, and asked his servant if it was ready?

'Quite sir.'

'What is there?'

'There's no soup.'

'Anything else?'

'There's no sosingers.'

'What more?'

'There's no pratees.'

'What next?'

'There's no visibles (vegetables).'

'So, it seems, go on.'

'There's no nothing.' '

Hum, a good negative dinner: you must borrow.'

'There's no time.'

'Buy.'

'There's no money.'

'Credit.'

'There's no tick.'

'Are there no rations?'

'Yes sir.'

I ate the beef.

Returning now to his correspondence, it is to be noted that several young London men, amongst them his cousin, Harry Fox, had attended the army during the retreat, and some of them had aided to carry him from Busaco. This kindness was spoken of with so much exaggeration afterwards in London, that Lady Sarah was disposed to manifest her sense of it in a way her son did not approve, hence the following letter.

November. A—— B—— C—— &c., were very kind, but not so as to demand particular thanks. They did what all persons, except my Coimbra physician, would do by a wounded man, but I had to shift for myself after the first half hour and went alone to Coimbra. They were not inattentive to me, but do not by writing thanks make them think me under an obligation to them: they only did what they would have been brutes not to have done, *i.e.* looked to the carrying a wounded man off, when near him. Black Charles indeed, like a true sailor, was active as possible, and personally assisted in carrying me.

All this was good-natured, and I am thankful; but it is displeasing that people should be told to think me bound in gratitude when I do not feel so. Gratitude is with me a sacred feeling, and it offends me to have it made common with thank you. I like Harry Fox and Charles Napier the better for not staying with me, and would not have thanked them if they had: I should have attributed it to dislike of returning into fire. My uneasiness was great lest George and William should come, though only five hundred yards off, yet I felt almost sure they would not: at the Coa I left William with the first surgeon and went back.

November. Black Charles is a queer fellow as ever crossed me, and as honest a one. He is going to Cadiz, we shall see him no more: this is a copy of his letter to the first Lord of the Admiralty on the occasion—

> Sir, my leave of absence is just out. I don't think it worth remaining here, for I expect you will give me a ship, as I am almost tired of campaigning, which is a damned rum concern.—C. N.

He is the delight of my life, and should live with me and be trusted with any enterprise, if I were a great man, he being just fit for a sailor; that is, bold, decided, and active: he will make a figure yet. Lord Wellington lately said to him, I could easily beat the French, but England has no other army, and it would cost me ten thousand men; so, we must have prudence, and fight when they must lose men and we not. Be comfortable therefore dear mother, no more Talaveras will shake you with fear. What does your friend Mrs. Adye mean about my good-nature to her sister Mrs. Hawker? She is not known to me by sight, though so pretty a voice as she has I never heard; and if my wound had not disabled me, I would have kicked a cursed physician, who told her in my hearing through a thin wall that her husband had been desperately wounded: he had fabricated the story to introduce himself, and she was half wild, poor thing! It was the same fellow who left me to cool my heels at Coimbra, but the wretch is, I believe, an idiot.

His sufferings were now dreadful, yet his light humour increased in the inverse ratio. In December he writes:

> My face is, luckily, not awry as well as my jaw; but the jawbone being broken to *smidereens*, has I fear lost its smoothness, and

won't turn in the socket. I want an anatomy book, and some fellow's skull, to see how things are made. Mrs.—— shall have a bit of my jawbone, which, with seven others, was lodged in the ball and came away with it. I offered it to a monk for a relic, saying it was a piece of St. Paul's wisdom tooth, given to me by the Virgin Mary in a dream. He was going to take it for his convent, but was told, that being a sinner with no other chance for salvation, it was impossible for me to part with it except for dollars! He never gave money for relics, he said. 'Devil doubt you' quoth I, and pocketed my bit of jaw.

Tell Susan Frost I am quite well, though talking such dreadful nonsense. No man dare talk sense here, the regency would think it plotting if a word of sense came from my mouth, and would send me to the Inquisition: they have sent numbers there for doing so, and are restoring all the pristine terrors of that institution under the countenance of the able humane British Government!

December. Why are you not yet gone to Ireland? What keeps you? Our health! You would hear of us just the same there as in London, and winter is a bad time for your journey, especially the water part. My fear is that they may drop you in your helpless state, in getting you on board. Wherefore tell Dick (his younger brother designed for the church, and then a fellow of All Souls) to have you swung in a chair, tied hand and foot. If he would put bladders to your fingers and toes, as boys do with cats before *projecting* them out of a garret window, it would be commendable, ingenious and laughable, though derogatory to the clerical character, and unbecoming the gravity of All Souls—he would prefer being the elect of all Psyches methinks. However, once done, flying our mothers might become fashionable. Ah! my God! as Louis Chabot says; my God! what nonsense I talk when the fit takes me. Is there any nostrum for it? if there is, the vendor should establish his shop near the parliament house.——

How I pity the poor old king, and all of them, they have much suffering; God restore their poor father to his senses. For the men my pity is less, they are said to have little feeling: but the princesses, and the poor old queen, who is believed to be very much attached to him! Well, no more. What part of a china tea service am I like? The major part, that is the teapot, because it is full of holes, and so am I. Three times dear mother has this letter been commenced in a most serious manner, and on the most serious subjects, but nonsense will come, and devil take me if I can stop for the life of me.

This tendency to joking when suffering in body or mind, was, indeed, inexpressible, for the examples given but faintly indicate the extent of the peculiarity. With Swift's humour however, he had nothing of his disgusting malignity of application to debase human nature; he provoked laughter only, not blushes. Even anger could not repress his mirth. His own terrible wound, and that of his brother ought now, he thought, to insure a promotion which was due to both before, and he claimed it from Sir David Dundas, but finding him callous, thus exhaled his indignation.

I want to have a rise out of old Pivot before he goes to the devil. My claim is good: every Coruña major except myself has been promoted; this is a stigma which only a medal, or a lieutenant-colonelcy can remove. If both are refused a court-martial must be asked for, to clear my character. The stiff old brush, I'll work him to death if possible. Writing in such a fury hurts my wounds, but really the flies and Sir D. Dundas would make Job angry. Those swarming flies get up my nose, and distract me, owing to my wound: five hundred a day is my average slaughter of them! This I never did before, but self-defence is human nature; war has been declared, and traps of gunpowder are laid to blow mine enemies up. Am I not a wretch! Brutality is our nature. When hit at Busaco, it gave me pleasure to be told George's men had just bayonetted a whole regiment. Strange! Strange! Strange!

Vexation of mind and the winter's cold and damp now caused very severe suffering, and more extravagance of humour: one example will suffice.

November. Being too cold to write much, know that I live; but in a house without a fireplace, hibernating like a bear in snow, rather than living like an alderman: happily, however not sucking my paws, for it would be an operation rather tasty than agreeable in this country; where constant bugicide &c. produces a second skin, equal perhaps to portable soup, though not quite a match for Quin's sauce. The Portuguese think fires are dangerous in the keen air of their country, and supply warmth by cherishing filth with a load of greasy cloaks on their shoulders: perhaps they are right, but I would willingly run the risk of a blazing fire, being quite perished, and my stiff jaws only hindering my teeth surpassing all the castanets in Spain. Not that there is much to complain of, but my two centre under teeth have necessarily a division between them, God having ordained that no two hills shall be without a valley. This division is exactly under the outer edge of the left great tooth in the upper jaw, so the twist is just the breadth of that large tooth. Meanwhile my general state is what it was a month ago, only with more freedom of opening and shutting my mouth. The swelled cheek is fixed for good and all 'tis said, and liable also to increase or diminish with heat or cold, which, being dead, it has no right to do. Electricity has been prescribed. Whether it will restore vitality is doubtful; for the living parts surrounding the dead are a great deal too sentimental, and flirt too much with the north-east wind: Mrs. M —— herself could not beat them. But all my teeth are shaken, and the feel is like a violent cold in them; it is worrying, but a shot through the face in its most amiable form is no joke. Often have I heard of a pig's foot in one's cheek, but believe no one ever before had a thermometer there. Stop! General Campbell of the guards got nearly the same wound at Talavera, only it did not pass through his nose, and he cannot yet open his mouth; whereas I can eat well, unless the food is hard.

There is nothing stirring here, not even my blood, which is almost congealed with writing to you in the cold, I wish to be in an oven. If Portugal be a hot country my nature is changed, for I have not been fairly warmed since landing last May. When other fellows were hanging out their tongues I was just comfortable, no more: my delight would be a shaved head, a vertical sun, a fiery horse, and no hat; the retreat through Galicia iced me, and I am not yet thawed. Shadrac and the other fellows, I can't spell their names, but the three salamanders, could not stand the fiery furnace better than me: the kindest thing that you can say to me, is go to the devil!

This extreme sensitiveness to cold continued all his life, a result of losing so much blood from wounds, and from that inveterate use of the lancet, which disgraced the surgery of the times: his abstemious habits also aided, for he never touched wine, and often adopted a purely vegetable diet.

His brother now left him and he felt his loneliness acutely, but it only produced more jokes.

December. I wish for someone to spend my Christmas with. My jaws are crooked and the doctors say, will always be so. My lip is very uneasy, and will always be so. My cheek is better and the swelling, *may* go away. Electricity used every morning, but the parts are insensible to sparks, while shocks would injure the parts around which do feel. My mouth opens but stiffly. My eye still stares, yet is stronger, more easily shut and sees further: it is said the sight may be lost, but it is not dim, and if it goes—why Hannibal had only one eye: I have a mind to pluck it out.

January 8th. My wound will always be inconvenient, having broken the gristle of my snout inside, one nostril has but little passage left, so my fate is to be always a snuffler, for the doctors say it will never be better. My surgeon is a good one, yet in truth little is due to them for recovery: nature and Charles Napier, that is me, myself, saved me. There needed to have been no lump in the snout had they used the spunge plug in time, and my wish was for it, but they said no! The jaw might have been set also; but in truth they were afraid of touching me, lest they should bring on inflammation. What a passion the devil must be in at being so often baulked!

However, it must please him to see what an ugly saint these clinks have made me! General Kellerman was thirty-two at the Battle of Vimiera, and had thirty-two wounds! My share is six in two years, hem! Kellerman take the prize: I am content not to get the twenty-six wanted in the next four years. What an animal I am! if my eye goes, but of that I have no hope, fear I mean, my resemblance to Captain Magan of song will be complete, *one eye was knocked out just over his snout.* Polyphemus forever.

CHAPTER 8

On Campaign

Lady Sarah Napier, from her powerful connections her blindness and her son's romantic escape was supposed to have much influence, and consequently was besieged by persons who could not conceive she had any object of interest greater than their welfare: hence the following letter.

February. My positive injunctions are to say nothing about me to the Duke of Richmond, speak only for George, and let no one interfere with his claims. Recollect what we found in my father's letter to M—— I cannot help you, because I have children, and my interest is very little to divide amongst them.' Now dear mother you have that simple answer for the applications made to you. Say, I cannot get my two eldest sons their just promotion, earned with their blood; a third son has also been wounded, and is a very old captain; a fourth, in the navy, requires much interest to get him on; a fifth is wholly unprovided for. If I can assist one of the five it is more than I expect, having been unsuccessful for two years: what then can strangers expect from me?

If Lord Moira comes in as commander in chief, I have his unsolicited promise to give me a lieutenant-colonelcy, and William a majority: between friends you should take all advantages, for our family have been too proud, it don't thrive, and 'tis time to change. We have worked through all for our own bread, and I would now have no conscience in asking. It is delightful to hear of Richard's success at college. Let me know how he likes All Souls, and if it is a pleasant college: he will understand me, you need not.

This success was the gaining of honours under a new statute at Oxford, by which at examinations, aspirants were classed according to their proficiency, without being pitted against each other. Sir Robert Peel's examination, in 1809, was the first under this rule, and he took the first honours, both in literature and mathematics. Richard Napier's examination was of the next year, and he took the first class in mathematics, though not in literature, and was elected a fellow of All Souls.

Charles Napier's anticipation of ministerial change, and hopes of promotion were alike vain; he and his brothers, had still to fight their way to fortune, winning rank, not through the aid of their high connections, nor the favour of the Horse Guards, but with sweat, and dust, and blood from Wellington, who was now leading the army to victories as incessant as they were glorious. For Massena, after exhausting all means of subsistence at Santarem, had retreated early in March 1811, with a skill which balanced the errors of his advance, justifying Napoleon's remark, that it was only in danger and difficulty he became a general.

On that retreat, day after day, Ney, the indomitable Ney, offered battle with the rear-guard, and a stream of fire run along the wasted valleys of Portugal from the Tagus to the Mondego, from the Mondego to the Coa. Combat followed combat, the light division led in pursuit, and Charles Napier, with his wound still bandaged, rode above ninety miles on one horse and in one course, to reach the army. His regiment being with the main body, he heard each morning the ever-recurring sound of the light division's combats in front, and had hourly to ask of wounded men if his brothers were living?

Thus advancing, on the 14th of March he met a litter of branches, borne by soldiers and covered with a blanket. What wounded officer is that? Captain Napier of the 52nd, a broken limb. Another litter followed. Who is that? Captain Napier 43rd mortally wounded:—it was thought so then. Charles Napier looked at them and passed on to the fight in front! But his story can now again be told from a journal, commenced two days before he heard of the retreat.

Lisbon, March 6th. Rode to Mafra. After Loures mountainous. Crossed Monte Chica, which is fortified and very strong from its precipitous features. Thence to Mafra, where the heights are strong and covered with works. The confidence inspired by these lines of Wellington must necessarily be great; but the danger to be feared is, that they must be defended in a great

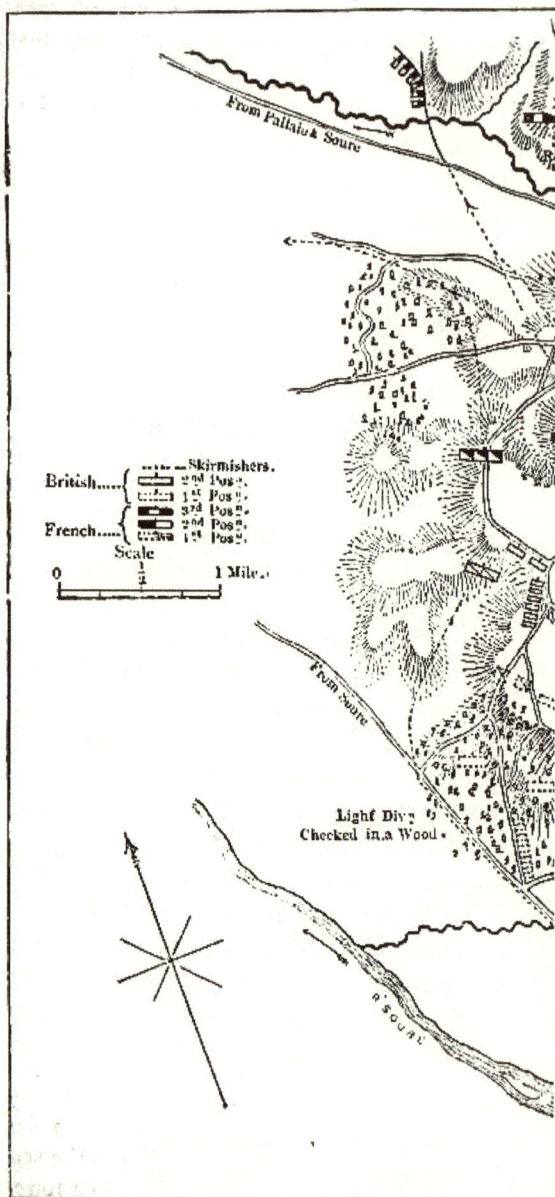

From Pallais & Soure

British.....{ ———— Skirmishers.
           ☐ 2ⁿᵈ Posⁿ.
           ⊏⋯⊐ 1ˢᵗ Posⁿ.
French.....{ ■ 3ʳᵈ Posⁿ.
            ▬ 2ⁿᵈ Posⁿ.
            ▭ 1ˢᵗ Posⁿ.

Scale

0   ½   1 Mile.

From Soure

Light Divⁿ
Checked in a Wood.

R⁰SOURE

PLAN OF THE AC

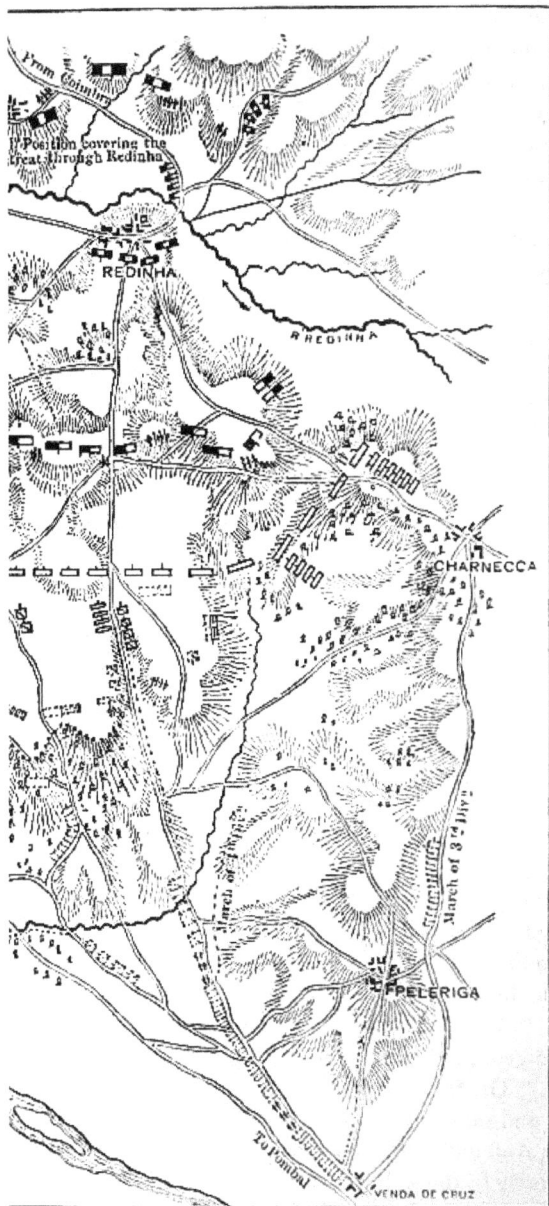

From Coimbra

Position covering the
retreat through Redinha

REDINHA

R. REDINHA

CHARNECCA

March of 3rd Div.

FPELERIGA

To Pombal

VENDA DE CRUZ

TION AT REDINHA.

measure by the *ordenanza* who are mere peasants; or by militia who are not better. Now regular troops, however confident at first, would be dismayed at seeing a French column penetrating where the works were deemed impregnable; consternation would then ensue, especially with the Portuguese troops. All lines have this drawback. A soldier who trusts to his firelock alone never despairs while he can use it; but he ever puts too much faith in works, and on seeing them forced thinks all is lost.

However, I only speak of what might occur if these lines were assailed by an army equal to the contest, and Lord Wellington says Massena's army is not so; and of that there is little doubt or Massena would have attacked: if ever lines were useful those of Torres Vedras are so. Mafra palace is, like all Portuguese buildings, wanting in consistency. Their structures have the most beautiful pillars, the handsomest porches, the finest statues, all worked in marble, or stone of the country, which is an inferior marble; their cornices, mouldings &c. are all highly finished and the Portuguese are excellent sculptors. But with all this the walls are of rubbish, or small stones plaistered, when with scarcely any trouble, they might be of marble blocks! Some parts are half finished and then filled up, anyhow: in one spot is a pilaster of marble in exquisite taste, its fellow is of painted wood, and so on.

8th March. Just heard of the French retreat, which I conclude is to seek subsistence in a country not yet exhausted, north of the Mondego; and perhaps to draw Lord Wellington from his lines, and then attack him in rear with the army now besieging Badajos. My wound is still open but I am off to join.

10th. Reached Villa Franca, five leagues: passed the plain where Junot was wounded.

12th and 13th. Rode all night, and having made ninety-two miles reached the army between Redinha and Condeixa. This distance was done, with only three hours' halt at Tom Napier's quarters, (the admiral's brother), who gave me a positive bad but comparative good dinner. My poor horse had 2 lbs. of Indian corn, on which he performed this severe journey in twenty-two hours, including the three hours' halt!

BREACHES

French Retrenchment

Sword blades

St. Maria · Holes O · Trinidad

Cunette

Cunette

Light Division · 5th. Division

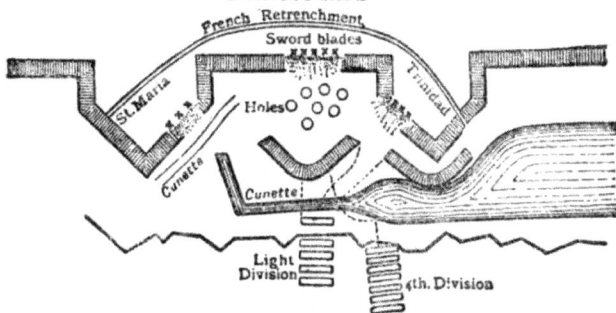

Siege of
BADAJOS
1812.

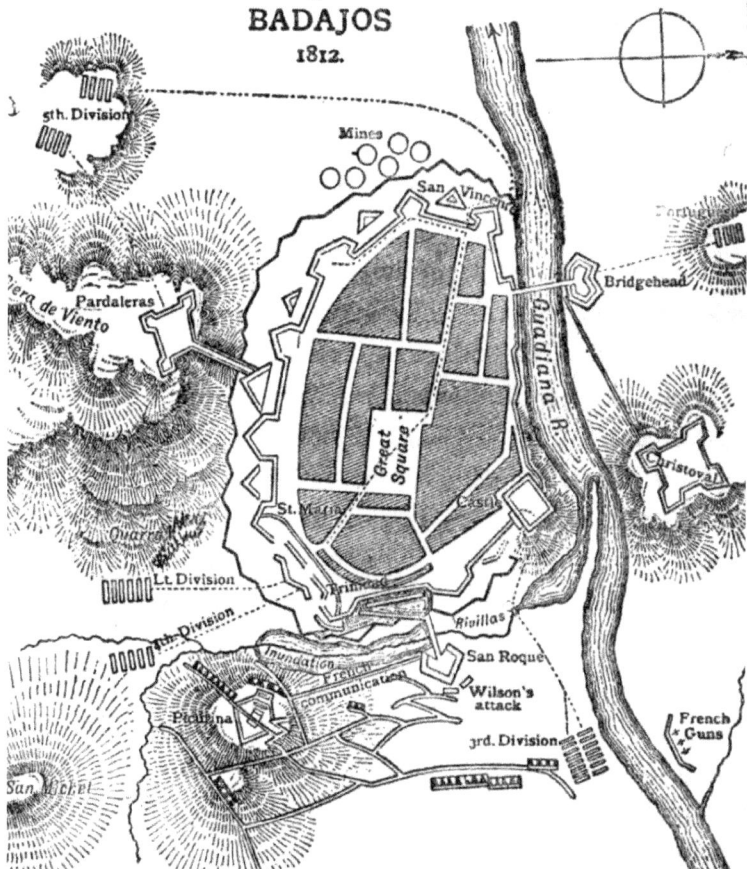

5th. Division

Mines

San Vincente

Bridgehead

Cerro de Viento · Pardaleras

Guadiana R.

Great Square

Casa

St. Maria

Cristoval

Quarries

Lt. Division

4th. Division

Trinidad

Rivillas

Inundation

Picurina

French communication

San Roque

Wilson's attack

San Michel

3rd. Division

French Guns

14th. A sharp affair between the light division and the enemy's rear-guard this day. We lost four hundred killed and wounded, here and at Redinha. My two brothers commanded the companies chiefly engaged, and are both severely wounded: the ignorance and imprudence of Sir Wm. Erskine said to have been conspicuous; and Colonel Drummond is not extolled for military qualities.

15th. Great want of provisions. Moved to Foz D'Aronce. At the end of the march, part of the light division was engaged sharply.

16th to 21st. Continued our route, enemy in full retreat.

22nd. Rode over the mountains to Coimbra to see George and William. Passed Ponte Murcella and saw Busaco at a distance. This Murcella is strong, the position finest on the left bank, but the ford and bridge best defended on the right bank. The ground on the left is very high, yet does not command the bridge, like that on the right bank, which though much lower is close and precipitous: the bridge is blown up, the town burnt.

23rd. Returning from Coimbra lost my way on the heath at night, and slept at the bivouac of the *Chasseurs Britanique.* Reached St. Romao the 26th—the village burnt. Cea the same. The fine palace of the Bishop of Guarda's brother, Don Bernardo, quite destroyed. Massena has used fire and sword with an unsparing hand. Numbers of peasants' bodies seen, many had been bayonetted, others shot; some were very old men, some were women! I did not think French gallantry would have suffered this: but Massena is an Italian.

28th, San Payo. Paid a visit to my old patron. At his former amusement, cracking vermin, on whom he seemed to revenge the wrongs of his country. This village has escaped better: in this very house, six months ago, stood with me, George and Giffard; now George is sadly wounded, and the amiable Giffard dead! Are these the pleasures of war? Does glory repay these losses and pains?

30th. In a delightful village. Colonel Stewart and a Portuguese are trying to cheat each other about a beautiful goat: Caledonia is too much for Lusitania!

2nd April. Marched to the village of Muselha, enemy close.

BATTLE OF
BARROSA
5th March 1811.

SCALES
Military Steps 2½ Feet each
English Mile

Positions before and after the battle coloured light

Retreat
of the
French

VIGIA DE LA BARROSA

Barossa

Bushes

Ruin

Graham

Dilkes

Wheatley

Bushes

Barrosa

Graham's column

Two Spanish Regiments

Casas de las Cuentas

French camp

French Lines

French camp

Bermeja

RIO DE SANTI PETRI

Molino de Almanza

Isla de la Torre

Punta del Boquon Puerco

Fuente Amarga

Punta de Santa Petri

Castᵒ de Sᵗ Petri

A T L A N T I C   O C E A N

3rd. The light division engaged near Sabugal, suffered much, but beat a whole *corps d'armée* and took a howitzer. Colonel Beckwith's conduct said to have been in a great measure the cause of such an extraordinary success: the fact is the French cannot stomach a British attack. Picton's division was slightly engaged towards the close. The three fighting regiments were the 43rd, 52nd and 95th.

5th, Ungera. We arrived last night, wet, tired, and no cover; cursing Portugal, and Portuguese names, and Frenchmen, and English generals, and quartermaster generals, fools and rogues, commissaries and medicos. The baggage of young Soult, who commands Regnier's cavalry, has been taken, and in it a book with copies of all his letters to Regnier, previous to Massena's penetrating Portugal. In one he says the English are at Ponte Murcella and Viseu, and generally supposed to be preparing for embarkation; they will immediately begin their retreat.

I did not see the letter, but this idea of our weakness is the only way to account for Massena's attack at Busaco, where he learned to his cost we were not ready to embark. He it is that flies, and we have this day been exactly one month in pursuit of him. Where will this interesting campaign close, and how? I can hardly think the French mean to re-enter Portugal, or they would not have destroyed the country so dreadfully. There was a horrible instance of brutality in this village; the French say it was the Italians. Massena is an Italian.

5th, Nava. The French left this village yesterday, followed by the light division. On our march, we passed the field of battle where the light division fought Regnier on the 3rd. The ground was a gentle slope and open, but this I think always good for us: the French stand fire for ever behind walls, but don't like close quarters. Dead horses and men were still unburied near a low wall, where the French cavalry charged our skirmishers and were driven back with great loss by the 43rd Regiment.

6th, Alfayates. We are making a flank movement to our left to force the enemy at Almeida. This must produce a general action or make Massena let go his hold of Portugal, leaving Lord Wellington master of the kingdom he has so skilfully and boldly defended. His whole conduct has been able: errors may have been committed, all generals commit errors, but this successful

142

COMBATE DO SABUGAL

NA

RETIRADA DE MASSENA

em 5 de abril de 1811.

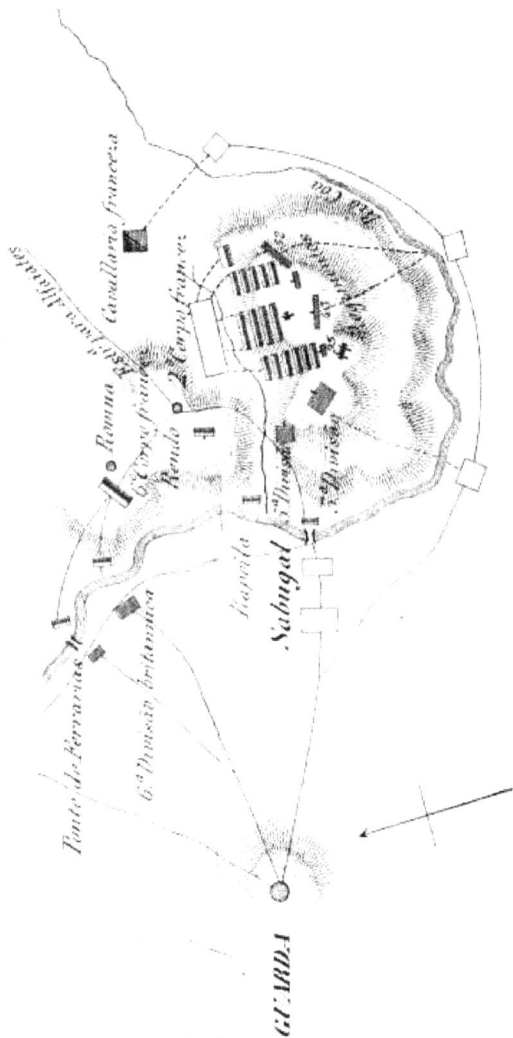

Ponte de Ferrarias

6ª Divisão britanica

GUARDA

Sabugal

Ruivós

Corpo principal

Ruina de

Cavallaria franceza

2ª Divisão franc.

Rio Côa

campaign renders him one of the first of his time. I regret that Buonaparte was not here in person; but perhaps it is better as it is: had he been here things would perhaps have been different. I can't help wishing for a general action near Almeida; the ground is perfectly open, and when that is the case our army is sure of victory. Our cavalry can then act, and though less numerous, is so superior that the combat would probably be in our favour. A total defeat of the French would put Ciudad Rodrigo into our hands and effectually stop a second invasion of Portugal for a long time. It would also save the Spaniards if anything can rouse their energies: perhaps it is too late but still worth trial.

Here the journal shall be momentarily abandoned for the never-neglected correspondence with his mother: the first letter is however addressed to his cousin, Lady Emily Berkely.

Ponte de Murcella. My brothers are at Condeixa. George was yesterday in great pain, not otherwise ill; William so much better as to be up: this is nearly proof positive that his inwards have not been injured by the ball, and the wound is therefore not dangerous. Twice have I written to my mother, but to meet accidents will you send this to her as a later account. The French have destroyed two arches of this bridge, and our light troops were warmly engaged last night; but we have no chance of a general action, which I am sorry for: my mother will probably not regret it so much.

My brothers' wounds will, I think, confine them a long time, for though it may be confidently said they are not dangerous, they are very bad clinks. George's poor subaltern, Lieutenant Giffard, was killed: his conduct was the admiration of every one; and that is the only consolation. George is so affected by his loss that it hurts his wound. Our skirmishers were retiring when the gallant young man was killed; my brother missed him, looked back, and saw him on the ground, a hundred yards behind. Four Frenchmen were plundering him, but George, sabre in hand, dashed back singly, beat the four men from their plunder, took his friend's bleeding corpse in his arms and bore it off from the midst of his enemies.

The company buried him on the spot with their bayonets, under a tremendous fire, gave three cheers and again attacked:

43RD AT SABUGAL

never was a soldier's death finer, or his burial more honourable! Giffard was so bravely conspicuous that the French officers called out many times, kill that officer. At last they succeeded— but we had shot for shot, they lost four hundred men.

In this account, there is an error. George Napier was followed by two men, but he did not know of their aid until they helped him to raise the body, still breathing, on to his shoulder. And while thus noting one fine display of feeling and gallantry, it will not be misplaced to set beside it other instances of fortitude and generosity, shewing what manner of men those were who bore England's standard from Lisbon to Toulouse.

First of William Light, a young cavalry officer. Son of Captain Edward Light, by the King of Quedah's daughter, who received for portion, Prince of Wales' Island. William was born to the rights and inheritance of an Eastern prince; but the court of directors, with that unvarying cupidity and oppression which has ever marked the East India Company's career, robbed his father of the island, by first forcing him to cede it for money, and then defrauded him of the compensation. The son entered the navy first, afterwards the army, and was now in the cavalry. William Light was a man of extraordinary accomplishments, soldier, seaman, musician, artist; and good in all: his disposition may be judged from the following action.

When nearly starved himself—all were so in the pursuit of Massena—he by some means obtained a loaf of bread, but hearing that George and William Napier were hurt, he stifled his own craving, and at the end of a long march, risked his life, and his horse's life, by riding some twenty miles across the wild mountains to Condeixa, where, entering the half-ruined house in which the wounded brothers were lying, he without a word threw down his loaf on one of their pallets, and rushing out returned to the army!

Now, one more heroic deed by a poor soldier, the noblest of all, and the circle will be complete.

A temporary bridge near the Murcella, had to be destroyed by powder, during Massena's advance; but the match failed, the enemy poured on and the passage seemed lost: then a man of Charles Napier's old corps, the Royal Artificers—would to God his name had been preserved for posterity—exclaimed *It shall not fail, they shall not pass*. So, saying, he deliberately walked along the structure, a floating one, to the mine, relighted the match, and bending his noble head over the spark, continued to watch its deadly progress until the explosion sent him from a world he was too heroic to live in! Why are young men told to look in ancient history for examples of heroism, when their own countrymen furnish such lessons?

Camp, Moita, 21st March. Both the wounded men are better mother. I make no apologies for the dirt of this note; for flead, bugged, centipeded, beetled, lizarded and earwigged, cleanliness is known to me only by name. Moreover, a furze bush makes a bad table for writing on, and a worse chair, when breeches are nearly worn out with glory, oh! oh! We have very little food, which forced us to halt: Massena has thus got two days' start, but he is pursued by the cavalry and light division.

We shall be dispersed in cantonments on the frontier, as Lord Wellington cannot, I think, muster men enough to follow into Spain, and probably more troops will be sent to the Alemtejo. Celorico again will be tiresome, but we are of Spencer's division, and it is to be feared will become headquarter pets, as the guards belong to us, and are favourites of his lordship; deservedly so. The light division are also great favourites, and most deservedly so. Lord Wellington has particularly thanked them, and is going to give three sergeants of the 43rd, 52nd and Rifles, each a commission for their conduct in the late pursuit of Massena.

He did give those commissions, and of eleven brevet majorities conferred on the whole army, two went to Charles Napier's wounded brothers; this left only his own promotion to press for: but he had yet to struggle hard for it, both in the field and by remonstrance: injustice reigned at the Horse Guards.

The distinguished animal now to be mentioned, was a half Arab, from Morocco, perfectly white, as indicated by his name, and of surprising sagacity.

Neither poor Blanco nor myself are much troubled with bile now. A hundred miles, with only three hours' rest and hardly a bit to eat, did he carry me coming up to the army, and my fear was it would kill him; but that was better than being too late for the action expected at Condeixa: he did not even tire! He is the strongest horse ever backed. Still he thinks a bivouac the worst amusement in the world, as he gets nothing but heath and hard riding. Poor fellow. I kiss and coax him, but it don't make up for *no oats*. He is the most delightful animal that ever was, but thinks being admired by the Lisbon ladies with a full stomach, better than my affection with heath.

Coimbra, March 23rd. Says I to Blanco yesterday, 'Suppose we walk over the mountains old boy and see the other boys:' no sooner said than done. William will be at his duty in two months, but he ought not for six; he suffers little pain and runs about in a go-cart like a child. As to George he suffers acute and constant pain, and cannot sleep without opium: however, the surgeons are positive he will not lose his hand, and think he will have the use of the two forefingers and thumb if not of all. Are we cats that we live and bear such wounds? But now having told you dear mother exactly the facts as usual, *adieu*; this is enough after a ride forty miles over the most rugged mountains in Portugal. Poor Blanco almost gives up the ghost.

24th. This country is ravaged by fire and sword, we get nothing for love or money, but pass through deserted tracks, the only symptoms of former habitations being the burned walls of villages and dead bodies. What a change in six months: England how little do you know of war! A dollar has been given for some biscuit; and two complete days and most part of a third I went without food: the boys at Coimbra stuffed me, for there they have plenty. We have also got a dinner here this day, and having been again two days without one I must make haste or it will be gone: we get no bread and the hard biscuit bothers my wounded jaw when there is not time for it to soak.

Alfayates, April 6th. No long agreeable letter, or even a civil one for you dear mother, civility is indeed a useless thing when one has neither food, nor drink, nor sleep. We have now, for one month, been up at three a.m. marching at four, and halting at seven o'clock at night, when we eat all we can get, from shoe soles to bread and butter. Writing is not agreeable, and done only to tell you how George and William are. The last is well now, and a brigade-major; and as George writes better with his left than his right hand he may do his own letters. You may rejoice at these fortunate recoveries from two as ugly wounds as could be, short of mortal ones. They are living well, we are on biscuits full of maggots, and though not a bad soldier, hang me if I can relish maggots. We suffer much in point of food, but the

French are nearly cleared out of the country.

Our late movement was to force the enemy from Almeida by turning their position there; they have run and the garrison of Almeida will blow that place up. Meanwhile our life for the last month has not been an easy one for a convalescent, yet I have worked through well, except a little rheumatism in the jaws: a splinter of bone protrudes still from the jaw, but very slowly. The first week, cold and sleeping out at night and severe riding made the wound bleed at the nose, but now all is right. Blanco is starving and curls his nose into a thousand wrinkles, cursing Buonaparte: there! my biscuit has run away on maggots' legs. We found many *Moniteurs* in the French camps and one had an account of Busaco, with this passage, *Le Major Napier, dejà bless*é *a la Corogne, reçu un coup de feu dans la figure.* (Major Napier, already wounded at La Coruña, received a shot in the face.)

Albergaria. Many thanks dear mother for your newspapers. You wonder at my carelessness about what you call a great public question—the regency. You shall have my reasons for calling it a trifling quibble of politicians, a dry and dull study. I may be wrong, no matter, I shall never have to settle a regency, unless with sharper things than Canning's wit or Lord Grenville's arguments. My first step is always to strip a subject of ornaments and leave my mind free for judgment.

Cobbett meets my notions here; he tells truth in plain language, giving his reasons for all he advances: now fact is fact, and his motives are to me nothing; our souls are not chained together like the bodies of Baird and his comrade. The king is mad, and cannot do his duty: he is therefore virtually dead. Were he really dead who would succeed? The prince. Madness and death are the same to kings, in the abstract; the prince should therefore have the place that real death would give him. If he is fit to rule as a king, he is fit to rule as regent: take away his powers and you impute unfitness to wield them. So much for the restriction.

Someone has sent me Prince Eugene's memoirs. It is agreeable to read anything written by a great man himself, and my hope is that these memoirs are authentic: they are amusing, with much fun and not too long. (This is also republished in book and kindle format by Leonaur, *Eugene of Savoy: Marlborough's Great Military Partner-Memoirs of Prince Eugene of Savoy &*

Prince Eugene-Soldier of Fortune by Alexander Innes Shand) As to style, my knowledge of French won't let me judge; but a style agreeable and clear cannot be very bad, for bad style would thus accomplish what good style aims at.

Towards books and people, I feel alike— if they give information or amusement their style is nothing to me. A good thing ill written is better than dullness with fine phrases; and an agreeable vulgarity is worth more than refined insipid gentility: who would not rather have fresh butter in *Jenny's brown jug*, than nothing in Lady Genteel's Grecian vase? I do not say a union is not best, when found; and in books this is generally the case, because refinement requires talent and study: but gentility, or what is called good breeding, carried beyond a certain point becomes trifling, and gives a bent to character.

Naturally I am civil, and therefore naturally trifling. I have indeed got pretty well rid of my breeding, it don't now trip me up often: would that I could also get rid of my trifling. Seriously: the habit of trying to please affects firmness, and a man often says yes instead of no, foolishly. A fellow comes smirking and smiling with 'Will you do me the favour of being so kind as to indulge me &c.' and you are conquered unless you get out 'I'll see you damned first:' that is generally decisive; but if you skirmish with. 'Indeed sir,' or ''Pon my life,' you are done at once.

Almeida will not surrender, Brennier refuses. All the majors have got brevet rank for Barrosa. Acheson is two years younger than me, and if they refuse me now my resignation shall go in to David Dundas; for this is insult added to injustice, and I will have justice or quit the service. I will write to him plainly, careless of a court-martial! for which indeed I wish, that the matter may become public. My intent is to have promotion or a trial, and if both are refused, appeal to the regent—if he supports Dundas, resign: exit in a rage.

April 29th. Under arms all day, because four or five poor devils of French battalions came from Ciudad Rodrigo to get food, perhaps to throw supplies into Almeida. Seventeen hours under arms for these ill-mannered knaves, who certainly came because it was post day. We shall be under arms again at three in the morning, being cruelly afraid of letting your friend Bren-

Battle of Fuentes Onoro

nier feed.

Lady Sarah had opened her house to him when a prisoner.

Suffering severely at this time from illness, Charles Napier treated his miseries with the broadest humour: but he had soon to meet new dangers. Lord Wellington having gone to correct Beresford's generalship in the south, Massena came down to relieve Almeida, Wellington returned immediately, the Battle of Fuentes Onoro was fought, and five days afterwards, Brennier broke out of Almeida, having first blown it up.

Journal, Albergaria, 9th to 16th May. This is my third entrance into Spain, and the cleanliness of the inhabitants is most striking on leaving Portuguese filth. Almeida still holds out, and Massena is said to have reached Salamanca; yet, I think, a threat to storm Almeida and put the garrison to the sword would make it surrender.

17th. How able we are in the art of war! Our army surrounds Almeida, the French are many marches from us, we thought we had blockaded the fortress, and daily expected its surrender from want of food. Now we hear that two days ago a convoy got into the place, it being on a plain, and we having plenty of cavalry, artillery, infantry, and means of all kinds! The French are our masters in war as to all but courage and bodily strength.

18th. The convoy got into Ciudad Rodrigo, not Almeida, and a reinforcement also, in face of the wonderful Sir Wm. Erskine, who is the laughing-stock of the army, and particularly of the light division. In the south, also we are exposing ourselves. A squadron of the 13th Light Dragoons under a major, has been surprised, and the whole made prisoners in the Alemtejo. What a pity our fine cavalry should have such officers as this, and others I know of: however, we have good ones in training. It is said heavy artillery is coming from Oporto to besiege Almeida. I hope this is true, the more work more glory. Lord Wellington is off to the Alemtejo, as Beresford has got in a fright and says, *'cock a doodle do, I don't know what to do.'*

19th. All majors in the action of Barrosa are made brevet lieutenant-colonels for their conduct. This is owing to their being brave, and their general not afraid to say so; nor selfish enough to take all reward, and leave those who saved him to shift for

Battle of
FUENTES D'ONORE
5th. May, 1811.

■■ *Allies* ▢ *French*

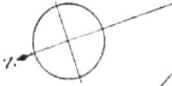

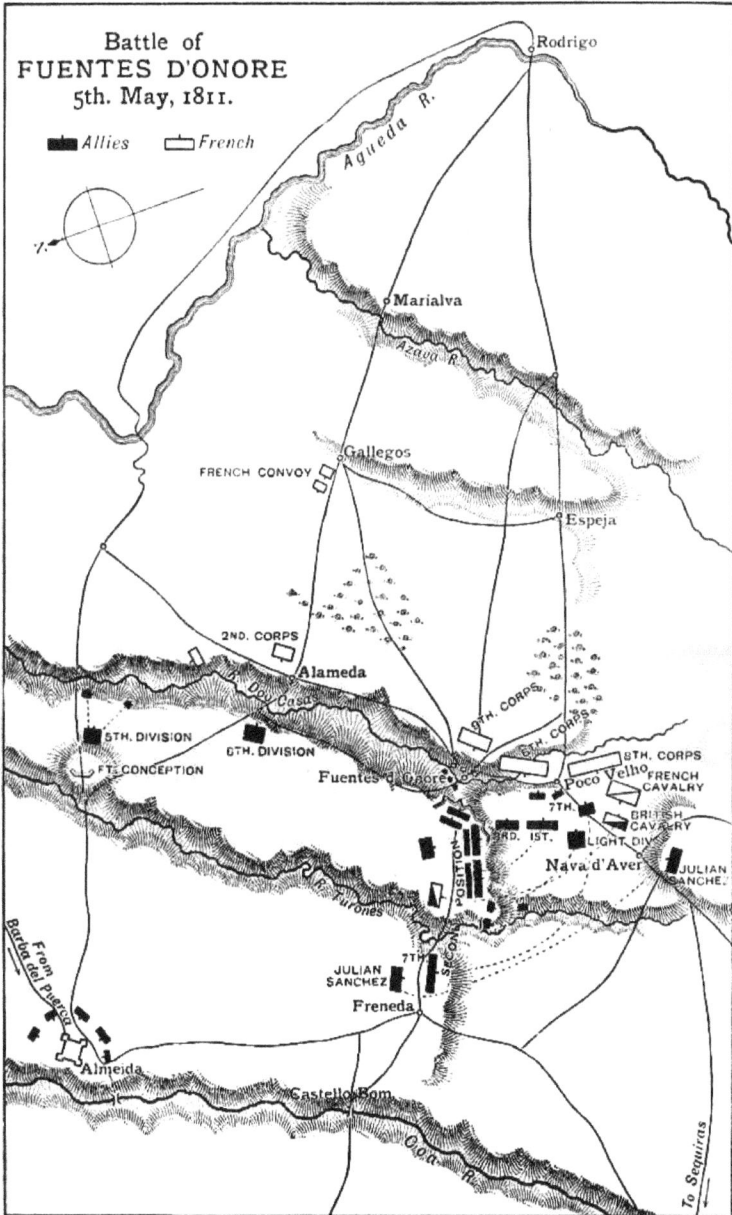

Rodrigo

Agueda R.

Marialva

Azava R.

Gallegos

FRENCH CONVOY

Espeja

2ND. CORPS

Alameda

R. Dos Casas

5TH. DIVISION

FT. CONCEPTION

6TH. DIVISION

9TH. CORPS

8TH. CORPS

8TH. CORPS

Fuentes d'Onore

Poco Velho

FRENCH CAVALRY

7TH.

BRITISH CAVALRY

3RD. 1ST.

LIGHT DIV.

SECOND POSITION

Nava d'Aver

JULIAN SANCHE.

R. Turones

7TH.

JULIAN SANCHEZ

Freneda

From Barba del Puerco

Almeida

Castello Bom

Coa R.

To Sequiras

themselves. Had Moore lived, or had Graham, or Lord Wellington, commanded at Coruña, I should have been now a lieutenant-colonel of two years' standing, instead of a major of five. General Hope neither gave my regiment deserved credit, nor mentioned me.

Of 480 privates and 23 officers, my regiment had 150 of the first and 10 of the last killed and wounded, total 160. This was as hard fighting as Barrosa; yet I am kept from promotion, because old David Dundas was jealous of Moore's glory. This is nothing strange. Have not the famous always been envied by the non-famous? But I must be patient for—*The commander in chief entertains the highest opinion of your meritorious services!* I have the military secretary's word for this; yet I don't believe it to be more true than that I have the highest opinion of the commander in chief's meritorious services.

Almeida still holds out. I wish Lord Wellington would give me 60 scaling ladders, and 200 volunteers with a supporting column, and the British standard should fly in Almeida in two hours without losing 50 men. The ditch is dry and not deep, the garrison is weak, and British volunteers are irresistible; they would be on the rampart in fifteen minutes. Once there the devil would not get them off again, and I should be a lieutenant-colonel, or lie in the ditch of the place.

May 14th. On the 2nd instant came a sudden order to march. We crossed the Turon River and bivouacked at Nava d'Aver, the French Army being in sight; at least their fires were distinctly seen. At daybreak, we found our army assembled, stretching from Nava to Fort Conception. Our division formed the right of the line. The two armies manoeuvred, the enemy to gain Almeida, the allies to cover it, and night brought both on to the plains about the villages of Villa Formosa and Fuentes Onoro, extending to Almeida, which lay in rear of our hue on the left. Headquarters were at Villa Formosa, about the centre of our line.

Two armies thus drawn up on a plain, each from thirty to thirty-five thousand strong, was a most beautiful sight; but the next day's sun was to shine on the graves of thousands who then beheld it set! No man knew his fate, but each anxiously awaited it in the coming combat, which all believed inevitable, and to be one of the bloodiest ever fought: one in which defeat to either side must be destruction.

Our right was on Nava d'Aver; our centre advanced to Fuentes Onoro; our left stretched to Fort Conception. There was much skirmishing at Fuentes this day, yet it ended towards night. We nearly lost some guns in the morning, but the enemy's cavalry fought shy and lost their advantage by timidity. At night, I was sent out with the picquets, and never did I see any worse posted, or more negligently; but there was no choice for me but to obey orders and keep good watch. On the 4th slight skirmishing at Fuentes Onoro. On the 5th at daybreak fighting began in the village of Fuentes, and soon after a bloody contest was sustained there.

The enemy then turned our right flank with his cavalry, and the 7th Division fell back to some high ground, nearly *en potence*, our cavalry keeping as far as they could in front: we lost many men in Pozzo Velho, so did the enemy. Then a heavy cannonade opened and continued in the centre for five hours, with smart skirmishing, so close as to knock down many in the line, which also suffered severely from grape shells and round shots: our guns however beat those of the enemy out of the field. Thus, closed the Battle of Fuentes Onoro, the 5th of May; a battle in which our loss was eighteen hundred, that of the enemy greater: both far short of what was expected, as everyone thought we should have had a severe general action.

Massena certainly drew out his army with the intention of saving Almeida and driving us into the Coa. Lord Wellington out-manoeuvred him and covered Almeida, presenting so formidable a line of battle as to oblige the Prince of Esling to give up his project. He retired, covered by his cavalry, on the 7th or 8th, after which our army was ordered into the surrounding cantonments. Our brigade marched first off the position, playing the British Grenadiers, which was a little like dunghill cock-crowing, but the men like it.

His correspondence from the field of battle will now display that elation which victory, notwithstanding the loss of friends, always produces in those who escape. A sense of safety united with an additional claim to our country's applause is irresistible.

May 7th, moonlight. Dearest mother, William and I are quite well, and the French, it is thought, will not try another general action again. We lost a good many men on the 5th. I was lucky, for we were many hours in a severe fire, and my bridle was hit by a grape shot. We are in mad spirits, and long to fight again, but Massena is not inclined. The 50th lost only a few more than thirty men by the cannonade; but we were obliged to be quiet all the time, and had no French lives in return. Remember now dearest mother, that fight more, or no more fight, a hundred thousand men are in the pickling tub with William and myself: it was our turn to escape, and we did so. This was proper, and though the fire of grape and shells was very heavy, I made it a point of honour not to be hit.

May 8th. The French are satisfied with the fillip we gave them on the 5th, and are retiring. We shall move close to Almeida, where poor Brennier has been firing and blustering in vain, he can't get out! he can't get out!

This was a Gilpin boast. Brennier broke out on the night of the 10th.

Albergaria, May 20th. You will hear of Almeida being blown up, and that your friend Brennier gave us the slip. Who is to blame we don't know, nor the particulars. Yesterday I went there. Never was there a more complete blow up; the achievement has been brilliant and marks Brennier for ever. Our generals, or whoever is in fault, ought to be shot; the whole army is disgraced. Lord Wellington must feel it deeply. To have all his operations for securing the town against a large army succeed, to see that army defeated and retire, and then to have the generals under him let the garrison out! It is enough to break his heart. England will begin to see that our generals are ———. Take Lord Wellington away and we are general-less.

It is said Sir Wm. Erskine is to blame, and next to him General Campbell. On my ride to see Almeida after the blow up, I passed the field where the two armies had fought, and saw such a multitude of eagles, vultures and kites, eating the carcases of man and beast, that I congratulated myself on not making a side dish at their feast: they would have gained little additional good by it, and to me it would have been a great inconvenience. So gorged they were, they could hardly fly, and I hunted some on Blanco, but he did not half like their looks, thinking they might

156

take to live flesh for a change.

Lord Wellington is again gone to the Alemtejo, to prevent disasters arising in the south from Marshal Beresford's blunders. In short, when Lord Wellington is in the south, we in the north grow frightened lest the French should advance; and when he is here, things go wrong in the south: he has to fly back and forward, like Lord Moira flying from Edinburgh to London, and does the journey in five days: hard work this for body and mind. So, Sir David is at last turned out! The Duke of York's advent will however do Napiers no good, and indeed Old Davy going to pot is luck enough for ten years.

Notwithstanding Lord Wellington's rapidity he was too late in the south; the first siege of Badajos had been raised, the Battle of Albuera fought, and so hardly won the master's hand was required to stamp it as success: hence, renewing the siege, he called troops from the north. With the first column went Charles Napier, and he was immediately charged with a confidential mission, his report of which was adopted by Lord Wellington as ground of action.

Talavera Real, June 10th. I am dear mother on a particular service; my post will likely be about Medellin. If you don't hear from me be not uneasy; for taking no baggage, means of writing may not be found. This mission displeases me. My duty will be to get information of the enemy, but I will not go near him to risk being taken, not being a spy. No danger, but great responsibility, which I don't like: be sure however of my keeping within safe bounds, not having the least desire to be taken in a ridiculous way, and my orders are not to risk anything.

I have only a new coat and a great-coat; the first was designed for smart days; but lest the Spaniards should think me a spy, I wear my blazing uniform, and so wear it out; Blanco and I are like meteors: we cannot go near the French, and so I send Spans. This however will only last the siege, and is because an active, intelligent officer was required. What a bore to be so clever!

Soon the siege was raised by Marmont and Soult, Wellington concentrated his force on the Caya, and with the sagacious daring which marked his whole career, so imposed on the French marshals that they retired at a moment when their superior numbers might have gone near to finish the war.

George Napier had now obtained a regimental majority by regular course of seniority, and the Duke of York, though not more friendly towards the sons than he had been towards the father, could not with decency longer withhold promotion from Charles, who had again pressed his claim strongly on him, and on the Prince Regent. It had also been separately urged by Lady Sarah through her friends, and was finally conceded. Yet a want of good-will was still evinced; for the promotion was to the 102nd Regiment, a colonial corps just returned from Botany Bay with the stigma of mutiny. Dreary, obscure, soul-sickening service was thus substituted for the glorious warfare in which he had been so distinguished, so wounded.

Still it was promotion. And as courts are proverbially far more vengeful than grateful, it was not surprizing that a man whose very existence had been an offence to royal pride, a man, of whose near kindred, one had severely checked royal indiscipline in the navy, a second had endangered royal life in a duel, a third had died an unsuccessful insurgent, and a fourth had been the most impassioned orator of his age in opposition to royal encroachment—it was not surprizing, or unnatural, that such a man should meet with disfavour, enmity it could scarcely be called. Moreover, to be noticed by Wellington, was then no recommendation to the new commander in chief; for whatever may be said, or supposed to the contrary, the writer of this work has sure knowledge, that no friendly feeling existed between the royal general who so signally failed in the early part of the war, and the great captain whose transcendant genius terminated it with a glory dazzling to contemplate.

Court favour, or court honours, it was never Charles Napier's fate to enjoy, nor his ambition to attain. Royalty was to him sacred, as the keystone of an arch spanning the turbulent waters of the social and political stream, but courts he regarded as mere pageants, unable to confer real glory: his aspirations were for that greatness which the applause of a nation sends down to posterity.

Strong however as his heroic impulses were, his letters, already quoted, and to be quoted, prove that the longings of his heart were always for beneficial labours; that he was averse to war, entirely opposed to cruelty, indignant at injustice, and careless of conventional honours. His sensibilities were indeed essentially domestic: like Sertorius he would have abandoned the greatest enterprises for his mother's sake. No wounds, no sufferings; no inconvenience of time or place; no privations or inclemency of weather, ever interrupted his efforts to relieve her anxieties, and assure her that she was always first in his thoughts.

CHAPTER 9

American War

Through new scenes and climates Charles Napier's career is now to be traced, but some circumstances attending his promotion must first be noticed. His Lisbon application to Sir David Dundas had been rejected; it was renewed more strongly from Albergaria, and as he then said he would, so he did appeal to the Prince Regent, when he found that Majors Gough, Acheson and Duncan, had been promoted for Barrosa.

April 1811. Sir. To address Your Royal Highness with respect, clearness and brevity, is difficult: the first I feel profoundly, the next I will attempt.

As every soldier holds his commission at the will of his sovereign, to speak of right would argue ignorance; but circumstances often give military men strong claims on the notice of their king, and to Your Royal Highness's gracious consideration I submit mine.

I commanded the 50th Regiment through the whole campaign under Sir John Moore, and in the Battle of Coruña, the brunt of which fell on that regiment. Every other major, or captain, who commanded either a regiment, detachment, or fort in action, has been promoted; and many of the majors were junior to me by several years: Majors Acheson and Duncan promoted in the last gazette were so.

To stand thus singly unfortunate, would seem to imply blame, but the enclosed letters from Lord William Bentinck and General Clinton will free me from that suspicion. I acknowledge myself strongly ambitious of military rank. Shall I be deemed unreasonable or impertinent, if I ask Your Royal Highness's favour to secure for me what has been bestowed upon others, *viz.* the brevet rank of lieutenant-colonel, bearing date from the Battle of Coruña, in which I commanded a regiment; or the lieutenant-colonelcy of a regiment. The want of interest has been my misfortune, and without Your Royal Highness be generously pleased to assist me, that is likely to continue.

This letter produced a gracious message from the prince to Lady Sarah, and at that time, to the great joy of the military world, the army was relieved from the offensive oppression of Sir David Dundas: the old man of the land was thrown off the neck of the soldier. Charles Napier then urged his claims on the Duke of York, stating his services and wounds and the recent promotions over his head. This was on the 27th of June, and on the 13th July, having heard of the regent's message to Lady Sarah, he thus again addressed that prince.

Sir. Labouring under a severe ague, and hardly able to hold my pen, I find scarce power to thank Your Royal Highness for your kind promise of promotion, expressed to my mother through Colonel McMahon.
The difficulties, by him mentioned, with regard to my standing, are to me inexplicable. That there are none real I can easily explain to Your Royal Highness.
In the latest gazette I believe there has hardly been a major promoted who was not junior to me in standing; many younger as men, I believe; nearly all younger as soldiers. Several have been subalterns since I held the rank of major: and I may say, none of them have been so unfortunate as to second their claims by six wounds received in the service, which is the case sir, with Your Royal Highness's faithful servant C. J. N.

His promotion followed, and with this introduction the following extracts from his letters and journal will be better understood. Meanwhile, having caught the Guadiana fever and ague, he went to Lisbon, suffering much, and having no comfort but that of—"not having medical attendance."

July 19th. Dearest mother read the following.

Sir, I am directed by the commander in chief to acquaint you, that previous to the receipt of yours of the 27th *ultimo.* His Royal Highness, hearing in mind your claims, had recommended you for a lieutenant-colonelcy in the

102nd Regiment, and the state of discipline in that corps requires that you should join it without loss of time.

H. Torrens.

Now which of the royal brothers has made me lieutenant-colonel? Or did they both jump together like gudgeons at a worm? That cannot be. Ergo one has done the deed, and the other takes credit: the higher power probably, for he took the credit of George's promotion as regimental major, though it was in the regular course, as they could not put any captain over his head with common decency. Now dear mother, I am not the least grateful to anyone but yourself for my promotion; to you I owe it entirely: gratitude to others there is no reason for.

Having been ill-used, the prince, or the Duke of York, has given me with loss of time, what without loss would have been only justice; for that much obliged, and thanks to both, but no gratitude to either: no more than to a jury for acquitting me of a crime never committed. I'll doff my beaver but no gratitude: it is giving royalty too great a hold of one's nose, and if royalty pulls, you can't resent. And these folks always have two holds:— gratitude as men, and loyalty as prince, or king. Hence, being less inclined to bear annoyances, exactly as the annoyer ranks among the mighty; and having returned zealous service for my pay, and a certain quantity of blood for promotion, besides two uniforms spoiled by the effusion, the balance seems clear between George Prince, and Charles Napier.

The impudence of whoever hinted to you that my promotion was a job is unbounded, and for the prince's sake, as well as my own, any man who says, or hints this, shall have a fair downright English box on the ear. He may fight me or let it alone, though the latter would be preferable, at least I think so; but a man is bloody-minded when feverish. Mark! The 102nd was at Botany Bay, where there was a party business, and they came home. The colonel died. The king would not give the step in the regiment. The next major was cashiered.

And now the Duke of York says the state of discipline requires the immediate presence of the new lieutenant-colonel. The job is therefore to teach scald scurvy knaves how to behave. Stop! These jokes won't do, they are probably very good fellows and may be touchy. If not good fellows they will have hot berths. I have a knack of annoying tricksters, and going to a young corps after an old one, is to drive two horses instead of eight. My reins are tight in hand, no fear of being run away with; and you know a good coachman uses reins, not the whip, unless with an old restive horse, which will indeed sometimes give coachee a confounded kick in return.

To get a regiment that is in bad order is agreeable; my fear was a good one, where no character could be gained and some might be lost. Caution is however necessary with these heroes; for, not making the regiment I unmake myself. My conviction has ever been, that more can be done with good-humoured than with angry men: if they will be angry, power will be an overmatch for them; but with sulky people, regiments cannot be made as much of as with good-humoured fellows.

Some people go to a regiment and commence drilling it at once, like Moore's brigade, forgetting that Moore put sugar into the lemon juice, and the mixture was good; he who puts lemon only causes wry faces: my way is clear enough, but my desire is not to see their faces for a year, staying quietly at home to recover my health. A little employment however, with eagerness and anxiety, does good to body and mind; and it is my nature to have both about everything, to a certain degree.

Lisbon, August 13th. Dearest mother, your ignorance of military matters leads you astray, and exposes you to the humbug of those who tell you the prince has done a job for me: they say so, from some disappointment to themselves. The duke will have no 'trouble to satisfy the army.' The army is here, not in England, and is very generally of opinion that I was one of the worst-used majors in it. The only observation made was, a damned shame he did not get it before! I agree that we are obliged to the prince, if he gave the step; and we must appear to think so to him and to others: but to you only am I grateful, for you only have worked.

Next comes Sir John Moore, for having given me the command of the 50th in Spain; then myself for fighting hard: lastly the Frenchmen who shot me, for that clenched the nail. Lord Wellington says, he won't let me have a Caçadore Regiment 'for the Napiers always get hit, and he will be killed: they have had enough of wounds'. Marshal Beresford told me this.

You have given me a long letter, settling all my doings till your arrival from Ireland. Now, if you ever knew of my following anybody's advice, or plans, you are acquitted of a silly waste of words. When in England the spirit must move; but I must move myself to Carlton House, for the spirit would never move me to the presence of king or prince. Had I lived in courts this would be like going to a camp; but to be condemned now to live in a court would send me from the world in a year.

I am better, a little, and have not had delirium the last two fits, otherwise no change; nor is any expected until home and quiet restore me: but if the voyage don't send away the fits I must shift about for new air. The doctor says three months will recover me after the fits go; I say he is wrong, and Bellarmin being thus confuted, I shall act on my own opinion. Lord March is well, yet requires two months of home for complete restoration, though he has had but three fits: I have had six weeks, that is, twenty-one fits.

On the 25th of August, he embarked in the *Fiorenza* frigate, and after a very tedious voyage, taking Blanco with him, landed in England, but continued ailing for a very long time; so roughly shaken was his constitution by his long sufferings and the hardships he had braved. At this time Lord Liverpool conferred on him the small sinecure government of the Virgin Isles, in consideration of his wounds and services, and he held it for a year or two; but when pensions for wounds were granted, resigned, saying, he could not take two rewards for the same service. Lord Bathurst, married to his cousin, Lady Georgina Lennox, was then minister, and strongly opposed this, but finding him immovable offered the government to George Napier, who had meanwhile lost his right arm leading the storming party at Ciudad Rodrigo: he however declined it on the same ground.

With the presentation of this government, Charles Napier received intelligence of George's misfortune; if a misfortune it can be called, to purchase with the loss of a limb, in a just war, the subjoined commendations, testifying that he emulated his brother in bravery as well as disinterestedness. Ciudad Rodrigo had been stormed in the night of the 19th of January 1812, and on the morning of the 20th, the following letters were written to Lady Sarah Napier, to Charles Napier, and to Lady Louisa Conolly.

Gallegos, January 21st. My dear Madam. I am sorry to tell you that your son George was again wounded in the right arm so badly last night, in the storm of Ciudad Rodrigo, as to make it necessary to amputate it above the elbow. He however bore the operation remarkably well, and I have seen him this morning quite well, free from pain and fever, and enjoying highly his success before he had received his wound: when he did receive it, he only desired that I might be told he had led his men to the top of the breach before he had fallen.

Having such sons, I am aware that you expect to hear of these misfortunes, which I have had more than once to communicate to you; and notwithstanding your affection for them, you have so just a notion of the value of the distinction which they are daily acquiring for themselves by their gallantry and good conduct, that their misfortunes do not make so great an impression upon you. Under these circumstances I perform the task I have taken on myself with less reluctance; hoping at the same time that this will be the last occasion on which I shall have to address you on such a subject, and that your brave sons will be spared to you.

Although the last was the most serious, it was not the only wound which George received during the siege of Ciudad Rodrigo, he was hit by the splinter of a shell in the shoulder on the 16th.

Ever my dear Madam yours most faithfully

Wellington.

My dear Lady Sarah. I am very sorry to tell you that George has had his arm amputated, in consequence of a musquet shot he received at the top of the breach of Ciudad Rodrigo; it has been done just above the elbow of the right arm. He suffers very little pain and is in high spirits. He volunteered leading three hundred as fine fellows as ever marched from the light division, and with them stormed the small breach. Everybody in the army admires his gallantry, and I trust they can't refuse to make him a lieutenant-colonel: his friend Lieut. Gurwood led the forlorn hope and they were the two first up the breach. I will let you know how he is by next mail, but I am convinced it will be a favourable account. He wanted to write to you but I told him I would. He is coming to my quarters, and I will take every care of him.

Believe me dear Lady Sarah ever yours affectionately

March.

(Now Duke of Richmond.)

P.S. Pray write to Charles, that I hope George will soon be a lieutenant-colonel, as he deserves it better than anyone in the army.

El Bodon, 21st January. My dear Napier, although the news I have to tell will shock you at first, yet, after all, it is more a subject for congratulation than condolence. You may rely upon my not deceiving you in any point, and therefore believe that poor George is as well as any man ever was who has sustained the loss of an arm. He has had an opportunity of distinguishing himself in a manner he has long sought for, by leading three hundred fine fellows up the breach at Ciudad Rodrigo; which he did in a style second to none that ever went up a breach. Before reaching the breach itself, they had to scale the walls of the *fausse bray*, and he planted the first ladder himself.

Nothing could resist such fellows and in a few minutes the place was our own. His wound was by a grape shot—in the elbow joint of the right arm; by which the bone was so much shattered as to render the loss of the arm inevitable, and for which he decided instantly. The operation was performed by Dr. Guthrie, and yesterday morning I saw him as well, and as unconcerned about it as if he had an arm to spare. I am going again to Ciudad Rodrigo, and until he chooses to write to you with his left arm I will always let you know how he is. I need not tell you he was a volunteer: a lieutenant-colonelcy will not half recompense his deserts.

Amongst others lost on this occasion is poor Dobbs; and Colonel Colborne, (now Lord Seaton) a great friend of George, is badly wounded. General Craufurd not expected to live. I now again repeat, that nothing is likely to happen to George; he appears so well you could not tell anything had happened to him. Of course, for many reasons he will go home as soon as the surgeons think it advisable to move. Believe me with the greatest veneration for everybody that bears your name most sincerely yours

Charles Rowan.

Gallegos, January 21st 1812. My dear Lady Louisa. Little did I imagine when I last addressed you, I should so soon have to communicate afflicting intelligence; but the gallant spirit of those Napiers leads them ever in the foremost ranks to danger; and honour is sure to be their just reward. George Napier, commanding three hundred as brave fellows as himself, stormed one of the breaches in the walls of Ciudad Rodrigo, and, sad to relate, received a wound in the right arm, which has been since amputated, and he is doing as well as possible.

His conduct equalled that of his brother Charles, to surpass it would be hard; but the gallantry of the Napiers is as proverbial in the army as the fame of our chief. God of his mercy be praised, we have not George to deplore as once we had, as we all supposed, his brother. Alas our victory has been attended with some cruel losses: that of General McKinnon is irreparable; and I have scarce a hope of my poor friend Craufurd. I write to you my dear Lady Louisa rather than to any other of the family, to break this intelligence to dear Lady Sarah. God Almighty bless you, believe me ever yours most affectionately

Charles Stewart.
(Late Lord Londonderry.)

Charles Napier had from his shrewd Colonel, Stewart of the 50th Regiment, caught many useful lessons; being in this remarkable, that where he found talent he became a pupil: yet only to strengthen, not control his own genius, for in action, relying solely on himself, his previous humility appeared as the stoop of a hawk to seize prey and then soar aloft again. It was therefore with good knowledge of regimental business he assumed command of the 102nd. Raised as "*The New South Wales Fencibles*" this regiment had gone out there by the Cape of Good Hope and returned by Cape Horn, and was probably the only corps that ever circumnavigated the globe. In January 1812, he joined it at Guernsey, and at first hoped to lead it to the Peninsula, but in June it was ordered to Bermuda, and his own letters must continue his story.

Guernsey, May. At a sham fight, our general in the flush of victory got with his *aide-de-camp* into a field where Blanco was feeding, and was immediately treated with horse tricks, the military drew their swords but to no purpose, Blanco jammed them up in a corner, and setting his ears back kept them prisoners while the fight went on: at last, they were found in durance, but could not be released, for the barb would only surrender them to my servant. Was there ever such a matchless horse! Not a word of your letter dear old lady will I answer, except rejoicing that you have sold Celbridge. You owe me nothing, pay others. *Je suis bien riche*, and am going to buy a cow for myself which will give suck on the voyage to some soldiers' wives and children—hang the imps! poor things!

It is said that not a day passes at Bermuda without opportunities of sending letters, and the ordinary run is but three weeks; two delightful things, for to be far from you is hateful, and with all my ill temper at the cross ways of London, never do I go to bed so happy as under your roof, if you are there. Take care of my other dear mother, Susan Frost, and make her go into the country. Thank Admiral Foley for his letter to Captain Bell, who is an excellent fellow; indeed, all seamen have been so to me. Some army bucks complain of them, because, forgetting they are in a man's house when in his ship, they give themselves airs, and are taken down.

Plymouth, 28th July. Forced in here by stress of weather, and my sea-sickness horrible: with enough to make the pot boil in England, no other country should see my pretty face. Unable to eat, my spirits are low, and six weeks, perhaps two months, of this before me: Oh murder! We have six ladies on board and two on the point of being confined. Wretched women! Why do I complain? Jonathan has declared war. We reckon ourselves equal to two frigates; three we should fight hard, and even four would have a tug: we have seven hundred men on board, and my left hand should go to board the *President* and smite Commodore Rogers with my right. I swear now, Jonathan lacks a licking, and an English line of battle ship is the thing to provide the needful. It would however please me more to delve for *pratees* at home, for an American war is a miserable thing.

Journal. While at Plymouth I procured bedding for the men, which idle official rascals had thought quite unnecessary. Whether the Admiralty or Transport Office are in fault is unknown, but the attempt to send five hundred soldiers on a voyage which may last two months, with only the deck to lie on, is shameful.

August 10th. This day 30 years old. In 1808 my birthday was spent in Lisbon: 1810 in the valley of the Douro; 1811 again in Lisbon; and now, 1812, in the midst of the Atlantic. Where next? perhaps at the bottom. Well, when not with those I love no matter where.

September 12th, Bermudas. This island beautiful to look at, but food, and all things but rogues, so scarce as to make a miserable quarter.

This long voyage in his debilitated state, hurt him severely, and for many months health did not return. Narrowly also was shipwreck escaped within a mile of the anchorage, for the ship made to land under a press of sail, her captain, unwitting of the sharp rocks below, was driving onward to destruction in sight of the garrison which, attracted by the sight of a war ship, looked from the shore trembling for the result, until a black pilot with shouts and gesticulations indicated the danger. They landed then in safety, but in that small disagreeable cluster of isles life was monotonous, and to him very depressing after the stirring scenes of the Peninsula.

His resolute pursuit of duty was however in no manner abated, and his mode of command so earnest, so peculiar and diligent, that it was felt by others as a reproof to their negligence, and gave offence. The governor. General Horsford, whose colonial irregularity was disturbed by an original mind, became his enemy, because the regulations of the service were enforced. No zeal! no zeal! was Talleyrand's advice to a young friend on entering a public office; and nothing is indeed more offensive to satisfied dullness than successful vivacity: Charles Napier was destined to feel the force of this truth all his life.

To be cut off from the great events convulsing Europe, and restricted to an island scarcely larger than a prison, and not more fertile of incident, was very chafing to such a fiery spirit, and his correspondence exhibits a mind preying on itself, perceptive of failings, and panting for action as a cure. Always uppermost however is the love of his mother, avowed with every variety of phrase that filial affection could suggest; but of this heaped tenderness only what is required for the story of his life at Bermuda shall be set down.

The nature of that life was thus epitomized on quitting it. From the 12th September 1812, to 23rd May 1813, there has been a series of yellow fever, starvation, and minor evils under the reign of King Horsford—a man extremely dull, and feeble of mind, and nearly as feeble of body. He seldom speaks, never to the purpose, and is indecisive on all occasions; no man ever gets yes or no from him. Yet he is very pompous, and as Colonel Lloyd, with Irish humour says of him. Poor man, he tries to look sensible, and no man can do more: he never succeeds indeed, but how can he help it?

His mother, October. We are waiting for accounts of the great Battle of Salamanca, of which we only know that the French have lost 25,000 men, with all their artillery and baggage; and that Marmont is killed. My anxiety is to know of a humbler man's fate: has my dear brother William escaped? This pleasant doubt has been mine since we encountered the Lisbon pacquet in August. These glorious deeds in Spain make me turn with disgust to the dulness of drill, and it is hard to rouse myself to duty: yet *duty must be done.* The example of colonial idleness here is very hard to stem, and many bad names are bestowed on my drilling, and my strictly conforming to the Duke of York's orders.

Entre nous, my great sin is giving all the bread to the men which the allowance of government flour will furnish, that is about 10 lbs. The 98th commanding officer gives only 8 lbs., the remainder being sold; and bread here will fetch always a shilling, sometimes two shillings a pound. What becomes of this large sum is to me unknown, but it would be easy to pocket £800 or £1,000 without detection. It is rumoured that my plan has given offence; for though I have said nothing, the 98th men complain: liking bread better than a *regimental fund.* Moreover, instead of buying bad fuel by contract, my quartermaster buys good clean wood, and thus baker Napier is famous in Bermuda. If you hear of my being a martinet, tyrant, &c., be assured it is this baking business.

My greatest dread is that the idleness of others will corrupt my *gents*; they are however now good, and proud of their military knowledge, which keeps up the military spirit. But to what end is all this work? To be starved in Bermuda, and become pioneers when tools come from England: it is hateful to think of. Every officer of mine, except three young ones, can now exercise a battalion: in one year of working parties they will be only thinking of making money and gardens, and the men will be ditchdiggers! How can we pester men with drill for that end? I only do it to keep them from drink and myself from rust. England would be my choice now but for those battles, which set me *cock a hoop* despite of reason which says fighting is bad for you, Charles Napier, and you don't like it: certainly, it appears pleasanter when only heard of.

November 29th. Bermuda is not unpleasant, if to be out of England is my fate; not from anything desirable in the place, but from my habits of occupation, which would keep me in spirits at any place. In Bermuda, or a jail, my books and drawings could be enjoyed as much as in a palace; that is if my seat was as soft, and my light as good. The having no other objection to Bermuda than the want of posts is however singular, as every other mortal hates it for itself. A wet climate, nothing to eat, no fruit, no vegetables, no wine, no good company; for the people, after cheating you in their shops all day, have the impudence to think they are to be your companions in the evening!

A good honest shopkeeper is to be liked and respected; but a knave, who weighs out his pound of bad butter at the modest price of three shillings, is quite affronted if you call his place a shop. No! you must screw up your mouth, make a bow, and 'Pray allow me to ask if I may be so bold as to take the liberty of inquiring if your stores contain eggs, or tallow candles?' He then makes you another bow and a long speech, and charges 500 *per cent,* profit.

A lady whose husband settled here after the American war, has lived sixty years in the Island of St. George, which is only three miles long, and not quite a quarter of a mile broad, with only a ferry dividing it from the large island. She has never seen the large island or been out of this little island since her birth, she told me; and added, or indeed out of the town except once, when I went to Saint David's—a smaller island! She is hale, strong, sane, and not singular.

Journal. This island is about thirty-five miles long, and from fifty yards to three miles broad. Taking the cluster as a whole, the main island is called the continent, and on the small island of St. George is the capital, St. George's town. This small island, with St. David's and some others, form a good harbour for merchantmen, but the approaches are through rocks, very narrow and difficult. There is good anchorage, and docks are being built at an island called Ireland. There is a large lake, seventeen fathoms deep in every part, and cutting away a little earth would render it one of the most perfect harbours in the world: it is called Harrington's Sound.

The population is about eleven thousand—five thousand whites; five thousand five hundred blacks, and five hundred strangers, who may be called the floating population. St. George is a free port. The soil is favourable for cultivation, but the indolence of the people is great, and as everyone lives by petty traffic no attention is paid to agriculture. In gardening, there is much trouble from the voracious green grub, and the keen sea air hurts vegetation: the chief product is cedar. The Gruper fish is delicious and plentiful, so are many other fishes. The whale season begins in April, and ends in June. About fourteen whales are caught each season, a good one being worth £300. The whale steak is like veal, some like it better, few find any difference, if not told what they are eating.

The slaves are not generally ill-treated. There are above fifty who have purchased their freedom within twenty years, and the freedmen gain ground. The blacks are ingenious, passionately fond of music, drunken, and idle: in short what slaves must be. Bermudian whites are very ill-looking, the men: the women are pretty. The climate is humid, and so changeable as to be destructive to consumptive people it is said, but I have doubts on that subject. The opinion is held chiefly by military medical men, and all consumptive soldiers do die; yet my belief is that constant drunkenness is more in fault than climate, the humidity of which in great measure is from the sea spray.

There are many law courts, and colonial regulations here, enacted by Parliament, which it is useless to learn, being all tricks to foster fraud, and without right to he called laws. The people are so confined in their ideas, and their curiosity so limited, from the nature of this small spot in the world of waters, that many old persons have never quitted the island they were born on: yet some of the islands are only one mile round!

The frigate in which his youngest brother Henry was a lieutenant arrived towards the end of the year, and he heard of his brother George's marriage.

December. Blessed mother, George's marriage delights me. You may now in time, have a dear animal of some kind with you, instead of being left in your old age by a pack of vagabond itinerant sons, getting wounded abroad, while you are grieving at home. The interest you have had about us has never been of much pleasure, and the little links of a chain to tie you to life may come, your lost great ones can only thus be supplied.

As to my being governor of Bermuda, my rank would not allow of it; and if to live out of England is my fate it would be better to send Lord Moira his written promise,—given unasked, to employ me in an advantageous situation when in his power. The time already spent here would in India have put £2,000 in my pocket; with this fatal objection however, that I would not sell the chance of getting near you for ten times that sum.

Yet if my fate is to be in a colony, an East Indian one is better than a West Indian one: there are indeed for India the drawbacks of distance and liver complaint; yet they are both in perfection at Bermuda, with the pleasure of living amongst dealers in rum, and nothing to pass time but books, which, though sufficient in part, do not make up for the want of curiosities to be seen in other countries.

We live in an island so small that the smell of cedar is overpowered by that of rum! Wherefore I am not disposed to be governor. Botany Bay would be more agreeable. A governor there can clear £2,000 a-year and live like a *nabob*. Three years of that would suit me, and then to come home for the rest of my life and drive old Blanco in a buggy: but of all governments the best would be an English house to put you into. Hang governments that is my answer.

Jan. 1st. A Happy New Year to you most precious mother, and old as you are a great many of them. Oh! may I have the delight of being within reach of you next New Year's Day. I would take another shot through the head to be as near you as I was in Lisbon last year. My broken jaw did not give me half the pain the life we lead here does; and so far from you. And to the displeasure of being abroad is added, that we see no new people, learn no strange language, no customs differing from our own: that is such customs as a huckster's shop at Portsmouth affords. We have the curses of banishment without its freedom, or its instruction, or the comfort of being 'suffering patriots.' Our officers and men sigh for Botany Bay; there every species of food was in perfection, carriages and horses in abundance, and excellent brick houses: everything man could desire, to make up for distance from England. A curious people too, whose wars and customs furnished food for observation, and savage nations furnish nearly as much of that as civilized nations do.

Two pacquets are due, and we fear they have been taken, for the Yankees swarm here: and when a frigate goes out to drive them off, by Jove they take her! Yankees fight well, and are gentlemen in their mode of warfare. Decatur refused Cardon's sword, saying, 'Sir you have used it so well I should be ashamed to take it from you'. These Yankees, though so much abused are really fine fellows. One, an acquaintance of mine, has just got the *Macedonian*; he was here, a prisoner and dined with me: he had taken one of our ships, but was himself captured by the *Poictiers*, seventy-four: being now in an English frigate, if he meets us we must take him, or we are no longer sovereign on the ocean.

Feb. 13th, 1813. The drunkenness of my regiment is beyond endurance. After doing all that was possible to stop it, I warned them that the lash would be used, for drink was killing them, and discipline was subverted. My boast had been that the young one should never see a bloody back, and the drummers here did not know how to go about it. Now it has fallen on them. Man! man! thou art certainly very vile: very vile and contemptible, let me therefore speak of my cow. She gave milk during the voyage for all the women and children on board the ship. She has a fine little calf, and there are hungry fellows about me who wish to kill it, but on no account, shall the little beastie be hurt: the mother has her own way.

This tenderness, to be justly appreciated, requires the addition of the following extract from another letter, showing what privations prompted to the death of the calf.—

Dr. Baily's treatment is exactly what suits me: but how can it be followed here, where we live on salt food: a little fresh pork indeed we do get sometimes, but not always. No part of his prescription can be adopted except regular hours and exercise.

Yellow fever now raged in the island, and he heard of the death, by consumption, of a lady, whose brother he had just nursed through the prevailing sickness, with imminent personal risk.

The shocking intelligence of Mrs. ———'s death has deprived me of the satisfaction which Henry's arrival had occasioned. Peace is not for us on earth: at least not for those who love more than themselves. Is not this enough to terrify one from marriage? Who can dare to be in love? What can make us fear death? I fear it, but my reason does not tell me why; and it is strange that a death which gives time for reflection is the one I could meet with least resolution, *viz.* an execution. But death appears more terrific to me when attacking others; there are those for whom my life could be readily given, with no regret save for their grief at losing me: so, says my mind at all times; but whether my nerves would second the impulse is another affair: yet more than once, when going off, as I believed, the thought of those left behind was present, not that of where I was going. But of all such efforts, that is greatest, which is called for in the midst of mortal disease. You cannot imagine the dread created here by the fever: terror is visible with the most determined fellows, terror even to ridicule. Not being one who expected to have the fever, my mind has not been tried like those who have; but even those who had no fear, were depressed in spirit beyond description. This was not constant, but the death of any one brought it down, and with me it was only thrown off by extreme pains to attain a conviction of its being disgraceful to let fear suppress reason.

One night we buried a poor ensign, and the ceremony, from being at night was more depressing. All present, except myself, went to a party afterwards to cheer their spirits; I put out one candle, and let the snuff of the other grow as long as my own nose, and at midnight my lowness was overcome: then quoth I, 'Lo! I am master, let me sleep.' It is easy to nerve myself in such cases, after Coruña: but I feel myself failing in self-command as to anger. It is good to be in a passion intentionally; very bad to be so unintentionally, and that has grown on me from the brutal drunkenness of my men.

February. All hope of reclaiming my men is not extinct. Severity of punishment, and disgracing all when one sins has had an effect, for Pat fears odium for getting his comrades into trouble, more than punishment. He does some *bloody mischief* in his cups, but it is horrible to flog him when you know he

175

is as sorry as possible himself There are however always some ruffians who may be flogged with satisfaction. One of the 98th was lately wounded by me with a bayonet, and beaten besides, which saved him from a flogging.

Before my eyes the ruffian, after beating his wife, gave her a kick which absolutely lifted her from the ground, and then, before he could be reached, jumped twice upon her breast with thick shoes, leaping high up to crush her! I laid open his head with a bayonet instead of stabbing him; but that, with another blow, served to make a show to the court and saved his back: however he was cut enough for any act short of the one he committed. He was so frightened at my striking him down that he conquered his passion; had he struck me I would have killed him on the spot, and even wished he had given me occasion.

Had you heard the horrible shrieks of the woman, till her breath was stamped out, and seen the rascal's violence and face, you would have thought, as I did, that her days were numbered. Mr. Burke of the 98th was the villain: he was not drunk, she had merely contradicted him. This kind of man it gives me pleasure to flog, and no regiment is without several. There were in the 50th Grenadiers two murderers. One of them murdered two wives: his name was Campbell, and he deliberately shot the last at Lisbon; how he escaped hanging is inconceivable: the first he strangled in bed.

This letter is filled with Paddy's tricks, which I hope to get out of him with as little flogging as possible. Poor fellows, with all their sins they are fine soldiers, and their blood should be kept for better use than being drawn with a cat-o'-nine-tails. I allow them to box, it is the best issue for the rum, and such a parade of black eyes was never before beheld. Oh! Pat thou art a very odd fish, very odd.

His efforts were successful. The sources of the evil were food and circumscribed quarters. Salt meat, and a monotonous existence when the world was everywhere else convulsed, were strong excitements to drink. But the state of the 98th must not be taken as a measure of its worth; regiments rise and fall according to circumstances. The 98th of Bermuda was disbanded at the peace, and its number fell to another corps, which, under the tuition of Major Hopkins, and the after-command of Sir Colin Campbell, has attained a character second to none in the army.

March.—No more symptoms of the fever, and we may live long for aught that yellow fever will do to help us. Strange, strange, that we dread the boat that tows us into the harbour of rest! But such is discontented man: he hates life he fears death! In God's name what do we wish for? What and who can satisfy us? *Adieu* my dearest best of mothers, when in better spirits I'll say more: would that we could remove anxiety like bile, but for the first there is only one cure. My friend Stewart is dead: I wonder how he likes it? I am alone, for Henry is on board, which is not amiss, as he makes me idle when business is necessary to keep me up; beside his mad spirits are too much: not that my lowness is apparent, others are not damped by me, if hanging is my fate you shall have a joke at the gallows, and probably not a decent one.

April 10th. Again, dearest mother my pen goes. I am not in better spirits but more master of them. Henry sails soon for Halifax. He is afraid of the cold, and it is rather cool there certainly, for people's eyes freeze, and they drink boiling water to avoid becoming icicles—at least so we hear and believe. If you hear of anybody coming here for consumption tell them they are mad: consumption's throne is here. The Bermudians all die of that hated, hateful, cursed disorder. Mother, dearest mother, would to God I was rid of this vagabond life of a felon. Peace! peace! when shall we have peace?

May. What a cursed life is a soldier's, no object, no end, without *appui* for head or heart, unless that unnatural one of military fame, which to a British soldier is so trifling that it is not worth gaining. A captain who wins the government of a country by his victories may sit down in peace, and have an interesting pursuit for the rest of his life, but war, eternal war is horrible.

Vain are the speculations of man: he who thus expressed his horror of war was doomed to war; and having won the government of a country by his victories, far from finding peace, was pursued to his grave, and beyond it, with all the malignity and falsehood and virulence that an infamous exercise of power could excite. But a change for his thoughts was now at hand; rumours of expeditions against the Americans were rife and his sentiments were thus poured forth as usual to his mother.

I would prefer fighting Americans with the 102nd, to fighting French with the 50th, for a while. What is truly hateful is, sojourning in Bermuda. I would rather fight neither, but stay quiet in England till in better bodily strength for a hard campaign: chance must decide, but for interest America is the game; and if made prisoner there it will not be eternal captivity as in France. This is an inexpressible advantage to me, who shudder at the idea of being taken again by the French. I have doubts as to accepting quarter, so great is my horror.

However, always on going into action my song is, that I shall be as well off as a canary bird, so it is a folly to fret. To be afloat with a thousand light infantry and two pieces of cannon, and allowed to land where it pleased me and be off again is my wish. A force of that kind might pay itself and save government the expense: not by plunder, which is horrid, and leads to every dreadful crime, but by contributions, levied by the magistrates. I would not take a man's purse myself, but would have no objection to make his own magistrate levy a tax and remit it to government.

This predatory warfare might easily be practised, but should be carried on by honest men, who would account honourably to government and never make a shilling for themselves: and who would rigidly preserve discipline, otherwise their men would plunder and commit every enormity, I would not take such a command without unrestricted power to execute on the spot any marauder. On expeditions of this kind there should be but one marauder, the king. He has a right to make the enemy defray the expenses of the war, and it would be delightful to have the Americans paying taxes for us.

I am not a hater of Yankees though, they are fine fellows, liars it is said, but so are we. You English wise ones, hold Yankee cheaper than he merits, you take him for a dollar when in truth he is a doubloon. My desire is to have command of the marines that are coming, and of the 102nd, and to land, to sack towns and commit all possible enormities on the coast: how delightful to deserve hell by command! By Jove! I am most amiably disposed to maraud and make money of the Yankees. But dearest, blessed mother, to return to you is the first wish of my heart: when this

American war is over I must go home or mad.

May. Have the English yet settled whether Buonaparte is to be boiled or roasted? Everybody says he is done for at last. A knowing wise grin, and, 'Well now, it is pretty clear he has fallen from his high estate'—'We now see he was not such a great general'—'Vaulting ambition that o'erleaps itself.' Such quotations are as common as fools, a very plentiful article. As to the Yankees: if you wish to know American politics, read Cobbett. All Americans acknowledge him to be master of the subject; and the Bermudians, who are judges also being so nearly connected, say he is correct in his estimate of American resources: his talent is great and his remarks are sound.

There is now no hope of my quitting this island before becoming black: however, my colour is already that of a well-browned tea-urn. To be an exile, deprived of the only comfort of an exile, the seeing new countries and manners is dreadful: here we look north and all is sea; south, and all is sea; on our right sea; on our left sea! it is a ship on the ocean without the feeling that the voyage must end. As to writing to you at landing-places if I go back, why no letter will go so fast. I'll fly! but when shall I go back? these colonies, like Willis' madhouse, are easily got into but hard to get out of.

May. Sir Sydney Beckwith has just come with a force, to whop the Yankees. I go second in command, and am in most excellent tranquil spirits, having much to do.

Such was his Bermuda life, but never was he without a dangerous adventure. His brother Henry frequently visited the island, and on one occasion when Charles went on board his frigate a hurricane suddenly raged; vessels were torn off the water and dashed about like feathers, some were even cast over the harbour banks far inland, and many went down. The captain was ashore, and Charles Napier always spoke with admiration of the skill and daring energy with which Henry saved the frigate, fondly anticipating reputation for him if opportunity occurred: but Henry also was destined to feel the leaden hand of factious power, and fortune was not kind. Ill-luck, ill-usage, and finally ill-health, drove him from active life, and it will be no impertinent digression here to give a sketch of his career; for though much separated during life, there was a bond of affection which never was broken between him and Charles, and nearly together they died!

Henry Napier's first service was in the *Spencer*, 74, under the late Admiral Stopford. He was then remarkable for his size and good looks, being fair even to womanish delicacy, with large blue eyes, short crisp hair, and round athletic limbs. His youthful comeliness could not be judged of in after life, when he was by long exposure to the extremes of heat and cold, and by the blights of mental and bodily suffering— incurable grief and incurable disease, withered in limb and form, presenting but a gaunt spectral resemblance of what nature had originally made him.

In 1806, he sailed from Deal to the Cape, and months afterwards, the handsome midshipman of the *Spencer* was a subject of conversation at the former place. From the Cape, his ship convoyed Whitelock's ill-fated expedition to the River Plate, and on the voyage Henry Napier saved a seaman's life by a surprising effort. Both were floating about half a mile from the ship when the sailor suddenly sunk, but Henry brought him up from a great depth, and finding him clutching wildly with insensate desperation, drew back, placed his feet against the poor struggling creature's shoulders and pushed him violently forward; then following swiftly he with a strong hand replaced him in an upright posture, and again dashed him forward as before: in this manner, never suffering him to sink, nor yet to fasten a deadly grasp, he drove him, exhausted, to the ship's side and both were saved, but it was a sore struggle.

In 1807, he was several times engaged in boats against the Danish sea batteries at the siege of Copenhagen, and used to relate an amusing anecdote of an Irish sailor under his orders. Being exposed to the fire of a powerful battery, the shot flew very thickly just above the boat's crew, and the man in question, a giant of known bravery, ducking his head kept it down. 'For shame, hold up your head' was thundered forth from the stern! 'I will sir when there is room for it' was the laughing response.

After the siege, the *Spencer* made a winter's cruise in the North Sea, off the coast of Norway, and assisted in a successful attack on the Castle of Fleckröoe; from thence it joined the blockade of Brest, but Henry Napier was soon transferred to the *Clorinde* frigate and sailed for the eastern seas, where he nearly lost his life from a liver attack. He however continued to serve there until promoted to the *Diomed* 50, in which he came home, and after passing through several other ships, sailed in 1818 for the western seas, first lieutenant of the frigate, which by fine seamanship he now saved from this hurricane at the Bermudas. During his service in the western waters he was made commander, and happened to be at Halifax when a fire broke out, which he assisted to quell with an energy publicly noticed at the time. One house was destroyed to stop the spreading conflagration, but a long narrow beam remained, connecting the burning quarter with the untouched buildings, and it was flaming, at a height of fifty or sixty feet: then from the roof of the menaced edifice Henry Napier was seen to step, axe in hand, upon the lofty blazing beam, and with a few powerful strokes at that dizzy elevation cut through the burning beam at his feet and dashed the flaming mass down, cheered by the gazing crowd below: certainly it was a very daring act.

As a commander, he was charged to protect the trade on the northern American coast, and for two successive winters cruised off Boston, watching to try his strength with some American ship, and being well prepared for an encounter, for he was an able seaman, a strict disciplinarian, and had with peculiar care trained his crew to gunnery, a branch of service at that time too much neglected. Intent to provoke a collision, he was so vigilant that the Vice-President of the United States, having ventured a little beyond harbour on a pleasure excursion with some ladies, hardly escaped capture by running his boat into shallow water.

The second winter Henry Napier's brig, the *Jasseur*, grounded during a fog in the Bay of Fundy, where the tide rises and falls suddenly, eighty feet; she seemed lost, but with incessant exertions was again floated, and by the court-martial which followed Napier was acquitted; his sword being returned by the president with a compliment. Nor was his service in the western waters without other honourable testimonies. More than once he was thanked by merchants and captains for his careful convoys, and his general urbane, though rigid command on such occasions; and also for his severely disinterested rejection of all irregular profits, which the times and customs furnished opportunities to obtain without incurring blame. For this a valuable testimonial of plate was offered to him, but sternly and even disdainfully he refused reward for having only adhered to duty.

In peace, he was denied service by Lord Melville, and a specific promise of promotion, twice made, was broken; wherefore, impatient like all his family, of injustice, he reproached that nobleman in a way to have debarred all future employment, or advancement, under the existing administration; but when Sir James Graham became first lord, he admitted the validity of the promise and the rank of post captain was given. Napier was however finally laid aside with many other excellent sea officers, who having served through the great French war, and being still able and willing to advance their country's greatness, were condemned to pine in hopeless inactivity while their former ships, become the prey of political and family interests, sailed under youths unborn, or at school, when the ousted men were heroically braving battle and tempest.

Being thus unjustly rejected from active service he for some time turned his mind to improvements of gunnery, of the lines of ships, and of the fastenings and machinery for stowing boats and lowering them in moments of danger; but being unable to get these things noticed he refrained from further pursuits of that nature, as a useless waste of time and talent.

In 1823, he married a lady whose extraordinary beauty attracted the admiration of every circle she entered, at home or abroad, and they had many children but three only survived, two sons and a daughter; these deaths induced him to reside near Florence for the sake of climate, and he remained there until his wife died suddenly of cholera. Attacked in the night she suppressed her fears and agony, lest he, who was lying ill in the next room, should be disturbed, and when her state became known succour was useless!

From that blow, he never recovered. His after life was one long suffering of mind and body, painful to behold, terrible to sustain. Yet his strong spirit did not shrink from the duties or occupations of society; his friendships were maintained firmly, his benevolence to the poor was active and flowing, and he was always prompt with energetic kindness to devote himself personally, entirely and indefatigably, without stint or stay, to the aid of suffering friends or relations—and to strangers also, when accident threw them on his care. Grief and pain were indeed the constant companions of his solitude, but always cast aside to save others from their withering contact.

While in Italy, at the suggestion of his young wife, who was ambitious of honest fame for him, he commenced a *History of Florence*, and after her death with devoted tenderness wrought at it as a sacred duty. It was finally published with a pecuniary risk which his moderate fortune could not have sustained, if his brother Charles, with that unhesitating generosity which marked his whole career, had not voluntarily came to his aid. Portions of Florentine history had been written before by celebrated men. Captain Napier's, founded on laborious and accurate researches, and drawn from rare and curious materials, obtained partly by accidental purchases, partly by industrious investigation of the archives, antiquities and public libraries of Italy, is the only complete story of the wonderful existence of that wonderful state, its rise, progress, and decay; its institutions, customs, manners; its wars, dissensions, vicissitudes, riches, greatness and crimes.

He died at the age of sixty-four, six weeks after his brother Charles was laid in the tomb, and no want of noble sentiment rendered him unworthy to be placed alongside those honoured remains; for he had struggled manfully and without shrinking, through his whole existence, against a lowering fortune; preserving a warm heart, benevolent feelings, and feelings of honour clear and sensitive in the extreme, and without abatement in thought or action, from the time he could first think until thought departed for ever.

CHAPTER 10

Craney Island

That two spiritual fountains constantly played within Charles Napier's breast is evident; the one sparkling to the light of glory, the other flowing full towards the tranquillity of private life. He could not repress his inward sense of genius and natural right to command; nor could he stifle the yearnings of gentle affection: and the last would certainly have prevailed, though his only worldly resource was his profession, if his country had not been plunged in such a terrible war.

Duty impelled him, and that duty must be done was as much his motto as the Duke of Wellington's; but it was not peculiar to either: how many times did that phrase burst from the lips of poor soldiers in the Peninsula when called to face danger, endure fatigue, and suffer privations from which nature shrunk! Duty must be done was their war cry, and the noblest ever raised in war. However, fate came on, and Napier's desire to have a brigade of marines and his own regiment was now gratified. To them were added a corps of Frenchmen, enlisted from the war prisons, but his command was not an independent one, and previous to relating the operations which followed, an impartial witness shall tell how vigorously he executed the duties of which his spirit was so weary, in Bermuda.

NOTES BY CAPTAIN ROBERTSON, ROYAL ARTILLERY.

When the 102nd landed in Bermuda, even casual observers perceived it was commanded by no common man; while those of his acquaintances who enjoyed the edification of his conversation on professional subjects, and he delighted to dwell on them, could not but entertain something like prophetic views of future greatness. There was such earnestness of character, such a high estimate of his profession, such enthusiastic stern devotion, that he could not fail to influence all who had a spark of chivalry in their nature. He made soldiers of all under him, and had the rare quality of rendering the most familiar intercourse compatible with absolute authority. His men he was wont to address individually as comrades, and this was no lip expression: it meant the fraternity that should exist among brother soldiers, be their grade what it may; but like him who was lord over Egypt, he held the true sceptre of command: mental superiority. The hills and cedar groves of Bermuda were his places of instruction, where men and officers were made to study ground and movements: and with infinite care, and a peculiar happy manner he taught. Instead of condemning mistakes, he would put questions as if seeking for information, yet so framed as to bring conviction of error where such existed, and to suggest improvement. It might be imagined that, in the Bermuda climate, exposing men for hours to extreme heat would prejudice their health; he held a different doctrine and put it to the test. The staff surgeon admitted its soundness, and the regiment had not only fewest men in hospital, but those who did duty were stronger and healthier than those of other regiments which followed the opposite plan of avoiding exercise. His was no adjutant's regiment; he was himself drill master, and master also of every detail: with exception of beating a drum, there was no part of a soldier's duty from the sentinel to the serjeant major's, which he could not teach, and do as smartly as the smartest non-commissioned officer. Nor was his knowledge restricted to his own arm: he was conversant with engineer's duties, and with those of artillery, whose practice he generally attended.

This testimony goes further than the author knew of. Napier's process of discipline was a reproduction of the Shorn Cliff system. Moore's genius thus vivified the British Army; wherever his officers gained command they kindled fires with Promethean sparks.

While thus so earnestly attentive to his own duties, Charles Napier could not but watch the demeanour of his officers, and with a light hand thus sketched some of their characters. A——— is a fine young fellow and will make a good soldier: a little of a spoiled child now, and don't like drill so well as the Opera; but you may tell mama that he is going on very well, and stands a fair chance of losing the genteel slouch he has at present. He is a very fine lad indeed, and no one is more convinced of that than himself: but I like him because he don't sulk at drill though clearly to him a bore. H—— grows tall, broad, fat, ruddy, attentive, and steady: he is one of the best subalterns in the regiment, makes a point of being seldom in the wrong, and of never admitting it if he is. I make counterpoints, of proving to him that he is in the wrong; which proofs though in black and white before his eyes he always rejects: but then he notes down for himself that he was in the wrong and does right another time which is just what I want. Of a third who wanted promotion he says K—— is one of the best officers in the regiment: he is nearly six feet high, is in love, and in debt: what greater claims can an ensign have? Of a fourth L—— is always wrong, but means to be always right, and he will be so at last.

June 1st. Beckwith has divided his force into two brigades, the largest under me; the other under Lieutenant-Colonel Williams of the Marines. My fear is that my gents maybe too eager; all young soldiers are dangerous in that way; but ours will be less so than the Americans, for they are young also and without even theory. My regiment will probably do right, but I must be much with the marines if we engage, and shall have all the anxiety of a lady *sending* her daughter to court the first time. Very anxious also I am to ascertain my own force in command of an awkward brigade; for the marines, being ever onboard ship, are necessarily undrilled, and the foreigners under me are *duberous.* Fight these last shall, all men will fight when they begin, but delay enables rogues to evaporate. My self-confidence makes me wish for the chief command; yet am I fearful of estimating my powers too high, and much I dislike sacking and burning of towns, it is bad employment for British troops. This authorised, perhaps needful plundering, though to think so is difficult, is very disgusting, and I will with my own hand kill any perpetrator of brutality under my command. Nevertheless, a pair of breeches must be plundered, for mine are worn out, and better it will be to take a pair than shock the Yankee dames by presenting myself as a *sans culotte.*

Of this expedition, the following account is slightly epitomized from a *Memoir* by Captain Albertson, who was on Sir Sydney Beckwith's staff.

Memoir.—It was current that Beckwith had advised an attack on New London, where an American frigate and the captured

Guerrière and *Macedonian* were blockaded by our squadron: honour and policy demanded this, and the execution was said to be easy. On the other hand, New Orleans was mentioned, and at that time an effectual blow could have been struck there. Soon however the Chesapeake Bay was adopted for action, and after five days of sailing, our anchors were cast in Lynehaven Bay, with a view to attack Norfolk and reach the adjacent dockyard of Portsmouth, but after some days of inactivity the fleet beat up to Hampton Roads in a terrific thunder-storm. Here was Elizabeth River, which, one mile from its mouth, was barred by Craney Island, while a shoal confined the navigable channel to the right bank, with only a depth of water for small frigates. Fourteen gun-boats were stretched across, and behind them were two forts, one on each bank.

Opposite the town of Norfolk the *Constellation* frigate, 28 guns, was anchored with springs on her cables, her broadside bearing down the channel. In these roads, the fleet remained three days inactive; but on the 22nd of June the troops and naval brigade were landed by boats on the left bank of the river under a distant cannonade from a 24-pounder to attack Craney Island. Fifty armed boats, after landing the troops, pushed on under the command of Captain Hanshard, and they shoaled their water rapidly; but one gig was ahead of all, and on its bow stood Captain Romilly of the Engineers, sounding with a boat-hook amidst showers of grape until his boat grounded three hundred yards from the island. Hanshard, following in a launch and holding an umbrella over his head as a mode of shewing contempt, was shot in the thigh, just as Romilly's boat grounded, and then suddenly all the boats pulled back: this it was said, happened because the grounding of the gig indicated difficulties ahead, and the passing of the wounded commander to the rear was mistaken for a signal. It was a fortunate error, if an error; good judgment if no error; for the enterprise was badly arranged and must have failed. One boat with thirty of the foreigners stranded with a shot through her, and the Americans, wading to it, deliberately massacred the poor men!

During this time Beckwith's force, which had lost by desertion an advanced party of twenty-five foreigners, moved through the woods to the shore opposite the island; but the water was too deep to ford, and the distance beyond musquetry. A man in coloured clothes, calling himself a deserter, offered to guide the troops to a wooden bridge, and they followed him a little way, but Beckwith, doubtful of his faith, soon returned; sending however a party under his *aide-de-camp* Captain Robertson to throw rockets into Craney Island and draw attention from the boats. Lieutenant-Colonel Napier went with this party, but nothing could be effected, and Beckwith soon recalled the party, which was under a sharp fire of grape and round shot. The officer employed, stopping far short of danger, vociferated 'You are to retire, you are to retreat.' Napier shouted in scornful reply, 'Come up and tell us so.'

After three or four days. Captains Romilly and Robertson were sent in a launch to take open cognisance of the Hampton defences; they grounded on a shoal, but brought a man off from shore, and in a smaller boat entered the harbour, thus provoking a fire which discovered the American position and preparations. At dawn, next morning the troops were again landed, and proceeded through the woods to get in rear of the Americans, Napier leading the advance, and the armed launches of the fleet entering the harbour to divert attention. Napier's column was met by the Yankees, who however fled after the first discharge, and were pursued by the flank companies and the Frenchmen. The last to revenge the massacre of their comrades in the stranded boat gave no quarter; they even deliberately shot an officer after taking off his epaulettes. Bullets from a hidden field piece now continued to drop into the main column, but Captain Robertson being detached with five rocket men, after an exchange of fire, seized the gun by a rush.

Two pieces and sixteen wounded men were captured and Hampton fell, but was, after three days' possession, evacuated in the night. Cruel outrages had been committed, and whilst the town was still occupied the American general Taylor sent a flag of truce from Norfolk, with a letter strongly reproaching Colonel Beckwith for the conduct of the foreigners. Beckwith expressed his deep regret, and notified Sir John Warren's predetermination to send away the foreign troops, as men too lawless to be trusted; but he told General Taylor they had been excited by the murder of their comrades in the stranded boat. To refute this. General Taylor sent the minutes of a court of enquiry, wherein every witness had sworn that nothing of the kind hap-

pened, but Beckwith sternly replied—'*I saw it with my own eyes!*'
Sir George Cockburn was now detached with a squadron, having Colonel Napier with troops on board, to the coast of North Carolina, to seize some American vessels with specie: contrary winds however prevailed off Cape Hatteras, and though the ships were taken the specie was not found.

Kent Island, separated from the mainland shore by a narrow strait, next became an object. Napier landing there, with his own regiment and the marine artillery, pushed across the island and seized the ferry. Beckwith followed with the main body, and the whole were hutted in the woods. This was an aimless enterprise, but a project was devised for the surprise of some militia encamped at Queen's Town, seven miles off: for this one battalion of marines with artillery was embarked in the night, to land high up in the bay and take their camp in reverse. The remainder of the troops, with two guns, were to pass the ferry at midnight and march straight against the town, guided by Captain Robertson, who had got acquainted with the road by going in with a flag of truce.

This combination failed entirely: the boats with the detachment missed the landing point and returned, and the officer with the advanced guard disobeyed Napier's orders, which were calculated to capture the American outpost without a shot being fired. He had come suddenly upon an American vidette, and irresolutely suffered him to fire and gallop off.

The vidette was followed by the picquet, which would otherwise have been surprised, and the English officer, in a disgracefully incapable state, ordered his men to fire, throwing himself on the ground: then the whole advanced guard commenced firing, which brought up Beckwith and Napier at a gallop, to ascertain the cause. This done, they ordered Captain Robertson to take command and stop the firing, while they went to restore order in the rear: but the mischief had already spread there; for the men seeing the road suddenly lighted up by the firing in front while the reverberating sounds seemed to spread around them, were panic stricken, and in column as they were, fired right and left, shooting each other.

"Beckwith ordered the hand to play and resumed the march, but at every turn the American picquets fired and the panic returned. Then a fresh company was pushed in front, and Beckwith and Napier took the advance. Beckwith's horse was shot and Napier was thus dangerously exposed as the only mounted man. Captain Robertson earnestly entreated him to alight, calling to his recollection what had happened at the Battle of Busaco; he however refused, saying, the state of the troops would not allow of care for himself.

At dawn Queenstown was reached, and a hundred American horsemen were seen half a mile to the left, but being plied by Captain Robertson with some shot and rockets fled: their infantry had previously gone off with two field guns. The enemy's captain of artillery who thus retired, had been a few days before received with a flag of truce, and on that occasion invited the British to fight, going so far as to offer single combat to Captain Robertson: he now fled without firing a shot, though he might have used his guns effectually, and safely, being beyond musquetry, and Beckwith had no cavalry. The projects of Sir J. Warren, at whose entire disposal Beckwith and the troops were placed, were now exhausted and he had done nothing.

General Beckwith was a man of genius, but being cramped here did not exert it: nor did he like his employment, being by nature very humane; morbidly so, for he would not punish to save. Charles Napier's spirit was still more fettered, and several daring propositions made by him were rejected as mere ebullitions of unthinking zeal: it was not for those above him to estimate the untried genius which afterwards broke through the Indian desert, scattered at Meeanee and Dubba the warriors of Beloochistan, and warred down the indomitable robbers of the Cutchee Hills.

One of those propositions was to raise a servile war, the means for which he had perfectly calculated, and looked upon the object as holy. The lie, the deep, damnable lie, that the slaves were well treated in America he always met, by the fact that the poor wretches who came to the British, absolutely crawled on their bellies and licked his shoes when asking for protection! Had he been permitted to descant on the iniquity as he desired, a lesson would have been given for the world to admire and applaud: but a more enlarged notice of his project written by himself, will be found in another portion of this biography.

During the expedition, he formed many intimacies with naval men, and contracted a firm friendship with Captain Robertson of the Artillery, whose intrepidity and military talent he always eulogized.

190

Captain Robertson, Captain Powel, and Captain Romilly of the Engineers, were all on Beckwith's staff, and deservedly mentioned with great praise in his dispatch; but as the armament was under a sea officer the dispatches went to the Admiralty, where the secretary, John Wilson Croker, wantonly struck out their names and deprived them of an honour fairly won by danger, and dearly prized by all soldiers: and this happened at a time when the same Mr. Croker, in the name of the Admiralty, had urged on Sir John Warren the sending of a frigate to act on the Canada lakes, oblivious of the Falls of Niagara!

Charles Napier's journal and letters touched but briefly on these operations, but from his observations are not devoid of interest.

Journal, June 22nd. Last night we got into the boats at twelve o'clock, pulled on shore by moonlight, and landed in tolerable confusion at daybreak without opposition. Craney Island was attacked by a force under Captain Pechel R.N. but a large creek stopped our progress by land, and shoal water stopped the boats by sea. A sharp cannonade from the works on the island cost us seventy-one men, without returning a shot! We lost some boats also, and re-embarked in the evening with about as much confusion as at landing. We despise the Yankee too much.

25th. Last night again landed in rather more confusion than on the 22nd; but with the advance we drove away some Yankees, with loss of a few men ourselves, killing many of them. They were inferior in force and of course were beat at every point, and lost their guns &c. They would have been all taken but for the extreme thickness of the wood, and our local ignorance. Yankee never shews himself, he keeps in the thickest wood, fires and runs off: he is quite right. Local knowledge is very hard to gain, yet we might gain more than we do. We go on badly, and it is hard to say with whom the blame lies; but I think one of our naval leaders is a little deficient in *gumption*; he has much hurry and little arrangement: on the night of the 26th we embarked in such a style that a hundred bold fellows would have shot one half of our people.

30th. I am going on a detached expedition, but with no great hopes of doing anything with such a coadjutor. I am to command the troops, and yet am kept in profound ignorance of the object and destination!

Returned from Ocracoke, where we took a 20-gun brig and

a schooner of 16 guns. Cockburn is no doubt an active good seaman, but has no idea of military arrangements; and he is so impetuous that he won't give time for others to do for him what he cannot or will not do himself. If he had the conducting of any military operation before an active enemy he would get his people cut to pieces. In landing at Ocracoke we were nearly all drowned; the same in coming off.

Luck is a good thing and I have it, but it will very quickly play a chief a trick that will ruin him, if he trusts to it without providing for its ceasing. Cockburn trusts all to luck, and makes no provision for failure: this may do with sailors, but not on shore, where hard fighting avails nothing if not directed by mind, and most accurate calculation. The services are very different. Sailors' business is mechanical, and they have no idea of order and system out of their ships. With them subordination does not really exist; tyranny not discipline is their system, generally speaking; and their habits of life appear to me to contract their ideas and destroy their judgment.

I find however more mind, more expansion of ideas in the younger officers of the navy, who have not been long enough in it to suffer from the system. I never perceived that any dependence could be placed in a naval captain's accurately fulfilling his orders: this may perhaps do at sea, but our service could not exist with such loose discipline. My regard for the navy officers in general is very great, they are open-hearted generous-spirited men; but their life is one calculated to injure the mental powers, and turn them from enlarged views of things, and judgment of human nature, to the *minutiae* of their profession. A captain rules, and all under him rule by force; no one speaks to, or dare be familiar with him: the terrible confinement of a ship renders this necessary they say.

In the army officers are eternally forced to use their judgment in command, and from habitual familiarity have to support themselves against wit and satire, and even impudence at times. A naval officer has only to enforce manual acts of obedience, and being ever in his ship has no eye to trust to but his own. A regimental commander has to convince those under him that his orders are wise, and to procure obedience to them when he is not present.

In fine a soldier's intellect is always exercised in the study of mankind, and a seaman's in the theory or practice of mechanical operations. A proof of this is, that a thousand soldiers on shipboard can be easily managed by their own officers; but put a thousand sailors on shore and their officers cannot manage them: the moment they can elude despotic sway, away they go into excesses.

I have however no intention of saying naval officers are less able men than army officers, the generality of men run very equal; but whatever talents a soldier has are called into constant action, whereas sailors sustain the disadvantage of being compelled to keep theirs dormant, which in the study of mankind is a very bad thing. I have no agreement however with those who think navy officers illiberal and self-interested: my feeling is that they are generally more open and generous than soldiers in moral character; and this in face of the advantage our service has as to mental enlargement, arising from habits incident to their respective professions.

August 12th. We left Kent Island to land near St. Michael's town. There were five hundred men there, and a few guns. I wanted to attack the place with the 102nd alone (250 men) to clear them of the Queen's Town business, and intending to make them do all with the bayonet: of success I had no doubt, and it would have been a brilliant close to the expedition. We were only four miles from the town, the men were steady and eager, and it might have been done in five hours. I would have attacked three times our number of Yankees with confidence, but Beckwith was resolved to let nothing take place; he would neither let me go with the 102nd and two field-pieces, nor yet with the whole of our force.

However, hearing they had a camp of five hundred men four miles on the other side, he placed himself with two battalions of marines and one gun on the road, and detached me with the 102nd and two companies of marines to attack it, meaning himself to intercept any attempts to unite with the camp from the town. This supposed camp proved to be a miserable picquet, which fled and I had still some hopes of a stroke at the town, but he would not consent, though the admiral pressed him strongly. We re-embarked, having landed for no purpose, done nothing, and retired to our ships with the Yankee videttes quietly following, to see us off!

I have never said anything publicly, but am inclined to think that more might have been done in the Chesapeake; but whether doing more would be doing good, is a point to dispute. Taking an extended view of the expedition, as a diversion in favour of Canada it was a complete one; but it ended too soon or too late—too late if the troops were to be afterwards sent to Canada for reinforcing Sir George Prevost; too soon if not to go there. With a different arrangement, we might have done both. The alarm on the coast might have been kept up with six hundred men, allowing the two marine battalions to go at first to the lakes: or, if a serious attack had been designed against Norfolk, the marines might have gone to Halifax, and regulars been drawn thence.

Again, leaving Halifax for a time to its militia, the whole military force might have united and have taken Norfolk easily. Our attack on Craney Island was silly. Had Norfolk been decently attacked it would not have resisted ten minutes; had we landed a gun Craney was gone; had we attacked at high tide it was gone: still it was the wrong place to attack, we should not have lost more men in striking at the town. But the faults of this expedition sprung from one simple cause—there were three commanders! It was a council of war, and what council of war ever achieved a great exploit?

Had either Sir John Warren, Sir Sydney Beckwith, or Admiral Cockburn acted singly and without consultation, we should not have done such foolish things. Sir Sydney wanted neither head, nor heart, nor hand for his business; but he was not free to do what he thought wise, and run sulky when required to do what he deemed silly, which in my opinion made it more silly. He is certainly a very clever fellow, but a very odd fish. I like him, yet do not like to serve under him in his Chesapeake fashion. He ought to have hanged several villains at little Hampton; had he so done, the Americans would not have complained: but every horror was committed with impunity, rape, murder, pillage: and not a man was punished!

I have learned much on this expedition; how to embark and disembark large bodies in face of an enemy; how useless it is to have more than one commander; how necessary it is that the commanders by sea and land should agree and have one view: finally, never to trust Admiral Cockburn. All this has been learned by seeing our faults, for we have done nothing but commit blunders. Nothing was done with method, all was hurry, confusion, and long orders. If the Yankees are worth their salt they will give us a thrashing yet in one of our landings, going as we do like a flock of sheep instead of rowing ashore in lines. I have always thrown myself into the woods with any men that could be first got together, to cover the formation of the others from the boats, which never has been effected under half an hour; and had Jonathan come down to the water's edge or to his waist in it, he would have destroyed half our men: our soldiers themselves grow frightened at the evident want of arrangement. Why not land in order of battle? it was so in Egypt. Well! whatever horrible acts were done at Hampton they were not done by the 102nd, for they were never let to quit their ranks, and they almost mutinied at my preventing them joining in the sack of that unfortunate town. The marine artillery behaved like soldiers; they had it in their power to join in the sack and refused. I said to that noble body of men, 'I cannot watch your conduct, but trust you will not join those miscreants.'

They called out, 'Colonel we are picked men, we blush for what we see, depend upon us, not a man of the marine artillery will plunder. We are well paid by his majesty and we will not disgrace him or ourselves by turning robbers and murderers. Whatever you order we will execute.' Never in my life have I met soldiers like the marine artillery. We suffered much fatigue and hardship, but never was seen anything not admirable in these glorious soldiers: should my life extend to antediluvian years, their conduct at Little Hampton will not be forgotten by me.

Here the American journal ends, but a marginal note dated Kurrachee 1844 runs thus.

I am now reading this record of olden times. Little Powell a superb soldier, who was then with me, lies dead in the burying-ground hard by my house. How strange! We last parted at Halifax in North America 1814, and in 1844 I stand here by his grave in a land then unknown!"

His sister. Potomac. We have nasty sort of fighting here, amongst creeks and bushes, and lose men without shew, altogether above a hundred with three officers. The Yankees however get their share, for at Hampton we killed on the spot above a hundred: it is an inglorious warfare. Seven thousand men are at Baltimore, and we have no such force; still my opinion is, that if we tuck up our sleeves and lay our ears back, we might thrash them: that is if we caught them out of their trees, so as to slap at them with the bayonet. They will not stand that.

But they fight unfairly, firing jagged pieces of iron and every sort of devilment, nails, broken pokers, old locks of guns, gun-barrels, everything that will do mischief. On board a 20-gun ship that we took, I found this sort of ammunition regularly prepared. This is wrong. Man delights to be killed according to the law of nations; and nothing so pleasant or correct: but to be *doused* against all rule is quite offensive. We don't then kick like gentlemen. A 24 lb. shot in the stomach is fine, we die hero-ically: but a brass candlestick for stuffing, with a garnish of rusty twopenny nails makes us die ungenteelly, and with the cholic.

The American coast is one great stretch of flat land covered with wood, so thick nothing can pass except in the cleared lanes between detached houses, and along the great roads. The fire-flies are beautiful; the mocking bird is pretty and his notes very sweet. Humming birds there are, but I have not seen any. There is a bird like a bat, covered with beautiful green plumage. Snakes are abundant, and some very large.

A shrub, *wopong* is the name I think, made into tea, is good for the health, particularly so in consumptive cases: if any seeds can be got they shall go to you. We have sent off our Frenchmen, who are the greatest rascals existing. Much I wished to shoot some, but had no opportunity. They really murdered without an object but the pleasure of murdering. One robbed a poor Yankee and pretended all sorts of anxiety for him: It was the custom of war he said to rob a prisoner, but he was sorry for him. When he had thus coaxed the man into confidence he told him to walk on before, as he must go to the general; the poor wretch obeyed, and when his back was turned the musket was fired into his brains.

This is one of many instances of their killing without any ob-ject but murder, and they intended to desert in a body. I would rather see ten of them shot than one American. It is quite shocking, to have men who speak our own language brought in wounded; one feels as if they were English peasants and that we are killing our own people.

The marines, though brave, are ill disciplined for shore. At Craney Island my brigade, on which the loss all fell, the other not having been brought up, was in a road when a battery opened, and the first shot, enfilading the road, killed a sergeant who was with me. I ordered the brigade to file into a wood where shot could not strike, and the 102nd executed this instantly and were safe, but the marines could not do it before the battery threw three rounds into the thick of them. Eight or nine were killed and wounded, all that were hurt that day, except two sergeants of the 102nd hit unavoidably. One of these recovered, the other was killed, both his legs being shot off close to his body. Good God! what a horrid sight it was!

Nothing can be more interesting than our landings, which have been always by moonlight. Numbers of boats filled with armed men gliding in silence over the smooth water, arms glittering in the moonshine, oars just breaking the stillness of night, the dark shade of the woods we are pushing for combining with expectation of danger to affect the mind.

Suddenly, 'Cast off' is heard, and the rapid dash of oars begins, with the quick 'hurrah! hurrah! hurrah!' as the sailors pull to shore. Then the soldiers rush into and through the water. We have generally had two or three miles to row, the boats tied together and moving slowly; but when in reach of shot every boat casts loose, and they pull furiously with shouts; the 102nd excepted, which no shouting hath! I forbid all noise until they can rush on the enemy: then they have leave to give a deadly screech and away! away!

There are numbers of officers, of the navy in particular, whose families are American, and their fathers in one or two instances are absolutely living in the very towns we are trying to burn. Even Sir Sydney Beckwith has relations in America: it is certainly a most unnatural war, a sort of bastard rebellion. At Ocracoke I put a stop to plunder; yet, though the people were treated too well, being paid nearly double for everything, and the soldiers kept in perfect order, it is said, the American papers will abuse me as a perfect savage. There was indeed one atrocious attempt at murder by a soldier of the 102nd, and unfortunately the villain could not be detected; but we took all care of the man who was hurt, and he and the whole of his family were grateful to us: we offered to take him on board, to cure and land him again where he chose, and the admiral gave him £8.

August 22nd. Strong is my dislike to what is perhaps a necessary part of our job, *viz.* plundering and ruining the peasantry. We drive all their cattle and of course ruin them; my hands are clean, but it is hateful to see the poor Yankees robbed, and to be the robber. If we could take fairly it would not be so bad, but the rich escape; for the loss of a few cows and oxen is nothing to a rich man, while you ruin a poor peasant if you take his only cow. If the American Government will repay them, and levy the whole loss like a tax my care goes: meanwhile I sorrow for the wretches we punish in so individual a manner.

However, no outrages have been authorised on persons, though much on property, unavoidably. I confess to stealing a dog though, because he would be stole, and had no master: he was very beautiful, and took a fancy to me, swimming a mile and a half after me when we came away, however my conscience grew *rusty* on the beach and so he was not taken. For this I am very sorry, and often wish my honesty at the devil; and if a boat goes on shore again, burn my wig but I'll steal doggie: he liked to come and has a right to choose his master.

His opinion of the system followed in this expedition was evinced in the following note, endorsed on a rejected proposal of his to prevent excesses at Ocracoke.

Ocracoke, 1813. A proposal to Admiral Cockburn, in the hope of preventing a second edition of the horrors of Little Hampton, equally disgraceful to the British name and to human nature.

Camp, Halifax, September 24th. We left Chesapeake Bay, after having been on board since the 8th of June, and on the 20th instant pitched our tents here on a hill, in Nova Scotia, with the thermometer at 38°; and this from close ships, with the thermometer at 96°, a week before, and never under 80° for the previous six months. If our constitutions weather this they are *elegant adamants.* In the morning, it is a concert to hear 1600 men's teeth chatter together, and it screws up my wounded cheek wickedly: yet, as soldiers can't choose climate, and though they don't live long now-a-days, methinks there is iron enough in me to knock off twenty years still, if lead don't shorten the date. This transatlantic service sickens me however, and to increase its delights my last letters from home date the 6th of April! After that two packets were taken, a third sailed from hence to Bermuda, with all our letters two days before we arrived here, and the fourth came in yesterday—twenty-nine days from England without a line for me. No! not even from a dun! I would have given a guinea for a tailor's bill.

In April 1814 I expect to move to the south with a brigade, as Beckwith goes to Quebec. This I should not dislike if there was hope of doing good; but if Beckwith was too weak with the whole to effect any action of consequence, what is to be done with a smaller force? He takes a marine battalion and a company of marine artillery, leaving me less than 1000 men, and but three pieces of artillery. Now wherever we land the Yankee runs away; but when he is, in his opinion, able to face us, he will have not less than 5000 men, with strong works and heavy artillery. These 5000 in the open field might be attacked, but behind works it would be throwing away lives: yet I speak as one willing to try much for his own sake, indeed for all our sakes, the men being tired of expecting a fight of consequence. It is perhaps good also to indulge John Bull's taste for blood, now and then. Had Moore sacrificed an army instead of saving one, he would have been perfect in the eyes of the country. Nothing but his unpardonable humanity, which made him fancy England cared as much for her soldiers as he did, caused him to act as he did act. Had he saved his own life and contrived to have 20,000 men bayoneted, and I firmly believe he was the only man in our army who could have saved us, he would have done a job for which England would have made him anything he wished. Alas for himself, he thought of everything but himself. Fortunately, another hero has come forth, but we want both.

I expect to be up the Missouri and Mississippi Rivers in three months, making a diversion in the south. So be it, but when my mind rests from the worry of business and people not cared for, and turns to all I love on earth, then their faces come and tell me a soldier is a miserable exile, labouring in a bloody vocation, living to destroy, destroying to live.

A commander should use his best troops at the outset; success then will give spirit, and though the loss of good men is to be regretted, yet the saving them for harder work creates that work, and in the sequel greater loss is incurred.

The value of this maxim was afterwards very lamentably shewn at New Orleans, where the worst troops were first employed and failed: the beaten regiments, and the generals who survived were then disheartened and the expedition failed.

If I go to the south, as Sir John Warren proposes, my intent is to give the 102nd the lead in every attack, they are better disciplined, more obedient and handy than the marine battalions, and will, if the first blow succeed, try anything. The marines will thus be excited to emulation, and will soon be well in hand, for they are willing to learn. The stupid Craney Island blundering has indeed damped us all, but the 102nd have a good spirit and will, like all young soldiers, dash boldly; they know I had nothing to do with Craney blunders, and their confidence in me is not lost. My design is to fall on some place where we can easily succeed, and then try some tougher job, for a successful skirmish gives the spirit which secures victory in a hotter day.

Our good admirals are such bad generals, there is little hope of doing more than being made prisoners on the best terms. We shall form three plans, or as many as there are admirals: and to these mine will be added. From all, perhaps all bad, a worse will be concocted and of course fail. We failed at Craney because two admirals and a general commanded, and a republic of commanders means defeat. I have seen enough to refuse a joint command if ever offered to me: it is certain disgrace and failure from the nature of things: the two services are incompatible.

A navy officer steps on shore, and his zeal, his courage, his ignorance of troops, and the very nature of a campaign, makes him think you are timid. Discontent follows, and if it does not alter your views, it certainly augments your difficulties to find an adviser, or opposer, in one whose rank entitles him to speak strongly, though his habits have not enabled him to be the judge he thinks himself. For the same reason, a landsman on board a ship has no right to speak or advise. If I command this expeditionary force my request to Sir John Warren shall be, not to let any naval officer land except one or two of my own choosing, who will, and who do, for I have my eye on them, think themselves sailors, not soldiers. A general in a blue coat or an admiral in a red one is mischief!

Reflection has strengthened my first resolution. If we attack New Orleans, or New London, on our road, as the general talk indicates, the 102nd shall lead everywhere. My regret will be keen at losing those fine fellows in greater proportion than the rest, but the first blow is half the battle. I will not however let them be used to attack armed vessels; let the sailors and marines work at their own trade. I have no prejudice against blue jackets, but hate to have men attempt what they cannot understand. We who spend our lives in trying to be soldiers make but bad ones; how can sailors suddenly start into generals?

Yet Cockburn thinks himself a Wellington! And Beckwith is sure the navy never produced such an admiral as himself! Between them we got beaten at Craney. But even now the notion of attacking New Orleans is only known to me from officers who hear it talked of in the streets. We always take care to knock at a man's door and say. Good sir barricade and load your blunderbuss, we are coming to rob and murder you at night. Great therefore as this command is for me my hope is not to go, being sure such bad arrangements as were made in the Chesapeake and at Ocracoke will not succeed.

I do not know if my head is strong for good arrangements, but it can certainly note bad, and their effects in perspective. Cockburn's confidence in his luck is the very thing most to be feared: it is worse than 1000 Yankees. Luck is a good thing on a pinch, but sometimes it gives a pinch! I suspect it is inclined to follow good arrangements.

Royal Marine 1815

Chapter 11

Exchange to 50th Regiment

No expedition from Halifax had taken place, and in September 1813, Charles Napier, having exchanged into the 50th Regiment, took leave of the 102nd, receiving from the officers a sword of honour as a mark of their attachment. This exchange had been sought when the 50th was fighting in the Pyrenees, but when he reached England the French war had ended, and the American war continued: however, the 102nd saw no more active service. With the 50th he remained until, in December 1814, he was reduced on half pay, and then entered the Military College at Farnham.

No correspondence tells the story of his sixteen months' renewed intercourse with the 50th; but after his arrival from America he had to contend for his just share of prize money, on account of the separate expedition to Ocracoke. He claimed as commander of the troops, but was opposed secretly by Admiral Cockburn, who yet held fair language to him, saying Sir Sydney Beckwith was the opponent; an assertion indignantly denied by Beckwith. Finally, a warrant was issued, so little in accord with received rules, that Charles Napier consulted Dr. Lushington, whose opinion was that he might sue in the Admiralty Court, which was the least expensive but the decision would inevitably be for the royal order; or he might sue at common law and probably succeed, but the costs would swallow up the prize money! From this agreeable choice, he was relieved by the prize agent's bankruptcy.

This suit was not his only legal process: another, curious in itself, exemplified his moral resolution. During his childhood, an old Scotch gentleman named Waddel, professing great admiration for Charles Napier's father, passed some days at Celbridge, where, picking up some peculiarly large nuts, he said, I will plant these in Scotland. You are old Waddel to expect fruit from the trees. Yes, but you may gather. Nothing more passed then; but years afterwards Mr. Waddel died, leaving his estate, first to his widow, and, in succession to Colonel Napier. The widow lived long, and at her death some persons being, or pretending to be, heirs at law, took possession, on the ground that an English legal word had been employed instead of a Scotch word, and vitiated the will. Charles Napier entered an action under legal advice, but limited the cost to £200. That sum was soon expended, and though eminent Scotch counsel earnestly urged the further prosecution, he could not be moved to break his resolution.

At Farnham, where his brother William joined him, his aim was not to pass a brilliant examination, as if that were the end to be attained, but to make his studies subserve his genius, knowing that science alone never made a great captain. In that spirit he also studied history, policy and civil government; adding for extension of matter, his own experience of British maladministration in the colonies. His opinions on legislation and civil government were therefore fixed long before he attained power to test them by practice.

In 1815, Napoleon's outburst from Elba, the most astounding exploit that ever established one man's mastery over the rest of his species, shook the world: Europe arose in arms. This commotion of war drew Charles Napier to Ghent, where he awaited the great impending battle, not called by duty but seeking it as a volunteer. Napoleon's rapidity baffled all calculations, and Waterloo was fought almost before the French passage of the Sambre was known at Ghent: thus the eager volunteer could only join in the storming of Cambray. But when the British army reached Paris, the French were still resistant, and Charles Napier assisted in a combat, where the superiority of the British infantry, officer and soldier, over allies and enemies, was signalized in the following remarkable manner.

A large body of Prussians attempted to drive the French from a suburb, where they occupied one side of a street. For hours, a fire from the windows went on, each side suffering severely without any marked advantage to either. The Prussians were then relieved by a much smaller number of British troops, under Sir Neil Campbell, with whom Charles Napier went as a volunteer. The continuous fire, before heard for hours, now ceased, but the blows of pickaxe and hatchet succeeded, mixed at times with a stifled sound of musketry and occasional shouts, and in an hour the French were driven away. Campbell had forced entrance to a house on the French side, broke through the partition walls and stormed each building in succession, thus gaining his object with a furious but calculated rapidity, and with far less loss than the Prussians had sustained without success.

In Paris Napier stayed but a few days, to see the remarkable objects of that interesting period, and then with a stoic's contempt for pleasure, returned to the military college. His usual fortune as to accidents did not fail. When sailing from Ostend the ship sunk at the mouth of the harbour. He swum to some great piles, grasped one and struggled for life, yet with little hope, for the beam was too large and slippery to climb and each swelling wave overwhelmed him: while thus slowly drowning, he was saved by a shore boat.

His letters describing this accident, the storming of Cambray and Campbell's combat, have been lost; and with them his keen observations on the events passing at that great epoch of the world's fate; but the writer of this biography can add to the story of the time some facts, shewing how entirely unsound was the stately-looking edifice of Tory policy, then exhibited with such insolence of boasting. Great and imposing the structure appeared, but it was only a *whited sepulchre*. Even their own soldiers secretly rejected the despotism so violently imposed on the world as a restoration of freedom! Imposed but not so accepted, as reform in England and revolutions in France, Spain, Portugal, Germany, and Italy, have since demonstrated.

As field officer in command of the British picquets, stationed at several barriers of Paris while the negotiations for the king's entrance went on, the writer, for two days and a night, saw how the public mind within the city was swayed to and fro. Multitudes were continually assembling and dispersing with all indications of violent emotion; single men would harangue crowds, and be replied to by opponents; shouts and scufflings were frequent; and political agents were constantly passing to and fro by the barriers, carrying information for the expectant royalists behind the allies' camp. More than once those persons seemed to be assailed by crowds, and on one occasion a tall man of remarkable appearance, evidently not a hired agent, he was too daring and vehement for that, was suddenly surrounded by a mob and apparently slain!

The feelings of the British soldiers were unequivocally shewn. Proud of their long victorious course against the French, they yet respected the latter as brave enemies, and had a profound admiration, even love, for Napoleon. They thought of him, not as a foe but as a hero standing alone; a soldier to be hailed by all soldiers; as a man who had enabled them to gain the greatest possible glory by fighting him: a master in war, and the fast friend of warriors. Their instinct as fighting men was for him, and as freemen against the Bourbons. When Louis the Eighteenth entered Paris, the writer, his post being at the head of the picquets guarding the Barrier of St. Denis, was asked by the captain on duty there, if he was to salute? 'I have no orders on that head and give none' was the reply. The king came up, crowds thronged forward, and the words *vive* and *Roi* were heard on all sides; but the last was generally preceded by the words *L'Empereur et*, pronounced in a low tone. The British soldiers being left to themselves brought down their musquets from the shoulder, and placing their hands on the muzzles, fiercely regarded the approaching king. He seemed sur-prized, but soon his countenance assumed a look of such malignant ferocity, so fixed, so peculiar, as never to be forgotten.

A number of *mousquetaires* in burnished *cuirasses*, their faces con-vulsed with anger, then rode up, shouting, gesticulating, and brandish-ing their swords: but close behind the picquet was a wall, and the swarthy veterans, hard as the steel of their bayonets, and with wits as sharp, knew the advantage. Keeping their bronzed faces bent over their hands, their eyes glared sternly, yet no movement indicated that they were even sensible of the *mousquetaires'* presence, until the latter closed within a few paces and seemed dangerous: then suddenly, all their heads were lifted and streams of tobacco juice flew towards the shining *cuirasses*, whereupon the courtier soldiers followed the chariot of the king. A shout of delight arose from the crowd, and many well-dressed women embraced the British veterans.

In England Charles Napier's life became very cheerless. War was over, he was on half-pay, and his future was unpromising.

However, in 1822, he was appointed to the Military President's post in Cephalonia, a post he held until 1830. After a period of co-mand in northern England during the Chartist agitations, Napier was sent to India in 1841 assigned to the Sind command. It was in India that Charles Napier earned his greatest fame and, perhaps, notority.

Napier provoked a war with the *emirs* of Sind (Scinde) which brought about permanent British annexation of the territory. He died in England in 1853, aged 71.

www.ingramcontent.com/pod-product-compliance
Lightning Source LLC
Chambersburg PA
CBHW031839090426

42741CB00005B/283